BUILDING EXCEl
HIGHER EDU(

Over the last 30 years, Singapore has developed a system of higher education that is the envy of many other countries and regions. How has Singapore developed such a highly performing education system? Was it planned? Was it mere luck?

Written by Arnoud De Meyer, who is widely regarded as one of the pre-eminent management educators and leaders in higher education, the book focuses on Singapore as an in-depth case study of how to build a system of higher education, specifically a portfolio of highly differentiated and diversified universities. He worked closely together with Jovina Ang during the preparation of the manuscript. This book is unique because it showcases several case studies of the emerging system of higher education, and it was written based on insights drawn from interviews with the key decision-makers and actors in the system from the past 20 years, including ministers and permanent secretaries of the Ministry of Education, and presidents and chairmen of the six universities. The success of this system can be attributed to several factors: the clarity of purpose of the decision-makers, with clear targets in cohort participation rate, commitment to significant funding for education and research, discipline of an intelligent and well-implemented governance system, flexibility in adjusting plans, and rapid and adaptive learning from overseas partners. In the last few chapters, the authors look at the future of the system and postulate how it should be adjusted to the changes in Singapore and the world.

This unique book on educational strategy would be of particular interest to educational specialists and policy-makers in emerging countries who want to build a system of higher education, policy-makers in mature industrialised countries who are faced with the challenge of revamping their system of higher education, strategists who are interested in dynamic capability building and philanthropists who want to use education as an equaliser of social status.

Arnoud De Meyer is a global academic leader who has held the top jobs at institutions including Singapore Management University (SMU), Judge Business School at the University of Cambridge (UK) and INSEAD. His notable appointments include President of SMU, Deputy Dean of INSEAD worldwide and the founding Dean of INSEAD in Asia (Singapore). He has authored over ten books.

Jovina Ang is Managing Director of Communicatio and formerly an award-winning corporate executive of multiple Fortune 500 companies including Microsoft, Dell and Cisco Systems. She launched Singapore's first inter-company mentoring programme for emerging female leaders in the IT industry. She is the author of *Leadership Communication: Connect. Engage. Inspire.* and *The Game Plan of Successful Career Sponsorship.*

BUILDING EXCELLENCE IN HIGHER EDUCATION

SINGAPORE'S EXPERIENCE

Arnoud De Meyer with Jovina Ang

Routledge
Taylor & Francis Group

LONDON AND NEW YORK

First published 2022
by Routledge
2 Park Square, Milton Park, Abingdon, Oxon OX14 4RN

and by Routledge
605 Third Avenue, New York, NY 10158

Routledge is an imprint of the Taylor & Francis Group, an informa business

British Library Cataloguing-in-Publicatio Data
A catalogue record for this book is available from the British Library

Library of Congress Cataloging-in-Publication Data
Names: Meyer, Arnoud de, author. | Ang, Jovina, 1965– author.
Title: Building excellence in higher education : Singapore's experience /
    Arnoud De Meyer, with Jovina Ang.
Description: First Edition. | New York : Routledge, 2021. |
    Includes bibliographical references and index.
Identifiers: LCCN 2021005602 (print) | LCCN 2021005603 (ebook) |
    ISBN 9780367539153 (Hardback) | ISBN 9780367539160 (Paperback) |
    ISBN 9781003083719 (eBook)
Subjects: LCSH: Education, Higher—Singapore. | Universities and colleges—
    Singapore—History. | National University of Singapore—History. |
    University of Singapore—History. | Nanyang Technological University—
    History. | Nanyang Technological Institute—History.
Classification: LCC LA1239.5 .M49 2021 (print) | LCC LA1239.5 (ebook) |
    DDC 370.95957—dc23
LC record available at https://lccn.loc.gov/2021005602
LC ebook record available at https://lccn.loc.gov/2021005603

ISBN: 978-0-367-53915-3 (hbk)
ISBN: 978-0-367-53916-0 (pbk)
ISBN: 978-1-003-08371-9 (ebk)

Typeset in New Baskerville
by Apex CoVantage, LLC

Contents

Figures

Tables

Foreword

Education has both a strong economic and social imperative. Economically, it develops skills and knowledge, unlocks human potential, opens up career choices. Socially, it continues to be the dominant means for a child from a humble background to excel in life and surpass their parents.

Of course, education does its job provided that the country is stable, and the economy is well-managed. But it has no doubt become the key policy lever of governments in the modern world to engender both economic vibrancy and social mobility.

It is with good foresight that since our independence, Singapore has invested in the development of an outstanding system of education. In the early years, the focus was mainly on primary and secondary education. But with industrialisation in the 1970s and 1980s, we needed more graduates from polytechnics and universities, which started a 30-year journey to develop a system of higher education.

When we became independent in 1965 we had two universities and two polytechnics; now we have a diverse and well-performing system of six universities, five polytechnics and an ITE with three campuses.

The system developed progressively and in tandem with the needs of the economy. It grew as the demand for graduates expanded, and the pathways widened as job opportunities diversified. Economic opportunities, development of higher education and aspirations of the young were three inter-dependent variables of a nation building equation. We did not make one factor dominant and the others subservient to it. Our approach was pragmatic and flexible.

In my years as Minister for Education, I saw even greater changes. Research came to the fore; a few of our universities rose in international repute; higher education assumed the public mandate of lifelong learning; experiential learning took on pedagogical prominence as institutions realised the importance of skills in a digitalised world; there was recognition of the importance of inter-disciplinary learning when young, complemented by acquisition of deeper expertise later on in adulthood; work-study pathways emerged.

More than two years ago Arnoud De Meyer, then President of Singapore Management University, mentioned to me that the development of the highly performing system of six universities and the analysis of the drivers of success was a case study that should be documented. He was convinced that many other countries could take reference from our experience in developing and improving their own systems.

I threw him the challenge of writing this up. I thought he was eminently qualified to do the job as an academic who is a double insider of our system of higher education. He had been President of one of our universities, but also the founder of INSEAD's successful campus in Singapore. He knew our system from different and important perspectives.

This book is the result of this conversation. It has benefited from more than 30 interviews and conversations with the decision-makers and leaders in higher education in Singapore, and in-depth desk research.

In the early chapters, Arnoud reflects on the development of our six universities and the drivers of their development. At the time when I wrote this foreword, we were in the midst of the COVID-19 pandemic. Our higher education system had to adjust quickly over the last few months to new ways of delivering education, to nurture our young and conduct research. The recommendations in the last three chapters will help us to reflect on how the system needs to evolve.

I thank Arnoud for writing this book, and am glad that I can be part of it. This book will no doubt be one chapter in the long, ongoing, exciting and illustrious journey of our higher education system.

Ong Ye Kung
Minister of Education October 2015 – July 2020

Introduction

Singapore's higher education system is one of Asia's success stories. Without doubt, the quality of higher education in Singapore is the envy of many nations. Few other countries have been able to develop a system of higher education of such outstanding quality in 40 years. There are other examples of rapid development of a system of higher education, such as in Japan, Korea, mainland China and Taiwan. But Singapore is a special case since it is a small city state with limited resources except for its people and location. It is also a relatively young country which gained independence only in 1965.

While it may have taken the United States and many European countries centuries to develop excellent universities, Singapore has been able to accelerate the development of its higher education system in a relatively short time. This development was determined by both objective and subjective factors. Using the analogy of a game of cards, the outcome of the development of a system of higher education is "shaped by the hand of cards that systems have been dealt (the objective factors) and how well they play those cards (the subjective factors)" (Marginson, 2011). The objective factors – the size of the population and a lack of skilled human resources – were not in favour of Singapore. But its leaders, who influenced the outcomes of the subjective factors, played their cards very well. Being able to rapidly build a successful system of higher education was the consequence of the leadership and choices made by the Singapore Government.

Higher education has always been a key lever for addressing two critical needs of any country and nation – to develop skilled human capital to build the nation and the economy; and to fulfil the aspirations of the citizens for obtaining their preferred tertiary education. According to a 2015 OECD report (Hanushek and Woessmann, 2015), access to education and providing skills enhancement can boost GDP by an average 28 percent per year in low income countries and 16 percent per year in high income countries for the next 80 years. Even though this prognosis was made fairly recently, the correlation between education and economic progress was noticed by the founding fathers of Singapore – Lee Kuan Yew and the first cabinet of the Singapore Government. This explains why there has been so much emphasis on educating the citizens.

One of the original characteristics of education in Singapore can be labelled as "strategic pragmatism" to support the development of the economy. In the early days, the focus of education was on developing skills for a labour-intensive manufacturing economy. In line with recent changes in the economic and competitive landscape, and globalisation, the focus of education is now on developing skills and an entrepreneurial mindset for Singapore to thrive in a knowledge-intensive and innovation-led economy.

The second critical need that education addresses is the aspiration of Singapore citizens for a better career and a better life. To this end, education is seen as a way for the citizens to achieve their full potential. As Marginson (2011) noted, countries and cultures with a "Sinic" civilisation and where the Confucian tradition is strong, attach great importance to education as a means of enhancing a person's worth and career. Other than fulfilling this aspiration and the latent need of the citizens, education is seen as a way of moving up the social ladder to a higher economic status – to help the citizens to get good jobs and have meaningful careers. Marginson (2015) also argued that countries with Post-Confucian systems – which combine Confucian tradition with rapid modernisation in the economy, government, education and science, rooted in the encounter with the West – all have achieved rapid expansion of participation in higher education, rapid growth of scientific research and world-class universities.

Singapore is a special case of this Post-Confucian development. As it does not have any natural resources or physical space, the only "natural" resource is its population. Thus, it is no surprise that the Singapore Government placed education as a top priority for the country. Singapore has invested heavily and consistently in education over the past 40 years. The overall expenditure on education has increased significantly over the decades from S\$0.9 billion in 1981 to S\$13.1 billion in 2018 (Singapore Government, 2019), averaging about 3 to 4 percent of the country's GDP (TheGlobalEconomy.com, 2019). The proportion of the recurrent government expenditure on university education as a proportion of the total education expenditure was about 21 to 25 percent from 1995–2005 (Lee and Gopinathan, 2008). However, given the government's current focus on the ageing population, healthcare and other shifting priorities, combined with a low birth rate, it is expected that the budget allocated for education could stabilise if not decrease in the next few years (Arndt, 2019).

The approach the Singapore Government took for education is a holistic and comprehensive one. It focuses on high-quality education at all levels from pre-school and primary school right through to higher education and lifelong learning. It recognises that to be successful, you need an intake of high-quality students and you need competent and dedicated teachers.

Given the speed of change that is driving the global economy and the nature of work, the government recognised early on that education and learning have to be lifelong – which ultimately led to the introduction of the SkillsFuture movement in 2015. In fact, Lee Kuan Yew mentioned in a speech in 1977: "My definition of an educated man is a man who never stops learning and wants to learn" (Yiannouka, 2015).

With high-quality education at all levels from primary education to higher education, Singapore was able to transform from a third world to a first world economy; from an underdeveloped island with a lack of natural resources and high unemployment to a globally competitive economy that thrives and is centred on a hub of finance, professional services, trade, transportation and high-end manufacturing.

A QUICK OVERVIEW OF THE SINGAPORE HIGHER EDUCATION SYSTEM

Since the early 1980s, the Singapore university system has evolved from one relatively unknown teaching university that was the merger of two universities established during the British colonial times, to a system that includes two highly ranked comprehensive universities and four more focused universities. Collectively, these six universities help to achieve a cohort participation rate of close to 40 percent (Ministry of Education, 2019b). The cohort participation rate is the proportion of each primary one cohort that obtains a publicly funded degree place at university. They graduate almost 19,000 students per year from their undergraduate programmes (Department of Statistics Singapore, 2019). In contrast, only 3,002 university students graduated back in 1980 (Ministry of Education, 2019b), and the cohort participation rate was as low as 5 percent then (Singapore Department of Statistics, 2006).

At the same time, Singapore universities have raised their international profile and have become more attractive both to local citizens and overseas students, partially due to the rising quality of undergraduate education they offer. And the government has been providing funding and assistance in the form of scholarships, bursaries and loans, particularly to help the students of lower to middle income families access higher education.

The two comprehensive universities – National University of Singapore (NUS), established in 1980, and Nanyang Technology University (NTU), which received university status in 1991 – are now highly ranked in the Quacquarelli Symonds (QS) or Times Higher Education rankings. In the 2020 rankings of Scientific Impact compiled by the Centre for Science and

Technology Studies at the Leiden University, NUS and NTU were ranked 38th and 68th respectively in the world. In Asia, they have been consistently placed in the top 30 of rankings, respectively at 16th and 26th (CWTS, 2020).[1]

NUS is truly a comprehensive university. NTU is slightly less so and is still very focused on technology even though the university expanded its offerings to include business, arts, humanities and social sciences, science and medicine. Since the rise in rankings, these two universities have attracted applications from a substantial number of foreign students from across the world.

To address the needs of the country and citizens, the number of universities has tripled from two universities to six universities in the past 20 years. Singapore now has two specialised research-intensive universities – Singapore Management University (SMU) and Singapore University of Technology and Design (SUTD) – and two applied universities – Singapore Institute of Technology (SIT) and Singapore University of Social Sciences (SUSS).

SMU and SUTD, the two specialised research-intensive universities, were established through collaboration with top-tier institutions. The Wharton School of the University of Pennsylvania was the partner to establish SMU. This partnership continued for more than 10 years. Massachusetts Institute of Technology (MIT) and subsequently, Zhejiang University were the original overseas partners of SUTD. While research collaboration with MIT is continuing, the agreement on education with MIT ended after seven years of collaboration. The partnership with Zhejiang University is still ongoing, and there's a constant stream of SUTD students going to Zhejiang University for exchange studies and research collaboration.

Recognising that more vocational and applied skills were needed for the Singapore economy, the Government established SIT in 2009, and reorganised it as an autonomous university in 2014. It also transformed a private university, UniSIM (SIM University) into SUSS in 2017. These newer universities were established to equip students with highly practical and applied skills to meet the needs of the industry. They also provide multiple pathways for the less academically oriented students who can first study in the polytechnics or work before pursuing higher education at one of the two more applied universities.

Additionally, the Singapore Government launched the "Global Schoolhouse" initiative in 2002 to further boost and enrich the higher education sector by attracting foreign institutions and foreign students to Singapore (Tan, 2016). The original intent of the Global Schoolhouse initiative was to attract up to 150,000 foreign students and boost the contribution of higher education to 5 percent of GDP by 2015. From the government's perspective, inviting foreign "world class universities" to establish a presence in the country would enable Singapore to augment capability development in specific industries through tertiary level education in niche areas that was otherwise not available there. The Global Schoolhouse initiative also signalled an intention of the Singapore Government to establish Singapore as a key education hub. In order to attract big names, the government provided incentives and financial assistance. Specifically, foreign universities were encouraged to augment the country's capability in specialised industries and niche areas. High-quality degree and diploma courses in specialised areas such as business, hospitality, digital media, and science and technology are examples of the courses offered by these foreign institutions. Many education providers took advantage of this initiative. The INSEAD Asia campus was established in 2000, and is still thriving; it attracts more than 350 full-time overseas students who come to study in Singapore annually (INSEAD, 2020). By 2008, the Global Schoolhouse initiative had attracted other institutions including Chicago Graduate School of Business, ESSEC, New York University Tisch School of the Arts, and the S.P. Jain Institute of Management to offer postgraduate education. Other institutions, for example, James Cook University, Curtin University, University of Nevada, Las Vegas (UNLV) and the DigiPen Institute of Technology, came to offer undergraduate degree programmes (Ministry of Education, 2008).

Singapore's proper system of higher learning is more than the six universities. The system also includes five vibrant polytechnics – Singapore Polytechnic, Ngee Ann Polytechnic, Nanyang Polytechnic, Temasek Polytechnic and Republic Polytechnic – and the Institutes of Technical Education (ITE), which evolved from the Vocational and Industrial Training Board, to give students who are less academically inclined an opportunity for their professional growth.

The portfolio of six universities that was set up between the mid-1980s and today, offers multiple pathways for Singaporeans to pursue a variety of careers and aims to achieve a targeted cohort participation rate of 40 percent. It intends to be inclusive, and it has started to incorporate non-academic entry requirements such as interviews for a place in the higher education system. It addresses the complete spectrum of learning abilities of its citizens, from the highly academically oriented students to the ones with a more practical and applied interest.

While the universities, polytechnics, institutes of technical education and the campuses of overseas institutions make up the complete and integrated Singapore higher education system, the focus of this book is on the development of the universities as the central feature of the sector.

THE CREATION OF AN OUTSTANDING UNIVERSITY SYSTEM FROM THE MID-1980S UNTIL NOW

The question as to how Singapore developed and evolved this university system in 40 years has been of significant interest to many policy-makers and academic leaders alike – which is why we have decided to write this book. The restructuring of the university sector was the result of major policy changes in the early 2000s. In 1999, an influential comparative study of university governance and funding systems was conducted in Canada, Hong Kong, the United Kingdom and the United States (Lee and Gopinathan, 2008). One of the main consequences of this study was for the top public universities to be given a significant level of autonomy combined with a high level of accountability – which was why the concept of autonomous universities was introduced in 2006. Several other committees and studies followed, and four new universities were created. In this book, we want to elaborate on the vision, strategy and thinking that fuelled the development of this university sector and document how this vision was implemented.

The book is divided into three parts. Part 1 focuses on how the university system in Singapore has evolved from the first medical school that was started during the British colonial rule to what it is in 2020. Part 2 discusses the vision, strategy, thinking and drivers behind the development of the university landscape. This part also refers to some of the key architects who played a key role in shaping the higher education landscape. Part 3 consists of three chapters with our personal views on how the universities in Singapore need to evolve over the coming years.

Many of the insights in this book are based on publicly available documents and written materials, for example, ministerial communications to the Parliament, reports by committees that studied specific aspects of the development of the system of higher education, as well as internal reports. We also had the privilege of interviewing the key architects of the higher education system including present and former ministers for education, current and former permanent secretaries, chairmen of the board of trustees of the six universities, and past and present presidents of the universities. We are deeply grateful for the candid way in which they answered our questions. We have used a few quotes from the interviews with the permission of the interviewees. But as we promised confidentiality, we have kept this to a minimum. While we've benefitted enormously from their insights and reflections, the content of this book is solely our interpretation.

NOTE

1 We prefer the CWTS Leiden rankings over the Shanghai Jiao Tong Academic Ranking of World Universities because the latter's methodology favours older universities outside Asia with a longer history of research.

BIBLIOGRAPHY

Arndt, C. (2019). Is healthcare spending disrupting the education system in Singapore? *AsiaOne*, 25 November. [Online] Available at: www.asiaone.com/money/

healthcare-spending-disrupting-education-system-singapore (Accessed: 20 March 2020).

CWTS (2020). *Leiden Ranking.* [Online] Available at: www.leidenranking.com/ranking/2020/list (Accessed: 17 September 2020).

Department of Statistics Singapore (2019). *Education, Language Spoken and Literacy.* [Online] Available at: www.singstat.gov.sg/find-data/search-by-theme/population/education-language-spoken-and-literacy/latest-data (Accessed: 20 February 2020).

Hanushek, E. A., & Woessmann, L. (2015). *Universal Basic Skills: What Countries Stand to Gain.* OECD. [Online] Available at: www.oecd.org/education/universal-basic-skills-9789264234833-en.htm (Accessed: 20 March 2020).

INSEAD (2020). *Student Life – MBA Programme.* [Online] Available at: www.insead.edu/master-programmes/mba/student-life (Accessed: 24 August 2020).

Lee, M. H., & Gopinathan, S. (2008). University restructuring in Singapore: Amazing or a maze? *Policy Futures in Education,* 6(5), p. 569–588.

Marginson, S. (2011). Higher education in East Asia and Singapore: Rise of the Confucian model. *Higher Education,* 61, p. 587–611.

Marginson, S. (2015). The strategic positioning of Australian research universities in the East Asian Region. *Higher Education,* 70, p. 265–281.

Ministry of Education (2008). *Report of the Committee on the Expansion of the University Sector – Greater Choice, More Room to Excel.* Singapore: Ministry of Education.

Ministry of Education Singapore (2019a). *Singapore's University Landscape.* [Online] Available at: www.moe.gov.sg/news/committee-on-university-education-pathways-beyond-2015/singapore-university-landscape (Accessed: 20 February 2020).

Ministry of Education Singapore (2019b). *Education Statistics Digest.* [Online] Available at: www.moe.gov.sg/docs/default-source/document/publications/education-statistics-digest/esd_2019.pdf (Accessed: 18 February 2020).

Singapore Department of Statistics (2006). *Singapore Statistical Highlight 2006.* Singapore: Department of Statistics.

Singapore Government (2019). *Government Total Expenditure on Education.* [Online] Available at: https://data.gov.sg/dataset/government-expenditure-on-education (Accessed: 20 March 2020).

Tan, J. (2016). What happened to the Global Schoolhouse? *University World News,* 16 September. [Online] Available at: www.universityworldnews.com/post.php?story=20160913131137765 (Accessed: 18 February 2020).

TheGlobalEconomy.com (2019). *Singapore: Education Spending, Percent of GDP.* [Online] Available at: www.theglobaleconomy.com/Singapore/Education_spending/ (Accessed: 20 March 2020).

Yiannouka, S. N. (2015). The secret of Singapore's success in education. *The Straits Times,* 11 April. [Online] Available at: www.straitstimes.com/opinion/the-secret-of-singapores-success-in-education (Accessed: 22 February 2020).

PART I

THE EVOLUTION OF THE
UNIVERSITIES IN SINGAPORE

Chapter 1

The development of Singapore's universities until 1991

Under British rule in Singapore, several institutions of higher learning were created. By the time of independence in 1965, this had culminated in two universities: the University of Singapore which had its roots in the University of Malaya and used English as the medium of instruction, and Nanyang University (Nantah) which used Chinese as the medium of instruction. In the late 1970s, Nantah was gradually losing its attractiveness and the government decided to merge the two universities into the National University of Singapore (NUS). But by the end of the decade, there was a need to educate more students, in particular in engineering. There was also the perception that competition could be beneficial for the education system. Nanyang Technological Institute was split from NUS and Singapore again had two universities. These two institutions have been developing rapidly into some of the best institutions in Asia.

THE ORIGINS OF THE (NATIONAL) UNIVERSITY OF SINGAPORE[1]

The origin of Singapore's higher education can be traced back to the establishment of Singapore's first medical school in September 1905. It was known as the Straits Settlements and Federated Malay States Government Medical School. This school was the start of Singapore's oldest university, the National University of Singapore. Before the establishment of this medical school in Singapore, medical assistants in Malaya were sent to Madras, India to be trained to be doctors. There were no other options available either in Singapore or Malaya. Even though a commission established by the Legislative Council proposed a higher education institution to provide technical and practical education and a medical school in 1902, this proposal did not go through due to opposition from some leading medical doctors (The Straits Times, 1902).

The medical school finally came about through the lobbying of Chinese businessmen and merchants, in particular Tan Jiak Kim, who raised S$80,000 to develop home-grown doctors to address the needs of the local community (Singapore Infopedia, 2019a). By 1905, the medical school started offering a five-year medical course in Medicine, Surgery and Midwifery (NUS b). Other than medicine, the school offered a one-year pharmacy course (NUS c). The medical school became the King Edward VII Medical School, which was subsequently renamed in 1921 to King Edward VII College of Medicine. In 1929, the school started offering a four-year dentistry course (NUS d). This medical school became a part of the medical faculty of the University of Malaya when the university was established in 1949.

The other early development in higher education was the creation of Raffles College in 1928. This college focused on the disciplines of arts and sciences (Singapore Infopedia, 2019b). It was set up to mark the centenary of the founding of Singapore by Sir Stamford Raffles. Both the Chinese and European communities contributed funds to set up Raffles College. The idea of establishing a college can be traced back to Raffles himself (Raffles, 1819). He first put forward a proposal to establish a college to educate and serve the native population of the Malay Peninsula in their "intellectual development". Raffles envisioned the development of a college with departments of English and local languages including Chinese, Malay and Siamese. This initial concept was later changed to a college that was focused on the arts and sciences.

Initially, there were some issues regarding the recognition of Raffles College diplomas. This led the students of the college to lobby for the college to be upgraded to a university. Even though this proposal was supported by the professors of the college, the implementation of this plan was interrupted by the outbreak of World War II. The college ceased to operate during the war, and it reopened in 1946.

The medical school and the arts and science college operated as two separate institutions until 1949 when they were combined to address a need from the community to form a local university, named the University of Malaya. When it opened in 1949, it had three faculties: Arts, Sciences and Medicine. Its academic and administrative system was modelled after the higher education institutions in the United Kingdom. The initial faculty of Arts included five departments – English, Geography, History, Economics and Statistics, and Mathematics. The Kuala Lumpur campus of the University of Malaya was established subsequently in 1957 when there was a further need to expand the university in Peninsular Malaya. The university operated with these two separate campuses in Kuala Lumpur and Singapore until 1962, when there was a landmark decision from the Malaya and Singapore governments to make these two universities independent from one another. Thus, they became the University of Malaya and University of Singapore respectively (The Straits Times, 1962).

When the University of Singapore was established, the courses offered included Arts, Dentistry, Law, Medicine, Pharmacy (which became a part of the Faculty of Science in 1974) and Science (Biological Sciences, Botany, Chemistry, Mathematics, Physics, Zoology). The university started offering Engineering courses in 1964 on the campus of Singapore Polytechnic. It had oversight over the standards of the curriculum and awarded the Bachelor of Engineering degree. By 1969, the School of Engineering in Singapore Polytechnic became the Faculty of Engineering of the University of Singapore offering Civil Engineering, Electrical Engineering and Mechanical Engineering. The Department of Industrial and Systems Engineering was established in 1972. Chemical Engineering, which started as the Department of Chemistry in the Faculty of Science in 1975, became a part of the Faculty of Engineering in 1979. Architecture was another course that was launched even though it was first established in 1958 as a programme in Singapore Polytechnic.

NANYANG UNIVERSITY[2]

Established in 1955, Nanyang University, or Nantah for short, was the first university outside China to cater to students from the Chinese stream of instruction. In just one year, Nantah started offering classes.

Before the establishment of Nantah, students who wanted to pursue higher education in Chinese went to China. There were no options available locally in Singapore or the Malay Peninsula. Embarking on higher education in China was an expensive option that only the rich Chinese families could afford. Tan Kah Kee, a prominent local Chinese businessman, philanthropist and Chinese nationalist, had given generously to establish many educational institutions in Singapore and China including Amoy University (now Xiamen University) in his native Fujian province (Singapore Infopedia, 2019d). Another factor that led to the establishment of Nantah was the growing number of students studying in Chinese. Switching to studying in English was not an option for them due to the language difficulties they faced.

Students who chose to further their education in China, especially at Amoy University, met with a roadblock in 1950 when tight migration controls were imposed by the British. This was the consequence of the insurgence of communism in Malaya following the success of the Chinese Communist Party in founding the People's Republic of China in 1949. Increased acts of violence and sabotage, extortion, shootings, murders and arson attacks were led by the Communist Party of Malaya across the Malay Peninsula. The "Malayan Emergency" (Singapore Infopedia, 2019e), which lasted for 12 years, was declared following the killing of three British planters in 1948. Violence grew during this time. There was also an assassination attempt of the former

Governor of Singapore, Franklin Gimson. These events explained why the British became readily suspicious of the students traveling to China for education as they were perceived to be potential communist agents.

The idea of starting a Chinese university was first mooted by Tan Lark Sye, a prominent businessman, who pledged a gift of S$5 million towards starting a university (Toh, 2017). The idea was received with a lot of enthusiasm and spurred many Chinese from Singapore and across the region, whether rich or poor, to donate generously to the project. Within a short time, a sum of S$10 million had been raised for the university (The Singapore Free Press, 1954). Furthermore, the Hokkien Huay Kuan donated 2 square kilometers of land in Jurong as the site for the new university. This was the start of Nantah.

The goals of the university were to (Nanyang University, 1958):

- Provide high school graduates in Malaya with opportunities for higher education;
- Train teachers for high schools in Malaya;
- Develop specialists for Singapore; and
- Train new leaders for Malaya.

This university was originally incorporated as Nanyang University Limited on 5 May 1953 under the Companies Ordinance. Initially, there were some issues with the conferring of degrees. Given that Nanyang University was incorporated as a company rather than a university, the British Colonial Government refused to grant permission for the creation of this university. The university status issue was resolved when Nanyang University Ordinance was passed in March 1959. The degrees that were subsequently conferred by Nantah were recognised by the Singapore Government in 1967 after a full review of the curriculum was conducted.

By the 1970s, there was a fall in student enrolment in Nantah as fewer students pursued a Chinese education at the primary and secondary levels. Enrolment in Chinese schools fell from 45.9 percent of the cohort in 1959 to 11.2 percent in 1978. The shift to English schools was driven by better job prospects for those with an English education (Singapore Infopedia, 2019f). This led many parents to choose English schools over Chinese or other vernacular schools for their children. The Chinese educated students, especially those with better grades, also opted to go to the University of Singapore as this led to better job prospects. The shift was markedly apparent in the period 1975 to 1979. Many faculty members also jumped ship in this time. It was evident that unless this was redressed, Nantah might cease to exist (Singapore Infopedia, 2019g).

Nantah was also believed to be rife with communist activities. For example, 51 students were arrested on the suspicion of involvement in "communist subversive activities" on 27 June 1964 (The Straits Times, 1964). It was believed that these students had been actively recruiting cadres and disseminating pro-communist propaganda and were anti-government. There was also entrenched communist influence in the university council, administrative body, hostel and canteen staff, and the student body. Tan Lark Sye, the founder of Nantah, was investigated and he had his Singapore citizenship revoked. The arrest was critical to the crackdown on communist influence in the university, as well as to clearing the way for Nantah to be developed as a recognised institution of learning that followed stringent quality education standards. Prior to this time, there had been no interference nor guidance from the government in the curriculum and the development of Chinese education at Nantah (Singapore Infopedia, 2019h).

The reasons above led then Prime Minister Lee Kuan Yew and the Cabinet to suggest that Nantah switch its medium of instruction from Chinese to English. Another initiative that was introduced, subsequently enabled the students from Nantah to take classes in English at a joint campus together with the students of the University of Singapore – this helped to level up the standards of Nanyang students.

MERGER OF THE UNIVERSITY OF SINGAPORE AND NANYANG UNIVERSITY TO BECOME THE NATIONAL UNIVERSITY OF SINGAPORE

The two original universities were finally merged to become National University of Singapore following a commissioned assessment by Sir Frederick Dainton, who was the Chancellor of Sheffield University and former chairman of the University Grants Committee in Britain (The Straits Times, 1980a). He argued that it was preferable to have one strong university rather than two separate universities to train the graduate manpower that was needed for the country. The merger happened despite significant opposition from the alumni and donors of Nantah in 1980 after the National University of Singapore Bill was passed in parliament. While the merger was generally accepted as a rational decision, there was also a sense of tension and uncertainty at the ground level. This was especially the case when the new university needed to rely on expatriate staff to raise its standards of education in engineering, science and medicine. The Chinese educated students and faculty were also believed to be uncomfortable about their prospects in the new university.

The National University of Singapore was inaugurated on 8 August 1980 with a student population of 9,000 students and an academic staff strength of 600 (The Straits Times, 1980b). By 1984, the staff strength of NUS had doubled to 1,200. In that time, student enrolment increased to 13,000 and S$212 million was invested to develop NUS' infrastructure and facilities at the Kent Ridge campus (Birger et al., 2008).

In the ten years after the merger, NUS continued to raise the quality of teaching to produce the required graduate manpower for Singapore to further climb the technological ladder of progress. The government also tripled the combined number of faculty members to produce more than triple the number of engineering students in five years following the merger. The number of students continued to increase in line with the Singapore Government's plan to increase the cohort participation rate from 5 percent in 1980 to 15 percent by 1990. In the same period, Singapore's GDP grew nearly three times.

NUS has been evolving and growing over the last 40 years – many new departments, schools and courses were added at both the undergraduate and graduate levels. Today, NUS is the largest and most comprehensive university in Singapore offering a wide range of disciplines in 17 faculties and schools at both the undergraduate and postgraduate levels (National University of Singapore, n.d. m).

DEVELOPMENT OF NANYANG TECHNOLOGICAL UNIVERSITY

After the merger, Nanyang University made way for the establishment of Nanyang Technological Institute in its existing premises in Jurong in 1981. Unlike what was offered at the newly minted National University of Singapore, the curriculum was tailored towards developing practice-oriented engineers for the growing Singapore economy. Consequently, NTI graduates were perceived to be more hands-on and job-ready. It also had a charter for training 75 percent of engineers required in Singapore. Three engineering disciplines – Civil and Structural, Electrical and Electronic, and Mechanical and Production Engineering – were initially offered at NTI. NTI also focused on recruiting engineering faculty with relevant industrial experience. By 1986, NTI was named as one of the best applied engineering institutions in the world because of the job-ready and practice-oriented graduates that it produced (Birger et al., 2008).

By 1990, NTI's student population had grown 11-fold to 6,832. Additionally, the Accountancy School from NUS was transferred to NTI in 1987. A school of Applied Science was also added. Singapore's second university took 10 years to nurture and was built on the strong foundation of engineering. Nanyang Technological University (NTU) was formed in 1991 to address the increasing demand for engineers and technologists in the economy. NTI became a part of NTU when it was established in 1991.

Frederick Dainton was invited again by Lee Kuan Yew to review the status of higher education. He postulated that Singapore should aim to have two strong universities by 2000 so that there would be healthy competition for students, and resources and grants for research and contracts with the industry (Birger et al., 2008). In 1990, the government announced that the Institute of Education would be merged with the College of Physical Education to form the National Institute of Education (NIE). NIE became a part of NTU when it was established in 1991. The Singapore Government was clear that it did not want NTU to be a clone of NUS. NTU became Singapore's "second" university with strengths in engineering and sciences, whereas NUS offered a comprehensive range of disciplines including law and medicine. The number of schools at NTU increased gradually. While its core strengths are still in sciences and engineering, it now has faculties and schools in business, humanities, arts and social sciences, communication and information, environment and medicine.

NOTES

1 For the description of the development of the National University of Singapore, we used the information provided on the websites of the different schools extensively, unless otherwise referenced.
2 For the description of the development of the Nanyang Technological University, we used the information provided on its website and Singapore Infopedia extensively, unless otherwise mentioned.

BIBLIOGRAPHY

Birger, F., Lee, S. K., & Goh, C. B. (2008). Toward a better future: Education and training for economic development in Singapore since 1965. *World Bank Publications*, 18 April. [Online] Available at: http://siteresources.worldbank.org/INTAFRREG-TOPEDUCATION/Resources/444659-1204656846740/4734984-1212686310562/Toward_a_better_future_Singapore.pdf (Accessed: 21 March 2020).

Davie, S. (2017). University places: To cap or not to cap. *Straits Times*, May 18. [Online] Available at: www.straitstimes.com/opinion/university-places-to-cap-or-not-to-cap (Accessed: 21 March 2020).

Lim, C. P. (2013). *The Evolution of Universities – A Singaporean Story* at the Times Higher Education World Academic Summit 3 October 2013, Nanyang Technological University. [Online] Available at: www.a-star.edu.sg/News-and-Events/News/Speeches/ID/1888 (Accessed: 15 November 2019).

Nanyang Technological University (n.d. a). *Corporate Information*. [Online] Available at: www.ntu.edu.sg/AboutNTU/CorporateInfo/Pages/OurHistory.aspx (Accessed: 15 November 2019).

Nanyang Technological University (n.d. b). *Organisation: Colleges, Schools & Institutes*. [Online] Available at: www.ntu.edu.sg/AboutNTU/organisation/Pages/Colleges andSchools.aspx (Accessed: 12 November 2019).

Nanyang University (1958). *A Brief Sketch of Nanyang University*. [Online] Available at: http://eservice.nlb.gov.sg/item_holding.aspx?bid=4980735 (Accessed: 12 December 2019).

National University of Singapore (n.d. a). *110 Years of Medical Milestones*. [Online] Available at: https://nusmedicine.nus.edu.sg/images/resources/content/about/milestones/110-Years-of-NUS-Medicine-Milestones_01-horz.pdf (Accessed: 18 February 2020).

National University of Singapore (n.d. b). *The Pharmacy History*. [Online] Available at: https://pharmacy.nus.edu.sg/our-history/ (Accessed: 18 February 2020).

National University of Singapore (n.d. c). *The History of FASS: From Humble Beginnings to a World-Class Institution*. [Online] Available at: www.fas.nus.edu.sg/about/history-of-fass.html (Accessed: 18 December 2019).

National University of Singapore (n.d. d). *History*. [Online] Available at: www.nus.edu.sg/nusbulletin/general-information/history/ (Accessed: 18 February 2020).

National University of Singapore (n.d. e). *History of the Faculty*. [Online] Available at: https://law.nus.edu.sg/about_us/history_milestones.html (Accessed: 15 December 2019).

National University of Singapore (n.d. f). *The Pharmacy History*. [Online] Available at: https://pharmacy.nus.edu.sg/our-history/ (Accessed: 15 December 2019).

National University of Singapore (n.d. g). *A Brief History: A Brief Walk Down Memory Lane*. [Online] Available at: www.dbs.nus.edu.sg/about-us/a-brief-history.html (Accessed: 15 December 2019).

National University of Singapore (n.d. h). *History*. [Online] Available at: www.chemistry.nus.edu.sg/about/BriefHistory.htm (Accessed: 15 December 2019).

National University of Singapore (n.d. i). *About Us*. [Online] Available at: http://ww1.math.nus.edu.sg/about.aspx (Accessed: 15 December 2019).

National University of Singapore (n.d. j). *A Brief History (1929–2015)*. [Online] Available at: www.physics.nus.edu.sg/aboutus/history.html (Accessed: 15 December 2019).

National University of Singapore (n.d. k). *History and Milestones*. [Online] Available at: www.eng.nus.edu.sg/about-us/history-and-milestones/ (Accessed: 15 December 2019).

National University of Singapore (n.d. l). *History*. [Online] Available at: www.sde.nus.edu.sg/arch/about/history/ (Accessed: 15 December 2019).

National University of Singapore (n.d. m). *17 Faculties and Schools*. [Online] Available at: www.nus.edu.sg/education (Accessed: 12 November 2020).

Raffles, T. S. (1819). *Minute by Sir TS Raffles on the Establishment of a Malay College at Singapore 1819*. [Online] Available at: http://eresources.nlb.gov.sg/printheritage/detail/ec629c60-58e9-40c6-847e-43d191dada47.aspx (Accessed: 18 December 2019).

Singapore Government (n.d.). *Parliamentary Debates: Official Report*. [Online] Available at: http://eservice.nlb.gov.sg/item_holding.aspx?bid=4826189 (Accessed: 21 March 2020).

Singapore Infopedia (2019a). *National University of Singapore*. [Online] Available at: http://eresources.nlb.gov.sg/infopedia/articles/SIP_50_2005-01-17.html (Accessed: 18 December 2019).

Singapore Infopedia (2019b). *Raffles College*. [Online] Available at: http://eresources.nlb.gov.sg/infopedia/articles/SIP_1797_2011-03-15.html (Accessed: 18 December 2019).

Singapore Infopedia (2019c). *Nanyang University*. [Online] Available at: http://eresources.nlb.gov.sg/infopedia/articles/SIP_91_2005-02-02.html (Accessed: 12 December 2019).

Singapore Infopedia (2019d). *Tan Kah Kee*. [Online] Available at: http://eresources. nlb.gov.sg/infopedia/articles/SIP_839_2004-12-28.html (Accessed: 12 December 2019).

Singapore Infopedia (2019e). *Malayan Emergency*. [Online] Available at: http:// eresources.nlb.gov.sg/infopedia/articles/SIP_2019-06-12_145539.html (Accessed: 21 March 2020).

Singapore Infopedia (2019f). *Vernacular Education*. [Online] Available at: http://eresources. nlb.gov.sg/infopedia/articles/SIP_2016-10-03_094744.html (Accessed: 12 December 2019).

Singapore Infopedia (2019g). *Bilingual Policy*. [Online] Available at: http:// eresources.nlb.gov.sg/infopedia/articles/SIP_2016-09-01_093402.html (Accessed: 12 December 2019).

Singapore Infopedia (2019h). *Nanyang University's Student Activism*. [Online] Available at: http://eresources.nlb.gov.sg/infopedia/articles/SIP_2014-04-10_153052. html (Accessed: 21 March 2020).

The Singapore Free Press (1954). Nanyang fund is over $10 mil. *The Singapore Free Press*, 19 May. [Online] Available at: http://eresources.nlb.gov.sg/newspapers/ Digitised/Article/freepress19540519.2.47 (Accessed: 21 March 2019).

The Straits Times (1902). The Legislative Council. *The Straits Times*, 22 January. [Online] Available at: http://eresources.nlb.gov.sg/newspapers/Digitised/ Article/straitstimes19020122-1.2.35 (Accessed: 14 December 2019).

The Straits Times (1962). S'pore varsity starts today. *The Straits Times*, 1 January. [Online] Available at: http://eresources.nlb.gov.sg/newspapers/Digitised/ Article/straitstimes19620101-1.2.60 (Accessed: 18 December 2019).

The Straits Times (1964). 3 a.m. crackdown: 51 held at Nanyang. *The Straits Times*, 28 June. [Online] Available at: https://eresources.nlb.gov.sg/newspapers/Digitised/ Article/straitstimes19640628-1.2.2 (Accessed: 15 November 2019).

The Straits Times (1980a). The conclusions and recommendations. *The Straits Times*, 16 March. [Online] Available at: http://eresources.nlb.gov.sg/newspapers/ Digitised/Article/straitstimes19800316-1.2.48 (Accessed: 21 March 2020).

The Straits Times (1980b). NUS to recruit 600 lecturers. *The Straits Times*, 7 May. [Online] Available at: http://eresources.nlb.gov.sg/newspapers/Digitised/Article/ straitstimes19800507.2.8 (Accessed: 21 March 2020).

Toh, E. (2017). Remembering Tan Lark Sye. *The Straits Times*, 21 September. [Online] Available at: www.straitstimes.com/opinion/remembering-tan-lark-sye (Accessed: 21 March 2020).

Chapter 2

Building universities for a knowledge economy

From 1991 to 2020, the number and nature of Singapore's universities changed dramatically. After NTU was established in 1991, four more universities were created. This was in response to the changing nature of Singapore's economy. In this chapter, we describe how the education system responded to the country's transformation from an industrial and manufacturing economy to a knowledge-based and service economy, and ultimately to an innovation-led economy. Based on our desk research and interviews, we provide some highlights of the evolution of NUS and NTU, and the creation of SMU, SUTD, SIT and SUSS.

FROM INDUSTRIAL ECONOMY TO KNOWLEDGE ECONOMY

For the pioneering Singapore Government, education had always been a priority. It saw human capital as the only real resource for the country. As an island city, there was no other natural resource for Singapore to bank on for its growth and advancement. Thus, investing in education was, and still is, a national imperative and not a choice. Education represented an essential part of the main policies for Singapore to progress from a third world country with a per capita GDP of slightly more than US$500 at independence in 1965 to one of the most successful city economies in the world, with a GDP per capita of more than US$58,000 in 2019.

In its approach to education, the Singapore Government always had as a guiding principle the idea that education had to lead to jobs and employment, and that it had to support the strategic thrusts for Singapore's economic development and growth. It is therefore important to understand the economic changes that took place in the 1980s to understand the changes in education policies.

Dr Albert Winsemius, an early Chief Economic Advisor to Singapore, estimated that Singapore would be short of 500 engineers and 1,000 technical workers annually in the period 1970–1975. In the initial decades from 1960 to 1980, the emphasis was thus on technical skills education, responding to the needs of four main industries: construction and building the infrastructure, petrochemicals, shipbuilding and ship maintenance, and electronics (both production and assembly). The role of the universities was primarily to train the graduates needed to meet the economic needs of the country, as well as to graduate a small group of middle managers and senior leaders, and a group of professionals including doctors and lawyers. This focused education policy ensured that there were cohorts of highly trained graduates for the various sectors of the economy. Despite this, there was a growing shortage of well-trained employees in the late 1970s and early 1980s (Lim, 2013).

In the early 1980s, wages started to rise, and Singapore began to lose some of its competitive advantage in terms of cost compared to the other emerging economies in the region. This trend was somewhat compensated for by an increase in foreign workers and the introduction of industrial policies to stimulate automation and computerisation. Thus the economy continued to flourish during this time, averaging a yearly growth of 8.5 percent of GDP.

The ongoing restructuring of the economy was interrupted by an economic recession in 1985, Singapore's first since independence. The recession was caused by a combination of external and internal factors. Externally, the economies of industrial nations were slowing down; there was a decreasing demand for Singapore's goods and services. This was combined with increased competition from countries in the region. Multinational corporations were also starting to optimise their global assets and supply networks, not always to the advantage of Singapore. Internally, there was an increase in wages and a decreasing rate of productivity improvement. A construction slump, high domestic savings rate and economic rigidity further weakened the economy (History SG, 2019a).

The severity of the recession led Dr Tony Tan, who was then Minister for Trade and Industry, to form an Economic Committee in March 1985. Under the chairmanship of Lee Hsien Loong, Acting Minister for Trade and Industry, the charter of the committee was to review the progress of the economy and identify new directions for future growth. The 1986 Economic Committee Report (EC report) focused mainly on short-term measures to get the economy out of the recession. But for the longer term, the 1986 Economic Committee recommended that Singapore find a new economic strategy because its positioning as an offshore production centre for the developed world would quickly erode as wages continued to rise, and cheaper options became available in the neighbouring countries and China. The authors of the EC report argued that Singapore had to move beyond a production base to become an international business centre. It should attract companies to establish operations headquarters to carry out product development, manage treasury activities, and provide administrative, technical and management services. Furthermore, it had to become an exporter of services that were not limited to Singapore-based activities such as tourism or banking, but also offshore-based activities (Economic Committee, 1986).

Once the economy recovered, the government drew up in 1991 the Strategic Economic Plan (SEP) to analyse and design the economic landscape for the next two to three decades. Its aim was to transform Singapore from an industrial economy to a knowledge-based economy. The SEP called for promoting and developing Singapore as a "total business centre" and developing high-technological (high-tech) and high-value-added manufacturing and services as the twin engines of growth. The SEP contained two strategic proposals. The first was to develop and grow highly developed manufacturing and service clusters. The second focused on upgrading the domestic sector, which had low productivity, to move up the value chain. The strategies of the SEP were grouped under Manufacturing 2000 and International Business Hub 2000, and their implementation was to be led by the Economic Development Board (Chia, 2014). The proposal to create manufacturing and services clusters adopted Michael Porter's framework for competitiveness – that thriving business enterprises need access to various suppliers, qualified manpower, competency centres in relevant technologies, and efficient infrastructure and other services (Economic Planning Committee, 1991).

Key to these developments were the adjustment of the skills of the workforce and upgrading of the Singapore employees into knowledge workers. In a knowledge-based economy people and their ideas and capabilities are the sources of competitive advantage. The needs of the employers, especially the foreign multinationals from the United States, Europe and Japan, were rapidly changing. These changes would be even more reinforced during the 1997–1998 Asian Financial Crisis. The Singapore Government became increasingly aware that it was losing competitiveness vis-à-vis the other economies in the region where currencies had devalued sharply against the Singapore dollar. Cost-cutting measures in existing industries were a short-term measure.

Moving up the value chain and rapidly transforming Singapore into a knowledge driven economy with a strong capacity for innovation was hindered by the lack of skills and education typical for a developed economy. For example, it lacked sufficient competence in information technology. While the revolution of information technology was not synonymous with the knowledge driven economy, the two were tightly integrated. Information technology provided the knowledge driven economy with a platform through which the production and distribution of knowledge could enhance productivity and innovation. Information technology could also spawn new industries, create new areas of demand and transform the world of work.

It became crystal clear that Singapore needed a new kind of human and intellectual capital to further its economic growth with more top-end professional, managerial, technical and specialist manpower. However, there were four main manpower challenges facing the government (Chia, 2014):

- Other than producing graduates with the required expertise, they needed to embrace the innovative and entrepreneurial mindset;
- There should be sufficient quantity and quality of manpower to support the growth industries;
- Structural unemployment should be minimised; and
- Singapore workers should be offered meaningful jobs for them to develop their full potential while giving them a good quality of life.

Another master plan – the 1998 Report of the Committee for Singapore's Competitiveness and the Economic Development Board's Industry 21 Master Plan – was drawn up to position Singapore as a globally competitive knowledge-driven economy. Key industry sectors, including high-value-added manufacturing services and high-growth exportable products and services, were identified as key engines of growth. It was acknowledged that the success of the knowledge-driven economy would require entre-preneurship and research to create new markets and opportunities, as well as new products and services (Chia, 2014).

At the same time, the Singapore youth had grown more sophisticated, having benefited from an ever-improving primary and secondary school system and excellent junior colleges. Thus, it was not unexpected for them to express a legitimate request for more choices in the curriculum so that they could pursue their interests and aspirations.

Having one university in the 1980s – and later with the creation of NTI, a second engineering and sciences institution – was insufficient to match the demands of the economy. Reaching the targeted cohort participation rate of 15 percent in 1990 was probably impossible with only one mainly teaching-oriented university (Lim, 2013). Meeting the demands of a sophis-ticated knowledge-based economy and at the same time matching the genuine aspirations of Singapore's young citizens would require more and different institutions. The system of higher education had to be transformed to meet the needs of the country and citizens.

In the coming sections, we will discuss how NUS and NTU were trans-formed, and how and why new institutions were created during the period from 1990 to 2020. We will elaborate on some of the key events and actions in more detail in the coming chapters.

NUS AND NTU IN THE 1990S

While the two universities increased their offerings to cover more disciplines, the initial education bias was still towards science and engineering. This was in line with the economic development and the industrial needs of Singapore, to drive towards the knowledge economy and domestic entre-preneurship (Seong & Foo, 2008). Both NUS and NTU embarked on an expansion plan to build knowledge through research and development, and close partnerships with the industry. It was evident that Lee Kuan Yew took a personal interest in shaping and developing the paths of the two universities. He often caught up with the presidents of NUS and NTU as he believed that the universities were a "production machine of sorts" to drive the economy of Singapore, until this role was handed over to Dr Tony Tan. After a brief period in the private sector, Dr Tony Tan had returned to the cabinet as Deputy Prime Minister in 1995. He was asked by Prime Minister Goh Chok Tong to head a task force to transform the higher education sector.

By the mid-1990s, both NUS and NTU were producing the relevant type of graduates to fuel the Singapore economy. However, in 1996, both universities were challenged by Prime Minister Goh Chok Tong to go beyond this role and be the "Harvard" and "MIT" of Asia. To realise this vision for NUS and NTU, Prime Minister Goh Chok Tong insisted on three goals for the two universities (Goh, 1996):

> First, they must provide excellence in teaching and a good, all round educa-tion. They must not only develop professional knowledge and skills, but also nurture future generations of leaders in all areas of national life.
>
> Second, they must become hubs of research and intellectual exchange in Asia, in line with Singapore's desire to be a catalyst and a gateway to the region. NUS and NTU must establish themselves as premier centres of scientific and technological innovation. They should also promote greater intellectual understanding between Asia and the West in politics, society and culture.
>
> Third, they must each develop a community of alumni with strong bonds among each other and strong attachments to their alma mater. Their gradu-ates must contribute their experience, expertise and resources to sustain and enhance the reputation of NUS and NTU. The alumni's contributions will reciprocate society's support in getting them to where they are.

To show its commitment to building the higher education sector, the Singapore Government allocated significant financial resources. The expen-diture for higher education, in particular for the expansion of the universities, grew from S$0.4 billion in 1985 to S$3.3 billion in 2018.[1] This expenditure was kept aligned to the expected increase in student numbers. Student subsidies were critical to attract talent into higher education and improve equality of opportunity. Even though the Singapore economy was affected by recessions in the late 1980s, 1997 and 2008, the expenditure allocated for

Table 2.1 Recurrent and development government expenditure on the universities (1985–2018)

Year	Recurring expenditure (S$ million)	Development expenditure (S$ million)	Total (S$ million)
1985	253.8	156.9	410.7
1990	351.5	74.9	426.3
1991	841.2	102.2	943.3
1992	412.5	164.0	576.5
1993	431.6	200.7	632.3
1995	520.3	154.3	674.6
1996	546.1	174.2	720.3
1997	656.6	165.0	821.6
1999	570.0	340.9	910.9
2000	898.5	329.6	1,228.1
2001	1114.6	332.0	1,446.5
2003	1034.8	302.3	1,337.1
2004	1029.9	453.9	1,483.8
2005	1058.2	247.4	1,305.6
2006	1719.2	137.5	1,856.7
2007	1491.4	153.6	1,644.9
2008	1809.0	118.3	1,927.3
2009	2014.8	163.4	2,178.2
2010	2305.9	224.7	2,530.6
2011	2973.8	168.6	3,142.4
2012	2537.0	192.0	2,728.9
2013	2969.9	352.8	3,322.7
2014	2736.6	251.6	2,988.2
2015	2897.8	185.7	3,083.4
2016	3138.3	71.6	3,209.9
2017	3046.7	80.2	3,126.9
2018	3254.8	21.1	3,275.9

Source: Singapore Department of Statistics (2018)

higher education remained high (see Table 2.1). This reflected the government's firm focus on raising the quality of tertiary education.

REINVENTING NUS[2]

Over the past 25 years, several leaders of NUS including Lim Pin, Chong Chi Tat, Shih Choon Fong, Jacob Phang and Tan Chorh Chuan played key roles in transforming NUS from a relatively unknown regional institution to one that is world-class and internationally acclaimed.

One of the first pivotal transformations of NUS can be traced back to 1995, when it changed the education system from the British system to include elements of the US system. The revised modular education system, which is still in place to this day, combined the rigour and depth of the British university system with the flexibility and breadth of the US system.

Recognising the importance of research for elevating NUS' position in the global landscape of universities, the university intentionally reinvented itself from a mainly teaching university into a research-intensive university. The piloting of the new promotion and tenure (P&T) system in 1998 in the Department of Mathematical Sciences was a first step to reinforce the importance of research. One of the pioneers of this initiative, Chong Chi Tat, then Vice Dean of Science, had observed how the P&T system had been instrumental in enhancing the status and position of UC Berkeley to one of the top universities in the world. When a rigorous P&T system was introduced to the whole university it had a big impact on the recruitment, retention, and promotion and tenure of the faculty members. Those who had not engaged in research were gradually moved on. It was believed that almost half of the faculty members were affected by the new P&T system.

When Shih Choon Fong, a Harvard-trained scientist with a background in industry and research and administration at Brown University, was appointed president of NUS, he put in place initiatives to transform NUS into a "Global Knowledge Enterprise". The first initiative involved "changing the mindsets of staff", "making room for entrepreneurial spirit", "shutting out the bureaucratic mindset", and "becoming resourceful, innovative and pioneering". The second initiative included building borderless departments and faculties to establish a borderless knowledge community within the university. Thirdly, he wanted NUS to lead in producing "citizens of the world" who are agile and responsive to local and global opportunities, and graduates who are lifelong learners who have a sense of personal responsibility and moral obligation towards society (Shih, 2000). The transformation of NUS garnered substantial support from the government. That said, the success of the transformation required the university faculty and staff to adopt a different, growth-oriented mindset while assuming responsibility to play a part in building Singapore as a knowledge and innovation hub.

Being a part of the government body and a statutory board, NUS' pay scale was based on the civil service system. President Shih took the P&T system further by institutionalising a performance- and market-based evaluation and compensation system (Marginson, 2009).

In response to the national narratives for building a "new economy", NUS needed to attract and recruit top academics from across the world to build its research capability. When the pension age was raised from 55 to 65, Shih took the opportunity to refresh and renew the faculty. Significant rejuvenation of the ranks was seen, and many new faculty members were hired.

Additionally, Shih attempted to introduce a group performance bonus plan as a way to break down silos and increase collaboration among faculty members. He also made a push for NUS to join APRU (The Association of Pacific Rim Universities) to further encourage faculty members to increase their collaboration outside the university. This collaboration initiative saw pockets of success with some departments embracing it more than others.

Entrepreneurship was the other transformation focus at NUS. Despite meeting initial resistance, Jacob Phang, then Professor of Engineering, was convinced that NUS needed an in-house outfit to translate technological innovation into practice. An Entrepreneurship Centre was established to promote and undertake research on entrepreneurship. To provide support to the students, staff and alumni engaging in innovation, a Venture Support Unit was set up. Students could also work as interns at start-up technology companies in Silicon Valley, Philadelphia, Shanghai, Stockholm and Bangalore as part of the Overseas College initiative (Wong et al., 2007). Today, this entrepreneurship initiative continues in the form of NUS Enterprise – incubating start-ups and driving industry-relevant innovation.

NUS became an autonomous university in 2006. This new system of governance and its impact on the universities' growth will be discussed in more detail in Chapter 5. With this "public to private" change in status, NUS became a not-for-profit public company limited by guarantee under the Ministry of Education (MOE).

The autonomous university status allowed NUS to influence its own direction and build on its areas of strength. NUS was no longer constrained by the operational regulations imposed on statutory boards or government departments, even though the government continued to provide large endowment funds and injected research funds. The university was given more administrative and financial autonomy to explore different ways to: (1) build up teaching and research excellence; (2) raise its international standing; and (3) enhance the students' experience. With the autonomy also came an enhanced accountability framework for the universities, comprising the existing Quality Assurance Framework for Universities (QAFU), and the signing of Policy and Performance Agreements between MOE and each university.

The increased focus on research may have relegated teaching and education somewhat to the back seat. When the third university, SMU, rolled out a successful new model of pedagogy that was focused on small-group teaching and intensive instructor-student interactions in 2000, NUS was not ready to react quickly. It took quite a few years before the teaching approach was changed and many of the seminar rooms were redesigned. But by August 2011, NUS had opened University Town and a set of four colleges – Tembusu College, Cinnamon College, College of Alice and Peter Tan, and Residential College 4, to promote integrated living and learning and show NUS' commitment to teaching and learning.

One key strategy that NUS embraced to raise its standards was forming partnerships with the world's best institutions. The first partnership was with the Peabody Institute of Johns Hopkins University. The agreement with Peabody was signed in 2001 to develop what was to be known as the Singapore Conservatory of Music. Steven Baxter, former Dean at the Peabody Institute, was appointed Founding Director, and Goh Yew Lin was appointed the founding Chairman of its Governing Board. In 2003, the conservatory was renamed Yong Siew Toh Conservatory of Music in recognition of a S\$25 million gift from the Yong Loo Lin Trust to honour the late Ms Yong Siew Toh. When the doors of the conservatory opened, it welcomed an inaugural class of students with majors in orchestral instruments, piano and composition.

Next in a list of major partnerships was the partnership with Duke University School of Medicine. Given Singapore's changing demography, it was recognised that Singapore needed to invest in clinical medicine to study and research the diseases of the East. Three leaders – Tan Chorh Chuan, then President of NUS, Lim Chuan Poh, then Permanent Secretary of Education, and Sandy Williams – contributed greatly to building a graduate medical school to develop clinician researchers.

The foray into liberal arts education was kick-started in 2007 when it was raised at a meeting of the International Academic Advisory Panel (IAAP), an advisory group to the Ministry of Education comprising prominent international academic leaders. Even though the quality of higher education was already robust and increasing in excellence, the members of the IAAP believed that liberal arts education was needed to further improve the education in Singapore. Liberal arts education was deemed to be critical for developing foundational and fundamental skills of reasoning and critical thinking. The Yale-NUS College was launched in 2011 and it became the first liberal arts college in Singapore and one of the few liberal arts colleges in the region. The details of how these partnerships were formed and nurtured will be discussed in Chapter 6.

By 2021, NUS has become a premier international university, recognised worldwide for the quality of its education and research. While international rankings are a limited proxy for the real standing of a university, they do give some indication. One of the indicators is the numbers of papers published by authors of the university. This data is collected by CWTS Leiden for its rankings. In Table 2.2, we provide the data for some selected universities. The raw data for the number of papers published by an author of a university for the period 2006–2009 and the period 2014–2017 are in the second and third columns of this table. The fractional count – that is, where a paper counts only for a fraction, thus accounting for multiple authorship – is in columns 5 and 6. Columns 4 and 7 provide the change in percentage.

The research output of NUS has risen quite significantly, even though the output of Peking University (as an example of a top Chinese university)

Table 2.2 Total number of papers published in a period of three years by selected universities (all sciences)

University	2006–2009	2014–2017	Change in %	2006–2009	2014–2017	Change in %
				Fractional count	Fractional count	
Harvard University	48652	74600	53.3	27422	33188	21.0
University of Cambridge	20237	30862	52.5	11401	13154	15.4
Tokyo University	27977	31805	13.7	14412	14602	1.3
Peking University	12997	31076	139.1	7808	16171	107.1
Hong Kong University	8729	14323	64.1	5397	7202	33.4
NUS	14979	25749	71.9	9199	11929	29.7
NTU	9066	18081	99.4	5931	9643	62.6

Source: CWTS Leiden

has risen even more rapidly. More importantly, this shows that NUS is now in a league close to some of the best universities in the world, like the University of Cambridge or the University of Tokyo. In the 2019 ranking (based on the period 2014–2017), NUS was number 38 worldwide and 16th in Asia (behind Tokyo University, Seoul National University and 13 Mainland Chinese universities).

PROJECTING NTU ONTO THE WORLD STAGE

Like at NUS, the transformation of NTU was to a large extent top-down driven. President Su Guaning and Bertil Andersson, who was Provost from 2007 to 2011 before he was appointed the third President of NTU, were instrumental in elevating NTU's ranking and position in the world.

Given that research represented a critical component of rankings, Andersson knew that the only way for him to accelerate NTU's ascend to the top was to jumpstart research excellence by importing talent from across the world, especially top researchers who knew how research was conducted and evaluated. He was given full autonomy almost without any limit in budgets to recruit the world's best in research excellence. At that time, the focus on research at NTU was limited even though many faculty members had trained abroad for their PhD.

Andersson approached many notable researchers in his network to help him accomplish the goal that was assigned to him by Tharman Shanmugaratnam, who was Minister for Education from 2003 to 2008. Singapore has the advantage of having English as its working language, thus, Andersson could recruit from the United States and Europe, as well as Japan and China. He was able to attract some of the world's best researchers from Imperial College in the United Kingdom and the California Institute of Technology (Caltech) and Massachusetts Institute of Technology (MIT) in the United States. We will discuss how he went about accomplishing this goal in more detail in Chapter 4.

Like NUS a few years prior, NTU implemented under Andersson a rigorous promotion and tenure system. Across the whole university, every faculty member was assessed on his or her research and teaching capability. Andersson in his initial three- to four-year period reportedly moved on more than a third of the faculty who did not focus on research nor could teach well. In so doing, Andersson signalled the equal emphasis on educating people and creating new knowledge to power Singapore's economy into the future.

Other than hiring full professors who were renowned for their research, this period also saw NTU hiring academics across the ranks from post-doctoral researchers to assistant professors and associate professors. It was believed that this practice of hiring across the ranks lowered the resistance from the existing faculty who were already feeling uncertain about their jobs due to a revamp of the promotion and tenure system and who feared that the newly hired research stars would dominate the university.

NTU went all-out for all the available grants to take advantage of all the funding that came from the government. Andersson also encouraged research across disciplines.

Given the focus on engineering, NTU rolled out a world-class engineering "renaissance" programme. The unique features of this programme combined engineering and business, and offered substantial overseas exposure for the students. This and other programmes helped NTU to grow student numbers by 7 to 8 percent a year while producing the necessary engineering talent for Singapore.

It was further recognised that NTU had to offer a more comprehensive education to its students. Engineers cannot operate in a vacuum and wait for people to define a problem or apply engineering solutions to them – which was why several other schools quickly sprouted. NTU created a School of Humanities and Social Sciences, and a School of Art, Design and Media. Four colleges were built, of which three – Nanyang Business School (College of Business), College of Humanities, Arts, and Social Sciences, and College of Science – are less than 20 years old.

The next big expansion that NTU undertook was the establishment of Lee Kong Chian School of Medicine. Unlike the bottom-up approach that was taken for other schools and colleges, the approach taken was to partner with a top medical school. NTU could see how the partnerships with top institutions had benefitted NUS, especially in accelerating time-to-launch courses and driving innovations in the higher education sector. After exploring partnerships with several institutions in Europe and Australia, the partnership with Imperial College from the United Kingdom was signed in 2010. Imperial College was chosen because of its medical education and research capability, and its similarity to NTU as a major engineering university. By 2013, the Lee Kong Chian School of Medicine welcomed its first class of students to provide more options for high-quality Singaporean students to pursue Medicine locally. This partnership also gave NTU an opportunity to experiment and innovate in how Medicine was taught. Unlike the traditional way of teaching, key features of this course included team-based learning using technology and giving students clinical experience from Year 1. And in research, NTU could differentiate itself by conducting research in the intersection of Medicine and Technology.

The autonomy that was granted to NTU in 2006 contributed equally to its success. It was only then that NTU's leadership and board could really transform, run and operate the university. The previous council of the university could not do much in contrast to the leverage and decisional power that was given to the board of trustees that is still in place today.

The progress of NTU as a comprehensive research university is illustrated by the rise of its number of publications, as reported in Table 2.2. But its greatest strength remains in engineering. Based on research publications, NTU was recently considered number two in the world in Materials Science. Only MIT was ahead of it. The other flagship of NTU is Chemistry, where it was ranked number three in the world. Electrical Engineering is another stronghold of NTU where the university is in the top ten list in the world. In Computer Science, NTU is among the top 20 in the world (Sharma, 2017).

SINGAPORE MANAGEMENT UNIVERSITY

The idea to establish a third university was mooted by Dr Tony Tan, then Minister for Trade and Industry, who mentioned in Parliament in 1997 that Singapore needed 17,000 university graduates in 2000. If Singapore continued with NUS and NTU only, the economy would be short of 7,000 to 8,000 graduates every year (Tan, 2015). Rather than establishing another comprehensive university, Dr Tony Tan's view was to develop a university that was focused on business and management, given the evolution of the economy towards finance, banking and services. The time was also right for Singapore to further develop the higher education sector for the universities to differentiate, provide variety and chart new directions for their growth.

Singapore Management University (SMU) became the third university to be established. Unlike NUS and NTU, SMU was set up as an autonomous university right from the beginning in 2000, following a North American model (Tan, 2015). SMU became the first university to focus exclusively on disciplines relevant to the newly developing service economy: Management, Business and Economics, Social Sciences and Information Systems. When SMU opened its doors for student intake in 2000, the cohort participation rate had reached 20 percent (Lim, 2013).

The initial plan was to transform a private institution, the Singapore Institute of Management (SIM), into the third university. The original vision of SMU was probably like what SUSS is now. SIM had been in operation since 1964 to train managers for the Singapore economy (Singapore Infopedia, 2019a). Since the 1980s, SIM had been offering degree courses in partnership with several overseas universities including the University of London (UOL), the Royal Melbourne Institute of Technology (RMIT) and the Open University. SIM was focused on providing part-time degree programmes to working adults. However, the plan to transform SIM did not go through as the pioneers of SMU felt that SIM was addressing an important niche need for Singapore working adults:

> Beyond the difficulty in converting SIM into the SIM University or SIMU, the working committee [preparing the new university], was also concerned that as an ongoing institution, SIM remained extremely relevant and important in providing tertiary education opportunities to working adults. If SIM was transformed into the third university, then another SIM-like institution would need to be created from scratch, and this would be a total waste of time.
>
> (Leong, 2010)

It had become clear that it was quite difficult to graft something new onto an already successful institution offering part-time degree courses. Hence, it was believed that it would be better and easier to start a completely new research-intensive university (Tan, 2015).

SMU's first Chairman of the Board of Trustees, Ho Kwon Ping, is a well-known businessperson with strong views about university education. He is the founder and executive chairman of Banyan Tree Holdings Ltd. He was "untainted" as he did not come with any experience in running an academic institution. He was joined by a task force of academics from NUS and NTU, in particular Tan Chin Tiong and Tan Teck Meng from NUS and NTU respectively, and Tharman Shanmugaratnam, who later became Minister for Education, to review a suitable model for the university.

In 1999, SMU signed a five-year agreement with the Wharton School of the University of Pennsylvania to build the university, including curriculum design for the four-year undergraduate course, and collaborate on research between the two universities. The decision to partner with a top-tier university was based on the belief that it would be faster to build a university with a partner than to build it from scratch. The partnership with the Wharton School helped SMU to quickly establish itself by building on the reputation of Wharton. It was a utilitarian decision to help drive up the cohort participation rate and produce graduates of a different mould than those from NUS or NTU. The collaboration also aimed to produce creative entrepreneurs and visionary business leaders. Janice Bellace, then Deputy Dean of Wharton, who was involved in the initial discussions on the creation of SMU, became SMU's first President when it was inaugurated as a university (Singapore Infopedia, 2019b).

SMU introduced several innovations. It became the first university in Singapore to practice a holistic and comprehensive assessment to ascertain the students' readiness for college. It also became the first university to offer seminar-style classes at undergraduate level that focused on student participation, significant team-based project work and presenting arguments in class to develop students' "hard" critical and analytical skills coupled with "soft" presentation and leadership skills. These innovations were believed to help students to develop the skills, knowledge, and experience that are necessary for leading in a rapidly changing and dynamic world.

Additionally, SMU emphasised the need for international exposure through exchange programmes and work experience through internships to produce more "work-ready" students. The success of SMU in producing a differentiated type of graduates led to eventual changes in how business education is taught at NUS and NTU – especially with the increased focus on building student confidence and voicing abilities.

SMU incorporated multiple criteria in its admissions process as the university recognised that "grades are not everything" to produce graduates that are well-rounded. The pioneer faculty who were recruited to start SMU were those who were willing to take a risk and try a new style of interactive teaching. The location of SMU in the city centre was also seen as a factor that differentiated SMU from NUS and NTU. Being a business and management university, SMU is strategically located to be close to the central business district and the law courts.

Starting with a Business School, SMU quickly developed schools in Accountancy, Economics, Information Systems, Economics and Social Sciences. The School of Law was established later in 2007, following the acceptance of the recommendations of the Third Committee on the Supply of Lawyers when it was found that yearly an additional 140–150 legal professionals would be required from 2010 to 2015 to meet the needs of Singapore's legal sector.

Today, SMU is recognised by its peers as one of the fastest growing business-oriented institutions. Its Lee Kong Chian School of Business was ranked number 33 in the UT Dallas research rankings of Business Schools in 2020, and depending whether you consider INSEAD as Asian or not, it is number 2 or 3 in Asia (behind INSEAD and Hong Kong University of Science and Technology).

SINGAPORE UNIVERSITY OF TECHNOLOGY AND DESIGN

While the idea of a fourth university had been mooted since 2002, the real trigger to start a new university came about when the "Committee on the Expansion of the University Sector (CEUS)" (MOE, 2008), chaired by then Senior Minister of State for Education Lui Tuck Yew, ascertained a need to develop an inter-disciplinary university, particularly to provide polytechnic graduates an opportunity to advance their studies in Singapore rather than venture overseas. At that time, Singapore did not have the right system in place for polytechnic diploma holders to upgrade, as only a handful of them were able to progress locally to obtain their degrees. There was demand beyond what NUS, NTU, SMU and the "polytechnics and foreign specialised institutions (Poly-FSI) partnerships" could offer. It was envisaged that the expansion of the higher education sector to include a fourth university would cater to a wider spectrum of students with different backgrounds, abilities, talents and learning orientations. Along with the intent to increase the cohort participation rate from 25 to 30 percent, CEUS recommended that 40 percent more places should be allocated to polytechnic diploma holders.

Given the acceleration towards a new economy that was knowledge-driven and centred on innovation, and which should take advantage of globalisation, the plan for the fourth university was modified to produce even more highly skilled workers at both graduate and postgraduate levels focusing on science and technology. In order to produce highly adaptable and resilient graduates, it was recognised that university education had to be cross-disciplinary in addition to inculcating specialised knowledge and skills in the key disciplines. It had to be different from the traditional engineering or science. The focus was to give students extensive real-world experience to better equip them with the knowledge and attributes required to make an immediate impact in the workplace. Inter-disciplinary learning was to be achieved through a variety of means including coursework and projects, structured internships and other programmes organised in collaboration with the industry. The new university would also equip students with entrepreneurial skills and inculcate a spirit of creativity and innovation to enable them to better grasp opportunities and create value in a fast-changing world. Students would be exposed to the importance of superior design, sound engineering and a savvy business and marketing plan in the development of new products or services.

The CEUS proposed that the new university would initially offer three disciplines:

- Design and Architecture;
- Engineering and Applied Sciences; and
- Business and Information Technology.

Prime Minister Lee Hsien Loong announced in 2010 (Lee, 2010):

> The Singapore University of Technology and Design will provide something different from the existing institutions – a very high quality education, not just an academic education, but also one, which is going to stimulate students to go beyond the book knowledge, to apply it to solving problems. It will teach students to be creative, not just in the technology and the design part, but also to be creative in bringing ideas out of the academic environment into the real world, into the business arena and into the real economy.

SUTD was officially inaugurated by Dr Tony Tan, then President of Singapore, on 7 May 2012 and it became Singapore's fourth autonomous university (History SG, 2019b). The primary aim of the university was and still is to inspire and motivate a new generation of innovative entrepreneurs with the potential to make significant breakthroughs in Singapore's architecture, engineering, technology, design and software industries. Taught in small-sized classrooms, SUTD's curriculum embraces a blend of teaching methods and approaches, and inculcates an opposable mind and a design thinking mentality to enable students to develop creative, human-centric and innovative technology solutions for Singapore. Another interesting aspect of SUTD is its focus on technology innovation, "Big-D" (Big-Design) and Humanities. The university also focuses on open-ended problem solving and active learning by providing hands-on experience where students are required to build prototypes to test their ideas and concepts.

Like SMU, SUTD was originally set up in collaboration with a partner from the United States, the Massachusetts Institute of Technology (MIT), to build an innovative curriculum that combined Technology, Design and Humanities. Soon, this became a three-way collaboration between SUTD, MIT and Zhejiang University as it was believed that the "syncretic fusion of East and West" would be useful to position the university for the 21st century in this globalised world. Zhejiang University is in Jiangsu province, a place known for promoting entrepreneurial activities – it is also where companies like Alibaba and thousands of technology start-ups are based. In recent years Zhejiang University has been ramping up its research capability, e.g., in the areas of automobile, search algorithms, visual or picture search algorithms, etc. The collaboration with Zhejiang University includes research, teaching, internships in Chinese companies and student exchanges. Up to 100 students from SUTD can be sent to Zhejiang per year. The collaboration with Zhejiang University saw the university helping to develop and teach courses aimed at giving students perspectives on Chinese entrepreneurial culture and urban planning, as well as architectural and product design.

MIT helped to develop SUTD's curriculum and research programmes, and created an International Design Centre that would serve as an incubator for design research and experimentation. At one time, there were up to 100 MIT faculty members helping SUTD to develop courses that are modelled after MIT with very high rigour, technology intensive yet combining design and humanities. SUTD is also leading in driving gender diversity in engineering education with 40 percent female students.

While it is difficult to judge the success of a university that has been operating for slightly more than 10 years, there are some early indications of its quality in education and research. In 2018, SUTD was the most cited university by international experts as an emerging leader in engineering education (Graham, 2018). Almost all SUTD's fresh graduates were employed within six months of completing their final examinations (Ang, 2019).

SINGAPORE INSTITUTE OF TECHNOLOGY

Unlike what had happened in the United Kingdom and Hong Kong, the Singapore Government resisted upgrading all the five polytechnics to universities. In so doing, the government ensured that the less academically inclined could have the opportunity to learn the technical skills needed for its economic system. When it was found that 40 to 50 percent of polytechnic diploma holders moved on to pursue degree programmes within five years of their graduation (MOE, 2009a), the government decided to establish the Singapore Institute of Technology (SIT). This institution gives polytechnic upgraders both "a bridge and a ladder" to meet their aspirations for obtaining degrees. This path of education allows polytechnic diploma holders to continue their specialisation at a degree level, instead of having to switch to a more general academic track in a comprehensive or a research-intensive university.

Before SIT was established, there were already three subsidised pathways for polytechnic diploma holders. They could upgrade themselves by enrolling in (1) NUS, NTU, SMU or SUTD; (2) UniSIM; or (3) Polytechnic-Foreign Specialised Institutions (Poly-FSI). However, these subsidised options did not quite meet the needs of these students. These options did not consider the time required to obtain the degree nor their learning aptitude. Studying in NUS, NTU, SMU or SUTD would require another three or four years of study. The offerings at UniSIM were limited mainly to part-time courses and business courses. The Poly-FSI degree programmes remained very niche, catering only to a small group of about 200 polytechnic upgraders. The polytechnic students were also actively pursued by many reputable universities in Australia and the United Kingdom (MOE, 2009a). Other polytechnic upgraders went to private education providers like the Kaplan Higher Education Academy, SIM Global Education, the Management Development Institute of Singapore, or some of the Global Schoolhouse institutions.

To cater for this insatiable demand for the polytechnic upgraders, SIT became the first autonomous university of applied learning in Singapore. Located in each of the five polytechnics, SIT started by offering joint degrees in partnership with the overseas Poly-FSIs. This enabled polytechnic upgraders to obtain degrees in a much shorter time. SIT also offered traditional degree courses that were offered by the foreign institutions. After becoming an autonomous university, SIT started offering its own programmes and conferring its own degrees.

A key change that SIT brought to the table was the establishment of the centralised administrative unit. Rather than have each polytechnic to coordinate with their Poly-FSI partners, SIT took over this function to enhance its negotiation power while minimising the risks of partners pulling out. The Poly-FSI partners that were not committed long-term or who did not share the vision of SIT were quickly terminated. The government also introduced financial incentives to attract and recruit top Poly-FSI partners to invest and commit long-term to Singapore. These incentives helped SIT to roll out courses expediently; for example, the nursing programme with Massey University was launched in less than one year.

Today, SIT's programmes focus on five clusters including Engineering, Chemical Engineering and Food Technology, Infocomm Technology, Health and Social Sciences, and Design and Specialised Businesses (SIT, 2009). These programmes give SIT students an edge because they build critical technical skills that are needed by the country – skills such as railway maintenance, building maintenance and aircraft maintenance. These skills are also not addressed by the other higher education institutions.

There is a key distinction differentiating the degrees offered by SIT from its overseas partners. The unique distinction of SIT degree programmes lies in the Integrated Work Study Programme (IWSP). Unlike the typical internship that is offered by the other universities, this work-study programme helps SIT students to apply their studies and immerse themselves at work, thus gaining substantial work experience while pursuing their degrees, both within Singapore and overseas. The IWSP is similar to what is being offered at the Rensselaer Polytechnic Institute (RPI) in the United States where academic credit is provided for structured job experience.

Students pursuing joint or overseas university undergraduate programmes have to take a compulsory Overseas Immersion Programme module in their curriculum which allows students to visit the home campus of the overseas partner. Similarly, this option is given to students of the FSI home campus to come to Singapore for exchange.

To give equal opportunities to the polytechnic students, the government increased the number of places equally between them and the junior college students. In so doing, the government was able to create a system of "ladders and bridges" for young citizens to pursue higher education.

Unlike the four other universities, there is no tenure system at SIT. The faculty members of the different disciplines and ranks are seated together in open offices to encourage collaboration and drive innovation in how courses are developed and taught.

Currently, SIT's campuses are spread out and co-located on the campuses of the five polytechnics. However by 2023, SIT will have its central campus located in the Punggol Digital District. Punggol was strategically chosen as the site for SIT because it is a part of a grand plan to create a thriving hub in the north east of Singapore combining an education hub, a clustering of industries and a business hub that is digitally linked, and a residential hub. A key organisation that is engaged in furthering the Smart Nation initiative, JTC is already based there (Smart Nation and Digital Government Office, 2019). With SIT relocating to Punggol and having its campus in JTC's business park, the government hopes to facilitate greater collaboration between industry and academia through the cross-fertilisation of ideas and knowledge among students, academics and industry professionals. It is hoped that the new technological or business ideas conceived in SIT could be prototyped, tested and adopted by businesses in Punggol Digital District, thus contributing to a higher rate of commercialisation success.

SINGAPORE UNIVERSITY OF SOCIAL SCIENCES

The origin of Singapore University of Social Sciences (SUSS) can be traced to the Singapore Institute of Management (SIM). When SIM started, it was the only private institution for higher education in Singapore. One of SIM's first partners was the Open University in the United Kingdom. This partnership started in 1992 when SIM was asked by the Ministry of Education to run the Open University Degree Programme (OUDP). By 1994, SIM started offering courses leading to Bachelor of Science in Mathematics, Bachelor of Science in Computer Science, and Bachelor of Arts in English Language and Literature degrees (Singapore Infopedia, 2019c).

SIM addressed a demand from people in their late 20s and early 30s, of whom many had polytechnic diplomas, to upgrade themselves to obtain a degree on a part-time basis. This option did not require them to disrupt their careers, and provided a choice and an alternative pathway for adult learners.

Thus, it can be argued that it was a forerunner in providing continuing education for working adults in Singapore.

In 2005, SIM was restructured into two entities. One entity continued to offer degree programmes in partnership with overseas universities. This entity was subsequently renamed SIM Global Education or SIM GE. The other entity, SIM University or UniSIM for short, was granted university status by the Ministry of Education. By 2006, UniSIM became Singapore's first private university to award its own degrees.

In 2017, UniSIM was revamped into SUSS and it became Singapore's sixth autonomous university, offering both full-time and part-time degree programmes. This university adopted Social Sciences in its name because it was believed that Social Sciences were important in every discipline and in the education of every student. While the former UniSIM differentiated itself by offering degree programmes for adult learners, by 2019, SUSS offered nine full-time degree courses in Accountancy, Finance, Marketing, Human Resource Management, Early Childhood Management, Social Work, Business Analytics, Supply Chain Management, and Public Safety and Security to give young Singaporeans another pathway towards obtaining their degrees (SUSS, n.d. m).

SUSS offers students a high level of flexibility in terms of the time required to complete their degrees. Many if not most classes are held in the evenings. Students need not interrupt their careers and can progress as fast or as slow as they would like to complete their courses. Another difference of SUSS is that both full-time and part-time students are required to take core modules together. These core modules form the foundation in Applied Humanities and Social Sciences, and teach students skills in critical thinking and reasoning, inquiry and impact, and storytelling and story-making. Having full-time and part-time students interact and work on projects together serves three purposes. One, it helps the full-time students to build their networks; two, it helps the students to build their teamwork and collaboration skills; and three, this way of learning mimics the workplace. Like SIT, the full-time SUSS students are also required to pursue work attachments.

Despite becoming an autonomous university, SUSS' operations for running the university have remained relatively unchanged as it already had strong and efficient governance systems, having operated as a private university since the mid-2000s.

CONCLUSION

In this chapter, we described how the system for higher education was adjusted to support the transition of Singapore from a production and assembly economy into a knowledge economy. A knowledge economy requires many more knowledge workers, thus, the cohort participation rate at the universities had to be increased significantly. While the cohort participation rate could be achieved by growing the two comprehensive universities, Singapore's leaders realised that there was a need for diversity to cater to the distinct needs and learning aptitudes of young Singapore citizens. Therefore, we saw the creation of a portfolio of six quite distinct institutions. We described briefly their creation and development during the period 1995–2020.

In the coming section, we will analyse what we see as the five most important success factors in the development of the university system as a whole: (1) the development of a system that is fit for purpose; (2) significant investment in R&D; (3) the autonomous university as a good system of governance; (4) active learning from overseas partners; and (5) flexibility in implementation. The emphasis of our analysis is on the system of higher education. It is not our intention to gauge the success of each individual institution.

NOTES

1 This refers to expenditure for universities only. The figures here exclude expenditure for the National Institutes of Education (NIEs), polytechnics and Institutes of Technical Education (ITEs).
2 The selective descriptions of the six universities that follow are based on desk research, interviews with the current and former leadership of the universities and representatives of the MOE, but the resulting descriptions are solely our interpretations.

BIBLIOGRAPHY

Ang, J. (2019). Higher starting pay, employment rates for SUTD fresh graduates in 2018: Survey. *The Straits Times*, 26 March. [Online] Available at: www.strait-stimes.com/singapore/education/higher-starting-pay-employment-rates-for-fresh-graduates-from-sutd-in-2018 (Accessed: 21 March 2020).

Chia, S. Y. (2014). *Singapore: Towards A Knowledge-Based Economy*. [Online] Available at: www.nomurafoundation.or.jp/en/wordpress/wp-content/uploads/2014/09/20000127-28_Siow-Yue_Chia.pdf (Accessed: 20 January 2020).

Economic Committee (1986). *The Singapore Economy: New Directions*. Singapore: Ministry of Trade and Industry.

Economic Planning Committee (1991). *The Strategic Economic Plan: Towards a Developed Nation*. Singapore: Ministry of Trade and Industry.

Goh, C. T. (1996). *Speech by Prime Minister Goh Chok Tong* at the National University of Singapore (NUS) Alumni Day and Exhibition at NUS Multi-purpose Hall, 21 September. [Online] Available at: www.nas.gov.sg/archivesonline/data/pdfdoc/19960921_0001.pdf (Accessed: 15 January 2020).

Graham, R. (2018). *The Global State of the Art in Engineering Education*. Massachusetts Institute of Technology. [Online] Available at: http://neet.mit.edu/wp-content/

uploads/2018/03/MIT_NEET_GlobalStateEngineeringEducation2018.pdf (Accessed: 7 February 2020).

History SG (2019a). *Singapore Experiences its First Post-Independence Recession: 1985.* [Online] Available at: http://eresources.nlb.gov.sg/history/events/9f9489cf-5432-4797-bf66-fd1b3bab7a2b (Accessed: 15 January 2020).

History SG (2019b). *Singapore University of Technology and Design is Inaugurated: 7 May 2012.* [Online] Available at: http://eresources.nlb.gov.sg/history/events/383d0744-3fac-43ee-9bd6-fbcc34f97e52 (Accessed: 15 November 2019).

Lee, H. L. (2010). *Prime Minister of Singapore – Mr Lee Hsien Loong,* 11 March. [Video] [Online] Available at: www.youtube.com/watch?v=8tEfk8_E9Dk (Accessed: 15 November 2019).

Leong, K. S. (2010). *Oral History Interview.* Li Ka Shing Library. SMU. 13 July.

Lim, C. P. (2013). *The Evolution of Universities – A Singaporean Story* at the Times Higher Education World Academic Summit, Nanyang Technological University, 3 October. [Online] Available at: www.a-star.edu.sg/News-and-Events/News/Speeches/ID/1888 (Accessed: 15 November 2019).

Marginson, S. (2009). *Global Perspectives and Strategies of Asia-Pacific Research Universities.* WCU-3, 2–4 November. [Online] Available at: www.shanghairanking.com/wcu/wcu3/03%20Marginson%20Global%20perspectives%20and%20strategies%20of%20Asia-Pacific%20research%20universities.pdf (Accessed: 15 January 2020).

Ministry of Education (2008). *Report of the Committee on the Expansion of the University Sector: Greater Choice, More Room to Excel.* Singapore: Ministry of Education.

Ministry of Education (2009a). *Report of Taskforce on Expanding Upgrading Opportunities for Polytechnic Graduates.* Singapore: Ministry of Education.

Ministry of Education (2009b). *Polytechnic Foreign Specialised Institutions (Poly-FSI) Initiative Factsheet.* [Online] Available at: https://web.archive.org/web/20100215021903/www.moe.gov.sg/media/press/files/2009/05/tertiary-landscape-annex-a.pdf (Accessed: 21 March 2020).

NUS (n.d.). *Modular System.* [Online] Available at: www.nus.edu.sg/registrar/education-at-nus/modular-system.html (Accessed: 20 November 2020).

Seong, D. N. F., & Foo, N. G. (2008). Strategic management of educational development in Singapore (1965–2005). In S. K. Lee (ed.). *Toward a Better Future: Education and Training for Economic Development in Singapore since 1965.* Washington, DC: World Bank, National Institute of Education. p. 39–68.

Sharma, Y. (2017). The story of how Singapore became a research nation. *University World News,* 15 December. [Online] Available at: www.universityworldnews.com/post.php?story=20171215122350628 (Accessed: 15 January 2020).

Shih, C. F. (2000). *NUS — A Global Knowledge Enterprise,* Inaugural Address by the Vice-Chancellor of the National University of Singapore, 1 June.

Singapore Infopedia (2019a). *Singapore Institute of Management.* [Online] Available at: http://eresources.nlb.gov.sg/infopedia/articles/SIP_2016-11-01_140500.html (Accessed: 17 November 2019).

Singapore Infopedia (2019b). *Singapore Management University.* [Online] Available at: http://eresources.nlb.gov.sg/infopedia/articles/SIP_500_2005-01-19.html (Accessed: 17 November 2019).

Singapore Infopedia (2019c). *Open University Degree Programme.* [Online] Available at: https://eresources.nlb.gov.sg/infopedia/articles/SIP_92_2004-12-30.html (Accessed: 7 February 2020).

Singapore Institute of Technology (2019). *Undergraduate Programmes*. [Online] Available at: www.singaporetech.edu.sg/undergraduate-programmes (Accessed: 15 November 2019).

Singapore University of Social Sciences (n.d.). *9 Programme(s)*. [Online] Available at: www.suss.edu.sg/programme-finder?page=1&area=all&schools=all&t=progra mmes&types=dft&sort=date (Accessed: 7 February 2020).

Smart Nation and Digital Government Office (2019). *Punggol District*. [Online] Available at: www.smartnation.sg/what-is-smart-nation/initiatives/Startups-and-Businesses/punggol-digital-district (Accessed: 21 January 2020).

Tan, K. Y. (2015). *Daringly Different: The Making of the Singapore Management University*. Singapore: Singapore Management University.

Tan, T. (2011). *Oral History Interview with Tony Tan Keng Yam: Conceptualising SMU*, Institutional Knowledge at Singapore Management University, 20 May. [Online] Available at: https://ink.library.smu.edu.sg/cgi/viewcontent.cgi?article=1012& context=smu_oh (Accessed: September 20, 2019).

Wong, P. K., Ho, Y. P., & Singh, A. (2007). Towards an entrepreneurial university model to support knowledge based economic development: The case of the National University of Singapore. *World Development*, 35(6), p. 941–958.

PART II

THE MAIN DRIVERS OF SUCCESS

Chapter 3

Fit for purpose

A main driver for the development of Singapore's university system was that it had to be "fit for purpose". From the early days of the Republic, the Singapore Government realised that people were its most important if not the only asset, and education was essential to building a successful nation. The universities have responded to the changing needs of the society and the economy, and have played a role in transforming the country from an industrial economy into a knowledge-based economy – and now an innovation-led economy. Significant investment in R&D from the late 1990s also contributed to the transformation of the economy. At the same time, the universities had to respond to the aspirations of young Singaporeans to pursue their interests and develop their capabilities.

INTRODUCTION

As suggested in the previous section, the first factor that may explain the success of the Singapore higher education system is that it is "fit for purpose" and well-integrated into the overall education system. The Singapore higher education system is a system that was both inspired by the experience and innovations in other countries as observed during the many study visits the decision-makers made to Europe, the United States and Australia, and driven by the best-in-class partnerships that the universities developed.

Fundamentally, Singapore's higher education system is pragmatic. It is intertwined with manpower planning and "fit for purpose" on two levels. The system was built and constantly tweaked to deliver the most effective impact for the nation and society. First, as we have described in the previous chapter, it was and is developed in response to the specific and evolving needs of building a robust Singapore economy. In other words, the system of higher education was core to nation building and the economic development of the country. Second, its structure and composition changed dynamically in line with the changing needs and aspirations of the society. As explained by Tharman Shanmugaratnam, when he was Minister for Education, the purpose of universities (Lim, 2013):

> is to ensure that they continue to contribute to the well-being of Singapore and its people, not just economically by producing graduate manpower to support the economy, but also in propelling Singapore up the curve of knowledge creation through a concerted investment in R&D capabilities.

It is important to note that the universities depended on market signals from the employers who hire their graduates, students and parents who choose their degree programmes, and the faculty in the various specialisations. During the early 1990s, there was an increasing demand for information technology and computer courses. By the late 1990s, there was a shift towards biotechnology. Then there was a shift towards banking and finance in the early 2000s. Today, the focus is on data analytics, artificial intelligence and robotics. The underlying assumption in developing the higher education sector was and is to align with the manpower requirements of the society.

As globalisation and digital disruption brought on new and increasingly complex problems, the leaders of Singapore realised that innovation would be critical for Singapore's continued economic growth – which was why the focus on research excellence at the universities gained importance from 2000 onwards. As we will discuss in the next chapter, since 1990, significant funding had already been directed towards building research capacity outside of the universities at the National Science and Technology Board (NSTB), which subsequently became the Agency for Science, Technology and Research (A*STAR). From the late 1990s onwards, research capabilities were developed at NUS, NTU and later on at SMU and SUTD. As a small nation, Singapore did not have all the talent necessary to develop these research capabilities. This led many universities to pursue an open talent strategy, attracting researchers from all over the world. They also constantly calibrated their system with the trends in higher education overseas.

The higher education system also responded to the changing aspirations of Singapore citizens to pursue the education of their choice. It catered to the variegated needs of the population for students with different abilities and aptitudes to pursue higher education at their own pace and chosen path of progression. This explains partially the diversity in the system – to provide a variety of choices other than Engineering, Technology and Sciences to young Singaporeans.

FOUNDATIONAL THINKING

The development of the universities goes back to the core thinking about the role and importance of education at the foundation of the country. When Singapore became an independent country in 1965, it had no natural resources or advantages, except for its location. As we have already mentioned, Prime Minister Lee Kuan Yew (PM Lee) was often quoted as having said that the strategy to develop Singapore was "to develop Singapore's only available natural resource: its people".

More specifically, in a speech he delivered in February 1966 (Lee, 1966), barely six months after Singapore's independence, at a seminar on the role of universities in economic and social development at the University of Singapore, PM Lee articulated his vision and mission for a university:

> It is first, to produce the teachers, the administrators, the men to fill the professions – your accountants, your architects, your lawyers, your techno- crats, just the people to do jobs in a modern civilised community. And next and even more important, it is to lead thinking – informed thinking – into the problems the nation faces.

Even in those early days, he expected the universities to pursue thought leadership beyond the teaching of the elite. In fact, he argued that if the role of the universities was for teaching and education only, it would prob- ably be more cost effective for Singapore

> to select men and pay for sending them abroad to universities elsewhere, established universities, to give them knowledge and skills so that they come back and fulfil a function. But for it to be a self-creative, a self-generating process, you must have your own university.

In the same speech, he raised two other important requirements for a university in Singapore to succeed. The first requirement was that educa- tion of an elite should not be limited to the tertiary stage of education; specifically, he argued that high quality education in science and technology starts in the secondary schools. In other words, a good system of higher education needs to be embedded in a comprehensive end-to-end system of education in general. The second requirement for a university was for it to benefit from being close to practice and the industry. He favoured the idea of swapping jobs and encouraging job fluidity between an academic environment and active work in economic development, industrial research, or engagement in the implementation of industrial plans. While we have not been able to see many examples of immersion of academics in the corporate world and vice versa, today, we would probably translate this vision of Lee Kuan Yew into a plea for close collaboration between the universities and the industry.

A last quote from the speech makes it clear what he expected from a "national" university and what he meant by "fit for purpose":

> I like to remind my nationalists that having a national university means more than just having nationals manning that university. It means an organism which responds to the needs and the challenges of our time in this particular part of the world and in this society.

RESPONDING TO THE NEEDS OF SOCIETY

From a pragmatic standpoint, the objective of education in general, and higher education in particular, was often seen as the creation of a workforce that was needed by the economy and society. In simplistic terms, you would expect the Ministry of Manpower to determine what kind of workforce Singapore would be needed in the coming decade. This information would then be shared with the Ministry of Education to determine which disciplines should be taught and how many students should be admitted in each of these disciplines. In reality, of course, it would be more complex. Accurate forecasting of the real needs in manpower is both a science and an art. Forecasting these needs would become more and more difficult with the increasing sophistication of the economy and society, and with the evolving expectations of the potential students who might want to pursue their studies based on their interests, in fields of specialisation other than the disciplines that were projected by the ministries. In conducting this forecasting exercise, it became increasingly clear that the multiple needs of society were constantly evolving. To stay relevant to meeting societal needs, the higher education system had to be constantly adjusted to match these needs.

What are some of these changes? First, Singapore has become a much more sophisticated society. This is well-illustrated with the evolution of the GDP per capita. In Table 3.1, you will see the evolution of GDP per capita in US dollars at its value in 2010. Over the 50 years since independence in 1965, GDP per capita in nominal terms has multiplied by more than 13 times. Singapore has evolved economically from a third world country to a first world country, with all the ensuing changes in societal demands such as for leisure, health services, cultural services and education. These demands are vastly different in a first world country compared to those in a third world country.

Table 3.1 *Evolution of nominal GDP per capita in 2010 US$ in Singapore*

Year	Nominal GDP/capita in US$
1965	4,087
1975	9,673
1985	16,632
1995	29,473
2005	40,498
2015	53,883

Source: World Bank

At the same time, the population of Singapore has been ageing rapidly in the last few decades and birth rates have fallen precipitously from 1.83 per woman in 1990 to 1.19 in 2019 (Darke, 2019; World Development Indicators, 2020) (Figure 3.1). All these factors have a significant impact on the needs of society and the type of workers and professionals Singapore needs in the future.

This is clearly illustrated in Table 3.2 and Table 3.3 where we provide a simple overview of the composition of the workforce per type of occupation and per sector. Forty years ago, the economic strategy was to attract multi-national companies (MNCs) to Singapore as foreign direct investments to set up factories and provide jobs. Consequently, the education aimed to

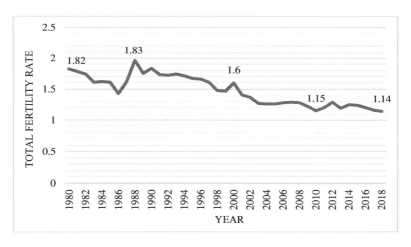

Figure 3.1 *Total fertility rate 1980–2018*

Source: Department of Statistics Singapore, www.singstat.gov.sg/modules/infographics/total-fertility-rate

Table 3.2 *Composition of the Singapore workforce by type 1980–2018*

Occupation	1980	1990	1999	2009	2018
Legislative, senior officials and managers	6.3	8.6	12.4	15.6	14.6
Professionals	0	4.2	9.9	16.1	20.4
Associate professionals and technicians	11.7	11.5	18	20.3	21.8
Clerical support workers	13.8	13.1	14	12.7	10.8
Service and sales workers	14.6	13.8	13.1	11.2	12.1
Craftsmen, trades workers, plant and machine operators, cleaners, labourers, etc.	46.3	44.5	29.1	20.7	17.1
Others (including agriculture and fishery)	7.4	4.3	3.5	3.4	3.2

Source: Several Yearbooks of Statistics, Singapore

Table 3.3 Composition of the Singapore workforce by sector 1980–2018

Sectorial employment	1980	1990	1999	2009	2018
Manufacturing	30.1	29.1	21.0	15.7	10.4
Construction	6.6	6.7	6.9	6.1	4.7
Services				77.1	83.9
Wholesale and trade	21.3	22.0	21.8	14.6	16.0
Transportation and Storage	11.2	9.5	9.5	9.6	9.0
Accommodation and food services				6.7	6.1
Information and communications				5.0	4.2
Financial and insurance activities				6.5	8.9
Business services	0.0			13.0	15.8
Community, social and personal services	0.0			21.6	23.9
Others	23.1	20.6		1.1	1.0

Source: Several Yearbooks of Statistics, Singapore

give the young citizens the knowledge and skills demanded by these MNCs. In Table 3.2, you will see that the demand for well-educated employees has increased as the economy evolved to be more knowledge-driven. Between 1980 and 2018, the group of senior officials, managers, professionals, associate professionals and technicians has risen from about 18 percent of the workforce to close to 57 percent. At the same time, the group of craftsmen, trades workers, plant and machine operators, cleaners and labourers has declined from 46.3 percent to 17.1 percent. The sectors in which these people were employed have also shifted considerably (Table 3.3). In 1980, more than 30 percent of the workforce was employed in manufacturing. That percentage has dropped to 10 percent by 2018. The number of people employed in services moved from slightly more than half of the population in 1980 to 84 percent by 2018. This evolution towards a higher educated workforce employed in services required an expansion of the university system, and an adjustment of the portfolio of disciplines.

This was translated in a clear planning parameter used by the Ministry of Education (MOE): the cohort participation rate or CPR. Since the mid-1980s, this CPR number has been a guiding indicator for the MOE in the implementation of its policies for higher education. MOE's position is that

> any increase in the number of university places will have to be sustainable and supported by the economy. Increasing places too quickly can lead to an over-supply of university graduates, who would then either become unemployed or under-employed. This has been the experience in some countries which have gone for very high CPRs or expanded university places too rapidly. Besides the overall increase in places, the mix of these places also matters. There is a need to ensure close alignment between the distribution of places across course disciplines, and the manpower needs of the economy. This will ensure that our graduates enjoy good employment outcomes.
>
> (MOE, 2020)

Thus, it is no surprise that the new institutions that were described in Chapter 2 were set up to respond to these societal needs. When Singapore's economy moved towards professional services, in particular financial and related services, SMU was created. A more complex society may require liberal arts graduates; thus, the Yale-NUS liberal arts programme was created. Investment in research in life sciences and pharmaceuticals required more medical schools which led to the establishment of Duke-NUS and the Lee Kong Chian School of Medicine with Imperial College. More sophisticated manufacturing and innovation required design capabilities, which are characteristics of the courses offered by SUTD. With the aspiration of raising CPR to 40 percent, i.e., beyond the total number of graduates of junior colleges, SIT was created to adapt to the more applied orientation of the polytechnic graduates. SUSS was created for adult learners to receive an applied education in the social sciences and in disciplines that have a strong impact on human and community development.

An interesting point to note in the evolution of the Singapore higher education system is the management of the polytechnic institutions. One of the easy ways to achieve a higher CPR would have been to transform the polytechnics into applied universities, as seen in the evolution of these institutions in the United Kingdom and Hong Kong in the 1990s. As the education system in Singapore has its roots in the British system, there were proposals and suggestions to follow the same route. However, as we have already mentioned in the previous chapter, the Singapore leaders recognised the continuing need in a highly industrialised society for highly skilled technicians and professionals graduating from the Institutes of Technical Education (ITEs) and the polytechnics. Experience and hindsight showed that the upgrading of the polytechnic institutions to universities in the United Kingdom has not necessarily transformed all of them into top notch academic institutions. A detrimental consequence of this decision was the deterioration and availability of highly skilled technicians in that country. The decision made in Singapore was to preserve and improve the polytechnics and ITEs. In so doing, the government was able to create multiple pathways comprising "bridges and ladders" between the polytechnics, ITEs and the universities for the ambitious and capable diploma holders to pursue their studies at the university.

PROVIDING CHOICE AND FULFILLING ASPIRATIONS OF SINGAPOREANS

Increasing the CPR could have been achieved by enlarging the existing universities. While NUS and NTU already had big intakes on an annual basis, the experience in, for example, China suggests that any given country can still have top universities of high quality with more than 60,000 students.

Diseconomies of scale is a problem that large academic institutions can overcome despite some difficulties. However, going down this route would not have responded to the legitimate demand by young Singapore citizens for choice. Singapore also needed a diverse set of institutions that could cater for the differences in abilities and talents.

The relative autonomy that is given to the six universities in Singapore (which we will discuss in Chapter 5) has enabled each university to develop its own style and culture and pursue its own distinctive path of excellence. Even though NTU is close to being a comprehensive university, it is no clone of NUS, as its core strength is still in engineering. SMU is differentiated with its very interactive style of teaching, and SUTD with its project-based learning. SIT remains focused on producing graduates with applied skills that are needed by the society while SUSS remains focused on adult learning and continuing education. Each university has its own unique approach to pedagogy. An applicant who wants to study undergraduate business, law or computer science can find different schools and programmes that offer different unique selling propositions: with or without accommodation; in a large somewhat isolated self-contained campus or in the city centre; with an interactive style of teaching in smaller groups or through more self-study or project work.

It was also clear that the needs of the society did not require five or six comprehensive research-oriented institutions with an intake of equally bright students. Some potential students are more applied in orientation and are looking for an appropriate education. Others may want to work first and start their university education at a later stage in life, perhaps on a part-time basis. They can find programmes adapted to their specific needs at SIT or SUSS. The introduction of compulsory internships and attachments by SMU and later by the other universities, and the work-study programmes introduced on a large scale by SIT, are examples of how the higher education system adjusted itself to the aspirations of Singapore students to have a more applied approach to education that makes them job-ready from day one in the workplace.

Education also provided a means for social mobility. Singapore has done relatively well in comparison to other countries in terms of social mobility. In the United States, among those who are born to lower income parents, only 7.5 percent make it to the top 20 percent. The trend in the United Kingdom is not that different. In Singapore, 14 percent of those with lower income parents end up in the top 20 percent of the income bracket. Mobility for Singapore's lower income children is higher than in Denmark, and almost twice as high as in the United States. This shows that Singapore is a relatively fluid society (Shanmugaratnam, 2015). A 2018 occasional paper by the Ministry of Social and Family Development mentioned that Singapore's Gini coefficient, using OECD's methodology, declined from 0.388 in 2007 to 0.356 in 2017 after taxes and transfers. Education is one of the several reasons highlighted in the paper for the lower Gini coefficient. It also lists government schemes and policies in employment, home ownership and healthcare as other major reasons for this social mobility.

BUILDING RESEARCH CAPABILITIES

As we have mentioned in the second chapter, the higher education system provided education for the professionals and produced the middle management needed for society. An emerging country like Singapore in the 1960s and 1970s did not need strong research capabilities. Singapore's manufacturing industry often worked as a subcontractor for multinational companies that were headquartered in the United States, Japan or Europe, and was focused on low-end manufacturing and assembly. Local innovation was limited and not necessarily needed.

This changed significantly in the early 1990s when Singapore started to transform itself into a knowledge-driven economy. The Economic Development Board (EDB) indicated that to attract the whole value chain from research to distribution, NUS and NTU had to upgrade their research capabilities and groom graduates who could perform research and development (R&D). Originally, the investment in government sponsored research went through the National Science and Technology Board (NSTB), the predecessor of A*STAR, the primary mission of which was to advance the economy and improve lives by growing the knowledge-intensive biomedical research, scientific and engineering fields. Most of the work conducted by NSTB was rather applied and focused on collaboration with the industry. Towards the end of the 1990s, there was a growing realisation that more fundamental research was needed, especially in biomedical sciences. In particular, Philip Yeo, first as Chairman of EDB, and later as Chairman of A*STAR, strongly advocated for funding biomedical research. Under the leadership of Dr Tony Tan, then Deputy Prime Minister (DPM), Singapore decided to invest heavily in R&D at the universities. This was done under the auspices of the five-year plans for investment in R&D, which were consolidated in 2006 by the creation of the National Research Foundation (NRF) and the Research Innovation and Enterprise (RIE) plans. In Figure 3.2, we summarised the R&D investments in the period 1996–2014 by the respective governments in the region as a percentage of GDP. Like several other countries in the region, for example Korea and the People's Republic of China, Singapore upped its game in R&D during that period. But unlike some other countries, the bulk of the growth in government R&D spending moved toward the universities, which we will discuss in more detail in the next chapter.

Building domestic research capability through a research-intensive culture in the universities was an ambitious goal, especially when the focus

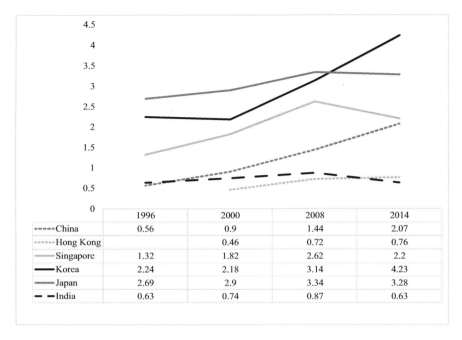

	1996	2000	2008	2014
••••••China	0.56	0.9	1.44	2.07
••••••Hong Kong		0.46	0.72	0.76
••••••Singapore	1.32	1.82	2.62	2.2
——Korea	2.24	2.18	3.14	4.23
••••••Japan	2.69	2.9	3.34	3.28
— —India	0.63	0.74	0.87	0.63

Figure 3.2 *Government expenditure on R&D 1996–2014 as a percent of GDP for selected countries in Asia*

Source: Compiled by author based on OECD statistics

of the universities was on teaching and the development of high quality undergraduate programmes. The promotion system that was in place also did not emphasise the importance of research. In order to level up research, the universities needed to establish research synergies and collaboration with globally positioned research institutions to emulate their success. The universities, especially NUS and NTU, were lacking professors, faculty and academic staff who were focused on conducting research. As we have briefly described in Chapter 2, this changed when Presidents Shih Choon Fung and Bertil Andersson were brought on board in NUS and NTU respectively. Not only did both presidents built an environment for research and changed the promotion and tenure system, both adopted an open talent policy. Andersson reached out actively to the world's best researchers to join NTU – which in a way, helped to set a benchmark and standard for global excellence of research there. Resources were allocated to attract academic staff who were among the best in their disciplines to build a culture of research excellence at the universities. Local academic staff were encouraged to model themselves on the foreign talent so that they could aspire to be the world's best. Academic staff were also encouraged to adopt an entrepreneurial mindset and develop strong links with the industry to commercialise the knowledge and drive innovation beyond the university environment.

HOLISTIC EDUCATION SYSTEM

While the focus of our book is on higher education and the universities, it is important to remember that higher education is a part of a larger system of education. Singapore's education system is a holistic one and managed under one ministry. In line with the important planning parameter CPR, the number of student intakes has been increasing progressively in all six universities. In Table 3.4, you will find the growth in intake from the 1960s until now.

As we have argued in the previous paragraphs, the universities are constantly challenged to educate graduates for today's and tomorrow's economy with new jobs and challenges that may not exist today. The education system as a whole incorporates multiple pathways that consist

Table 3.4 *University intake from 1980 to 2018*

Year	NUS	Nanyang University	NTU	SMU	SIT	SUTD	SUSS	Total
1960	532	651	–	–	–	–	–	1183
1970	1390	685	–	–	–	–	–	2075
1980	3002	–	–	–	–	–	–	3002
1990	5053	–	1875	–	–	–	–	6928
2000	6421	–	4506	305	–	–	–	11232
2009	6775	–	6719	1770	–	–	–	15264
2010	6568	–	6132	1686	523	–	–	14909
2011	6724	–	6177	1729	936	–	–	15566
2012	6733	–	5905	1930	1304	327	–	16199
2013	6892	–	6660	1924	1510	265	–	17251
2014	7108	–	6480	1912	1836	317	217	17870
2015	6935	–	6525	1944	2076	362	284	18126
2016	7011	–	6138	1961	2559	460	423	18552
2017	7121	–	5955	2004	2589	424	575	18668
2018	7856	–	6160	2161	2660	437	767	20041

Source: Education Statistics Digest 2019, MOE, www.moe.gov.sg/docs/default-source/document/publications/education-statistics-digest/esd_2019.pdf

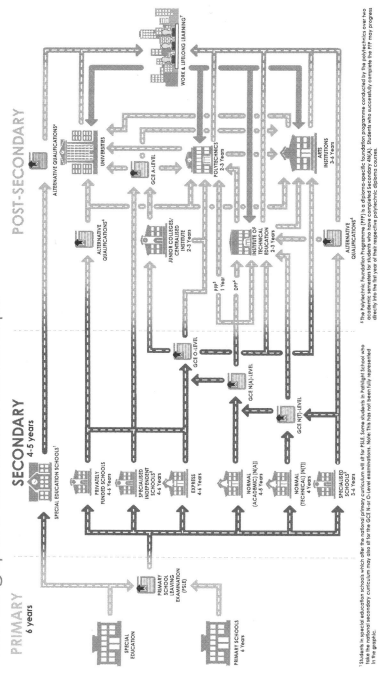

Figure 3.3 *Comprehensive landscape of the Singapore education system*

of bridges and ladders for every young Singaporean who completes primary school. As explained by the Ministry of Education (MOE, 2019):

> Singapore's education system aims to bring out the best in every child by enabling students to discover their talents, realise their full potential, and develop a passion for lifelong learning. We seek to nurture the whole child, and help them develop an enduring core of competencies, values and character, to thrive in the 21st century. Our multiple educational pathways cater to the different strengths, interests and learning styles of every student... our students also benefit from Applied Learning experiences, where they (1) learn by doing; (2) learn about the real world; and (3) learn for life.

Even as early as 11 years of age, the schools offer education and career guidance to help the students discover and recognise their interests and strengths, and choose the pathways that allow them to achieve their fullest potential. Figure 3.3 further illustrates the comprehensiveness of the Singapore education system. The striking and perhaps typical feature of this figure produced by the Ministry of Education is the ultimate goal of education – that is, preparing for "Work and Lifelong Learning". The education system as a whole and higher education in particular has a very utilitarian objective.

EVOLVING "FITNESS OF USE": EXTENDING EDUCATION INTO LIFELONG LEARNING

The universities have successfully proven that they address "fit for purpose" in producing graduates for the economy. But as explained by Prime Minister Lee Hsien Loong, there is a real challenge in how the universities can address "fit for purpose" for continuing education. He expanded on this issue at a ministerial forum at SUSS in 2019 (Prime Minister's Office, Singapore, 2019):

> We know what to do for the phase of pre-employment education: schools, colleges, universities, ITEs. These will be kept updated with courses changing as necessary and the teaching is improved. However, the challenge is in creating a system that is effective for adults in their 50s, 60s or even 70s who want to go back to school for a refresher or who want to pick up new skills. How do we run a course, run an education system which can meet their needs and suit their style of learning? It is not easy. It is not just a matter of money or running the courses. I must have people with the experience, and I must have a whole support system for them.

While SkillsFuture, a national movement to promote lifelong learning and continuous education was launched in 2015, it's still too early to determine its success. Continuous education and training have become core to the

Singapore education system – it is a way for Singaporeans to constantly upskill and remain competitive and prepare themselves for the globalised work environment. It is also a way for Singaporeans to learn about how to innovate in the way they work and enhance their productivity.

SkillsFuture encapsulates the impetus for Singapore to move towards an advanced economy and society, where individuals go beyond competence to attaining expertise and mastery of skills, motivated not just by current demands of their job but by a dedication to excellence and passion in their own areas of strength and interest. It embodies the spirit of lifelong learning, respect for skills in every job, and it celebrates the skills and growth of every individual, no matter their background, age or qualifications. We will cover the topic of continuing education and SkillsFuture in more detail in Chapter 9.

Since the increasing focus on continuing education, the universities have started to rise to this challenge. A range of short, industry-relevant courses are available at the six autonomous universities, five polytechnics and the ITEs. These short courses provide adult learners with a more flexible and bite-sized learning option to acquire skills to help them stay responsive to a changing workplace. Four out of the six universities, namely NUS, NTU, SIT and SUSS, offer SkillsFuture Work Study Degrees, which feature integrated institution-based learning with structured on-the-job training, in partnership with companies to co-develop and co-deliver these programmes.

Short industry-relevant courses have also been developed to meet the needs of adult learners to minimise disruption to work. Some of these courses lead to academic credentials including Graduate Certificates, Micro Master's and Master's courses. The universities are also expanding lifelong learning support for their alumni. One example is NUS's Lifelong Learners (L3) programme which aims to support its alumni for 20 years from the point of enrolment.

CONCLUSION

The first factor that contributes to the success of the system of higher education is no doubt the clarity of the objectives: building the nation, matching the needs of Singapore, and offering a variegated choice to young Singapore citizens. As you will read in Chapter 7, this objective was implemented in a very flexible way. But the overall vision was very clear. In the recent developments towards focusing more on continuing education, the basic tenets of education remain the same.

It is important to reiterate that the higher education system is not isolated from the rest of the education system. As shown in Figure 3.3, it is very well integrated with the whole system. The whole system is designed to be fit for use and beneficial for Singapore society.

BIBLIOGRAPHY

Darke, A. (2019). Number of babies born in Singapore falls to lowest in 8 years. *CNA*, 22 July. [Online] Available at: www.channelnewsasia.com/news/singapore/ number-of-babies-born-in-singapore-falls-to-lowest-in-8-years-11743722 (Accessed: 21 March 2020).

Department of Statistics (2019). *Total Fertility Rate.* [Online] Available at: www. singstat.gov.sg/modules/infographics/total-fertility-rate (Accessed: 21 November 2019).

Lee, K. Y. (1966). *Speech by the Prime Minister Mr Lee Kuan Yew* when he opened the seminar on "The role of universities in economic and social development", at the University of Singapore, 7 February. *National Archives.* [Online] Available at: www.nas.gov.sg/archivesonline/data/pdfdoc/lky19660207.pdf (Accessed: 21 March 2020).

Lim, C. P. (2013). *The Evolution of Universities – A Singaporean Story* at the Times Higher Education World Academic Summit, Nanyang Technological University, 3 October. [Online] Available at: www.a-star.edu.sg/News-and-Events/News/ Speeches/ID/1888 (Accessed: 15 November 2019).

Ministry of Education (2019). *Education Statistics Digest 2019.* Singapore: Ministry of Education. [Online] Available at: www.moe.gov.sg/docs/default-source/document/ publications/education-statistics-digest/esd_2019.pdf (Accessed: 2 December 2019).

Ministry of Education (2020). *Singapore University Landscape.* [Online] Available at: www.moe.gov.sg/news/committee-on-university-education-pathways-beyond-2015/singapore-university-landscape (Accessed: 24 August 2020).

Prime Minister's Office, Singapore. (2019). *PM Lee Hsien Loong speaking at the Singapore University of Social Sciences (SUSS) Ministerial Forum on 4 September,* 4 September. [Video] [Online] Available at: www.youtube.com/watch?v=81fo 9MZTZHg&list=PLqvAkd0-laMfGbPj9YtS2zPFiPd0SlRyq&index=1 (Accessed: 9 April 2021).

Shanmugaratnam, T. (2015). *The Economic Society of Singapore SG5*, Distinguished Lecture by Deputy Prime Minister and Minister for Finance Tharman Shan-mugaratnam. [Online] Available at: www.mof.gov.sg/Newsroom/Speeches/The-Economic-Society-of-Singapore-SG50-Distinguished-Lecture-by-Deputy-Prime-Minister-and-Minister-for-Finance-Tharman-Shanmugaratnam (Accessed: 2 December 2019).

World Development Indicators (2020). *World Bank.* [Online] Available at: http:// datatopics.worldbank.org/world-development-indicators/ (Accessed: 21 March 2020).

Chapter 4

Ample research funding for the universities

One of the key factors leading to the creation of a successful system of universities in Singapore has been the availability of ample resources for research at the universities. But it was more than money. The government wanted to engineer the creation of an innovation hub around the universities. Other than financial resources, the imperatives for building a strong research capability at the universities included having a strong community of experienced top researchers who were willing to contribute to the development of the R&D landscape in Singapore, and a drastic change in academic performance evaluation, promotion and tenure processes. A non-trivial factor in the success of this transformation was the careful management of public opinion to explain the relevance of R&D to the society.

The second factor that contributed significantly to the success of the university system in Singapore was the steep increase from the late 1990s onwards in the investment in applied and blue-sky research and development at NUS and NTU, and subsequently at the other two research-intensive universities, SMU and SUTD. Investing in science and technology (S&T) was not exclusive to Singapore. Across the world, governments believe that investing in S&T, especially in research, eventually leads to innovation and economic progress and development. Whilst there is no direct correlation between investment in research and innovation, or a linear path from research to commercially successful innovations, it is generally accepted that it provides the foundation for driving innovation and moving an economy up the value chain towards a knowledge-driven innovative economy.

Unlike many other governments in the world, Singapore has had a stable and an integrated governance system that focused on the long term since its independence. The current government is convinced that research plays an important role in building Singapore's future as a smart nation. As explained by then Deputy PM and Chairman of the National Research Foundation Teo Chee Hean (National Research Foundation, 2020a):

> R&D is an investment in our own future. It's an expression of belief in Singapore and Singapore's future. If we want to be a knowledge-based economy, which thrives on innovation and enterprise, we must build this knowledge base on which we can build the future of Singapore – then R&D is where we have to invest.

For the past 25 years, the investment in research has grown significantly. In the Research, Innovation and Enterprise (RIE) 2015 Plan, the Singapore Government committed S$16 billion to research, innovation and enterprise in 2011–2015, especially to building Singapore as a global research and development hub. The investment in research was increased to S$19 billion in the RIE 2020 Plan, covering the period 2016 to 2020 and for the period 2021–2025 the planned investment is about S$25 billion (National Research Foundation, 2020a).

According to the OECD, the top nations across the world invest over 2 percent of their GDP in R&D (OECD, 2019). The latest available data shows that R&D intensity (expenditure on R&D as a percentage of Gross Domestic Product or GERD) in OECD countries increased slightly from 2.34 percent in 2016 to 2.37 percent in 2017. The R&D intensity in Singapore has been around 2 percent except in 2008 when it peaked at 2.62 percent. Figure 4.1 shows the trends in the development of GERD in selected countries.

The potential importance of R&D was recognised early in the history of Singapore. Even in the 1960s, the ambition for Singapore to be a leader in S&T in Southeast Asia was expressed publicly. In 1966, at the opening of the Science Tower at the University of Singapore, then Prime Minister Lee Kuan Yew (PM Lee) said that "our population is the one thing we have which makes up for our lack of size and numbers, and it is of utmost importance that, in the field of science and technology we should lead the field in this part of the world" (Josey, 2012). In 1967, a Science Council was established through an Act of Parliament to nurture the human resources in the various aspects of R&D including training and establishing official relations with the other scientific organisations (Singapore Statutes Online, 2020). In 1968, Dr Toh Chin Chye was appointed Minister for Science and Technology.

As Ng et al. (2018) commented:

> the sixties were a time when S&T were seeded as a means to leapfrog [Singapore's] R&D capabilities. In the seventies, Singapore struggled with a lack of skilled labour and in the eighties, there was a conscious effort to attract foreign talent and investments to boost S&T capabilities as there has been difficulty in attracting Singaporeans into research. In 1981, the Ministry of Science and Technology was subsumed under the Ministry of Trade and Industry; clearly signalling that the primary role of R&D was applied and focused on economic development.

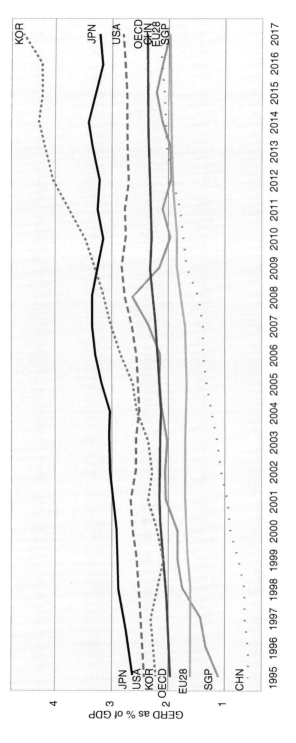

Figure 4.1 *R&D intensity in Singapore and selected countries*

Source: OECD (2019) Main Science and Technology Indicators, www.oecd.org/sti/msti.htm

In the 1980s, there were other initiatives to develop a better performing research environment. Sydney Brenner, the 1992 Nobel Prize winner in Physiology and Medicine, first visited Singapore in 1984 to advise the government on what it would take for the Republic to create a biotechnology industry. During this visit, Brenner met PM Lee and wrote a short proposal to set up a research institute in molecular and cell biology to train Singaporeans at the PhD level who could then provide the country with the necessary biotechnology infrastructure. When PM Lee remarked that Singapore was a nation of technicians and not scientists, it was believed that Dr Brenner candidly replied: "Prime Minister, if you don't do something like this, you will remain a nation of technicians" (Khew, 2015). He suggested the creation of Singapore's first biomedical research institute – the Institute of Molecular and Cell Biology. This became a crucial step for Singapore's foray into biomedical sciences. Brenner was associated with the institute since its inception in 1985 until his passing in 2019.

In 1990, the National Science and Technology Board (NSTB) was established to enhance Singapore's R&D capabilities and develop a strategy for S&T. In 1991, the NSTB developed a blueprint for transforming Singapore into a centre of excellence for S&T and its first five-year National Technology Plan. It was the pivotal point for a structured approach, with a significant investment in R&D, that led to the crystallisation of the S&T strategies. In the same year, a budget of S$2 billion was set aside for the National Technology Plan 1995. In 1995, the government announced the National Science & Technology Plan 2000 with a budget that doubled to S$4 billion. In Table 4.1, we summarised the planned investments for the successive five-year plans.

This massive research investment helped to attract top research talent to Singapore, through both the NSTB (which later became A*STAR) and the autonomous universities. New recruitment policies were shaped to

Table 4.1 Singapore's planned public R&D budget from 1991 until 2020

Technology plans	Planned public R&D budget in S$ billion
National Technology Plan 1991–1995	2.0
National Science and Technology Plan 1996–2000	4.0
Science and Technology 2005 Plan (2001–2005)	6.0
Science and technology 2010 Plan (2006–2010)	13.5
Research, Innovation and Enterprise 2015 Plan (2011–2015)	16.0
Research, Innovation and Enterprise 2020 Plan (2016–2020)	19.0

Source: National Research Foundation, www.nrf.gov.sg/research/rie2020

attract the top researchers from overseas. This helped to fill the void of Singaporean researchers. Within a short timeframe, Singapore was able to leap forward and position itself as one of the world's most attractive places to do research.

In January 2002, the NSTB was transformed into A*STAR or the Agency for Science, Technology and Research. Under the leadership of its first chairman, Philip Yeo, there was a relative shift of investments towards the biomedical sciences.

Singapore also built the physical infrastructure for scientific research; examples included the investment in One-North, where the Biopolis and Fusionopolis hubs for biomedical and physical sciences respectively were created. The intention of these hubs was to co-locate the researchers from the private and public sectors to further the progress of research.

THE SHIFT OF R&D SPENDING TOWARDS THE UNIVERSITIES

Until 2002, public R&D was to a large extent carried out in government laboratories, following to some extent the approach seen in southern Europe. Some of these research institutes were physically co-located within the universities. Professor Chong Tow Chong, now President of SUTD, commented about his early days as a faculty member:

> When I returned in 1989 from doing my PhD in the USA, I started as a full-time faculty member at the university. The main purpose was teaching, education. But starting from 1990 onwards, the government established NSTB, and for the first time, there was real money for research. That was when research became more visible, and you could see a stronger research orientation. I was quite lucky. My research required pretty expensive equipment. At that time, I needed S$1.2 to 1.5 million. I imagine that 5 years earlier, I would not have been able to get that kind of money, as there was no research funding available. But with the establishment of NSTB, there were suddenly resources available.

Until the end of the 1990s, the universities were largely teaching-oriented institutions even though they conducted some research. As former NUS President Tan Chorh Chuan said:

> Prior to the 2000s, research funding was pretty low with research concentrated in engineering. After 2000, there was a rising tide that lifted both A*STAR and the universities. When research spending was increased, there was a discussion whether the universities were the right place to locate some of the large research centres proposed. But we know that all thriving technology hubs are anchored by major universities. Universities attract an ecosystem. But most of these hubs have grown organically. Was it possible to engineer one? We were convinced it

was possible. That reflection led finally to embedding the Research Centres of Excellence at the universities.

According to the Department of Statistics Singapore, the spending on research at Institutes of Higher Learning was a mere 11.2 percent of the total spending on R&D in 2000, while research by the government and public research institutions was 26.8 percent of the total R&D spending. By 2017, this was adjusted: the higher education institutions represented 18.7 percent of the R&D spending while R&D spending from the government sector and public research institutions dropped to 21.6 percent. Put simply, higher education R&D spending rose at a faster proportional rate than government/public R&D spending, against the backdrop of a significant overall increase in R&D spending in Singapore. As seen in Table 4.2, the total spending on R&D had risen by a factor of slightly more than 3. Considering the rise in absolute spending from S$3,009 million in 2000 to S$9,086 million in 2017, the higher education sector saw an increase by a factor of more than 5 from 2000 to 2017. The rise in actual total spending was aligned with the increase of the total GDP of Singapore in current terms by a factor of 2.96. As mentioned in several of our interviews, specifically with Professor Bertil Andersson, Professor Tan Chorh Chuan and former Permanent Secretary Lim Chuan Poh, this rebalancing of relative research spending towards the higher education sector had been quite painless for the other government or public research institutions given the steep rise in total spending.

THE CREATION OF THE NATIONAL RESEARCH FOUNDATION

In Table 4.3, you can see that the rise in spending at the universities really took off after 2005. This rise coincided with the creation of the National Research Foundation (NRF), initially under the purview of then DPM Dr

Table 4.2 *Evolution of spending on R&D in S$ millions*

Actors in R&D	2000	2005	2010	2015	2017
Total	3,009	4,569	6,315	9,239	9,086
Private sector	1,866	3,018	3,774	5,512	5,423
Higher education	338	478	968	1,573	1,704
Government sector	424	443	672	1,028	997
Public research institutes	381	630	901	1,127	962

Source: Several Singapore Statistical Yearbooks

Table 4.3 Multiplier of investment in R&D per sector

Actors in R&D	2000–2005	2005–2010	2010–2015	2015–2017
Total	1.52	1.38	1.46	3.02
Private sector	1.62	1.25	1.46	2.91
Higher education	1.41	2.03	1.62	5.04
Government sector	1.04	1.52	1.53	2.35
Public research institutes	1.65	1.42	1.25	2.52

Source: Compilation by author based on Table 4.2

Tony Tan, who was NRF's inaugural Chairman when NRF was established in 2006. NRF's mission (National Research Foundation, 2020b) is:

- To develop policies, plans and strategies for research, innovation and enterprise;
- To fund initiatives that strengthen research and scientific capabilities, and achieve economic and national impact;
- To build up R&D capabilities and capacities through nurturing Singaporeans and attracting foreign researchers and scientists; and
- To coordinate the research agenda of different agencies to transform Singapore into a knowledge-intensive, innovative and entrepreneurial economy.

In 2007, NRF, in collaboration with the Ministry of Education, allocated a significant part of the available resources to establish the Research Centres of Excellence (RCE), to jumpstart top quality research that was conducted locally. This programme saw the creation of five research centres within NUS and NTU. The RCEs were expected to carry out world-class investigator-led research aligned with the long-term strategic interests of Singapore. At the same time, these RCEs aimed to attract, retain and support world-class academic investigators; enhance graduate education in the universities and train quality research manpower; and create new knowledge in the specific areas of focus of each centre. White papers and subsequently full proposals were submitted for peer review and evaluated by the MOE's Academic Research Council (ARC), comprising a committee of distinguished international scientists and academics. While this was a somewhat competitive process, it was clear that in a small country like Singapore, there wasn't a multitude of teams that could develop large research programmes.

The five RCEs that were established are:

- Earth Observatory of Singapore;
- Centre for Quantum Technologies;

- Cancer Science Institute of Singapore;
- Mechanobiology Institute, Singapore; and
- Singapore Centre for Environmental Life Sciences Engineering.

NRF also initiated a few other schemes and programmes, which we will not describe in this book. The details can be found on their website (see www.nrf.gov.sg/). That said, we would like to illustrate with one example how NRF has played an instrumental role in fostering the development of R&D capabilities at the universities, as well as coordinating with the other initiatives by the government and the public research institutions.

The programme that deserves special attention is CREATE or the "Campus for Research Excellence and Technological Enterprise". This is an international "collaboratory" that houses research centres set up by top universities. At CREATE, researchers from diverse disciplines and backgrounds work closely together to perform cutting-edge research in strategic areas of interest for translation into practical applications that can lead to positive economic and societal outcomes for Singapore. CREATE has been successful at recruitment at the institutional level. The universities and institutions with research centres at CREATE that collaborate with Singapore investigators are:

- Swiss Federal Institute of Technology, Zurich;
- Massachusetts Institute of Technology;
- Technical University of Munich;
- Hebrew University of Jerusalem;
- University of California, Berkeley;
- Shanghai Jiao Tong University;
- Cambridge University;
- University of Illinois at Urbana-Champaign; and
- French National Centre for Scientific Research.

While we will not discuss the successes and shortcomings of the individual programmes carried out at CREATE, a major contribution of CREATE was the fast development of a research community of top quality researchers with whom Singapore-based faculty could interact and collaborate. This research community was critical to the creation of a culture that promotes excellence in research and development.

DEVELOPING THE HUMAN CAPITAL FOR RESEARCH

Having the right leadership to develop policies and allocating financial resources for R&D was not sufficient to transform the universities into research powerhouses. The universities needed scientists and academic researchers who could use these resources in a productive way. The leadership at the two incumbent universities realised that two priorities had to be in place: (1) attracting top quality researchers and improving the performance of the local staff through better performance evaluation systems; and (2) putting in place an international benchmark to determine the quality of the research output.

Both NUS and NTU responded quickly to the rapidly increasing funding by recruiting top researchers from overseas. Bertil Andersson, former President of NTU said:

> ...when this big investment in research started, we at NTU were [...] hungry. We really went for all the grants and we recruited top level people from Caltech, MIT, Imperial College, Germany and Switzerland. So, in a sense, NTU changed from a mainly engineering college to a top research-oriented broader university. We recruited two types of people – the big whales, the superstars, and we recruited a lot of young investigators in Europe who competed for the European Research Council grants.

NRF helped in attracting foreign scientists to Singapore rapidly through two highly competitive programmes – the NRF Fellowship and NRF Investigatorship initiatives. The first programme provided very attractive fellowships for early career researchers to carry out independent research in Singapore over a five-year period. The second programme provided opportunities for established, innovative and active scientists and researchers in their mid-career to pursue ground-breaking, high-risk research. It was designed to support a small number of excellent Principal Investigators who had a track record of research achievements and who were leaders in their respective field(s) of research.

By the 2000s, when SMU was established, all three universities had the advantage of the Singapore brand to leverage and help them in attracting foreign talent. Asia had become attractive to many researchers in Europe and the United States. Singapore had also raised its profile as a country that was committed to excellent basic scientific research – its commitment to research measured in terms of research intensity was on par with the top countries in the OECD, e.g., the United States and Japan. As mentioned in some of the interviews, apart from the forces that attracted researchers to Asia and Singapore, there were perhaps some repulsive forces in the United States and Europe: during the Bush era, some research such as that related to stem-cells was perhaps not fully embraced in the United States; and in Europe, there was often a lack of sufficient funding for R&D at the universities.

The leadership at NUS and NTU recognised that a culture change was needed at their institutions. As we have mentioned in Chapter 2, both President Shih Choon Fung at NUS and President Su Guaning, and Bertil Andersson in his role as Provost at NTU, changed the performance evaluation and promotion system at their institutions. The performance and evaluation system at SMU, and later at SUTD, were less of an issue as they were greenfield universities. These two universities could implement the evaluation and promotion system adapted from the Wharton School of the University of Pennsylvania and MIT respectively.

Around 2000, President Shih initiated significant reforms to transform NUS from a university based on the British model to a university based on the US model. As SMU President Lily Kong, who was then at the geography department at NUS, mentioned:

> Some of the ideas he proposed, like the introduction of nine-month salaries, as is common in US universities, could not work in the Singapore context. But he brought in a group of professors from the US to help reform the promotion and tenure system that did shift the standards. That was really hard: the kinds of evaluations that were to take place, the standards that were expected – there was a step change. And people who could not meet those standards left academia. [...] He also experimented with different things. He tried to get people to work in groups, as a department rather than in silos, and he introduced the concept of a group performance bonus. [...] He very quickly turned it around and decided it was too difficult to implement [...]. But, for some departments, it worked quite well. In my own department, for example, we sat down and we thought for ourselves what would distinguish us as a discipline, as a department in Asia. What is it that we bring intellectually that would make a difference in our discipline?

Implementing this at NUS had significant consequences, and many academics left the university.

A few years later, a similar process was implemented at NTU. As Bertil Andersson mentioned (Sharma, 2017): "The first thing I did was to recruit top professors from all over the world, but I also terminated many professors' positions. It was a big transformation of the faculty". The NTU leadership discontinued around 25 percent of the faculty. It set up a strict evaluation system based on Stanford University's approach. Andersson stated in our conversation:

> As somebody said, we changed the engine of the car. [...]. The 25 percent that had to go were typically those who hadn't done any research for ten years and who were not particularly good teachers. We also succeeded in recruiting superstars to replace the 25 percent. [...] And I changed the culture: people started to know that if you are going to get tenure, you have to be able to do research, you have to be able to win grants. The top people we recruited led to a big reinvigoration of the place. In fact, the faculty that stayed had potential. They had done PhDs in foreign universities, but they had never been encouraged to do research. [...] We have been lucky. We recruited people who were top notch cadre.

Along with recruiting foreign talent and raising the internal standards for promotion and tenure, the university leadership also recognised that the benchmark for research performance had to be levelled up to international standards. In our conversation with the current NTU President Subra Suresh, he recalled that in the late 1990s, he was a member of a review panel to answer the question whether NUS and NTU had an Engineering department that was world-class. The review panel didn't think so then, and provided a number of recommendations including the revision of the performance evaluation system.

Professor Shih Choon Fong also invested in the internationalisation of NUS. For example, in 2000, he decided that NUS should join APRU, the Association of Pacific Rim Universities, a consortium of 50 leading research universities. APRU might have lost some of its relevance to NUS today, but in the words of one NUS faculty member: "it generated a vehicle for international collaboration in research. It was a platform to find collaborators".

RISKS OF THE TRANSFORMATION INTO RESEARCH-ORIENTED UNIVERSITIES

A first risk in emphasising research meant that teaching would be relegated to a less important activity. Some of our interviewees commented that the incumbent universities, in particular NUS, were not paying enough attention to teaching. In contrast, the newcomer SMU focused strongly on small-group teaching and emphasised new ways of learning. Instilling competition among the universities did work, and the incumbent universities quickly realised that they had to keep up with the quality of the teaching and learning environment through which SMU had been able to differentiate itself quickly. Consequently, this led to the building of University Town at NUS and initiatives like the Hive at NTU. In today's environment, all the universities realise that they need to push the research agenda, as well as pay attention to the quality of the education they offer.

A second risk was centred on the Singaporeans' mindset. Singapore citizens might not understand the large investment of taxpayers' money in research and might wonder about the need for recruiting large numbers of foreign talent. That said, Singapore has had a longstanding tradition of bringing in foreign specialists where necessary. In a speech to NUS staff at the time of the merger with NTU in 1980, PM Lee Kuan Yew said:

> In a ministry, some sensitive work needs to be done by Singaporeans; in a university, it does not matter what colour of skin the teacher has: white, black, yellow, brown or mixed, they are all important. The importance is whether they are able and enthusiastic. Can they engage the students' interest?
>
> (Lee, 2003)

There were some rumblings amongst the wider population and some negative comments were made about the foreigners holding the top positions at the universities – I personally have experienced this when I became President of SMU. Overall, these comments were handled well by the government, particularly in ensuring that there were sufficient places at the universities to respond to the aspirations of Singapore citizens. By 2010, about 60 percent of the active research faculty at the main universities had foreign passports.

The real problem was not so much that foreign researchers had an advantage, but that there were insufficient numbers of Singapore citizens who opted for an academic career. To overcome the relative dearth of Singapore citizens among the academic staff, at least two programmes were launched. One was a set of prestigious and generous scholarships developed collaboratively between the Ministry of Education and the universities. These scholarships aim to attract and encourage talented young Singaporeans to embark on an academic career by providing financial support for an overseas PhD or terminal degree programme, as well as academic guidance and mentorship. The scholarships were made available to the applicants who had just completed their undergraduate studies, or had completed a Bachelor's degree or a Master's programme and had worked for several years. They were also offered to those who were enrolled in a PhD programme overseas. Generally speaking, the beneficiaries of these scholarships were offered positions as assistant professors after the completion of their studies at the university providing them with the scholarship. A second scheme was the "Returning Singapore Scientist Scheme" that sought to attract outstanding overseas-based Singaporean research scientists to come back home to take up leadership positions in Singapore's autonomous universities and publicly funded research institutes. As the availability of a sufficiently large pool of Singaporeans who choose an academic career remains a critical issue for the future development of the universities, we will address this in more detail in Chapter 10.

A fourth issue that was often raised was whether the increased investment in R&D has translated into economic success for the country. The answer to that issue is complex and not straightforward. To some extent, it is still too early to judge. The research rankings of NUS and NTU, as well as SMU in some of its disciplines, such as Business, Accountancy, Econometrics and Computer Science, are a testimony to the quality and quantity of the research that is carried out in Singapore. Some case studies (De Meyer and Bhattacharya, 2020; De Meyer and Chan, 2020) provide evidence showing that the quality of the research environment has attracted multinational companies (MNCs), for example Johnson and Johnson or Schneider Electric, to locate their innovation centres in Singapore. The rise of collaborations between the universities and industry, for example the corporate labs of Rolls Royce with NTU, Keppel and Sembcorp with NUS, Fujitsu with SMU and ST Engineering with both SUTD and NTU, are another strong indicators that the industry is genuinely interested in the research capabilities of the universities. These MNCs have been able to provide high-quality employment for the highly educated and research-driven workforce who wanted to further their careers in a business environment instead of an academic environment. Some early stage start-ups have benefitted from the research outcomes and results, even though it is still too early to evaluate the success of these ventures. In some cases, particularly in biosciences, it has been argued that the absorptive capacity of the companies in Singapore for the research output has been limited. The value captured from the research has occurred elsewhere, for example in China and the United States where the MNCs are based. The value migration to other countries is also partially due to some foreign PhD students returning to their home countries after obtaining their degrees. Thus, these students have enriched the research environment in their own countries rather than in Singapore.

In the early 2000s, there were some voices criticising the lack of funding for Social Sciences research. Already in the 2007 International Academic Advisory Panel it was noted that

> Singapore's R&D strategy was driven by economic growth, which had led to a heavy emphasis on Science and Technology... research in the humanities and social sciences was also important as it had much to contribute to intellectual discourse about scientific and technological advances... a Foundation for humanities research similar to the NRF could be considered.

Indeed, almost all of the funding administered by NRF or by other agencies in the RIE ecosystem was for STEM research. Several contentious questions remained in the minds of some researchers: "Could the implementation of the results of STEM research be effective without a deep understanding of the societal and business context in Southeast Asia?" "Should Singapore invest more in research on societal issues, for example, ageing, demographics, urbanisation, etc.?" These questions were brought to the attention of the government. By the end of 2016, then DPM Tharman Shanmugaratnam announced that the government would make S$350 million available for Social Sciences research through the Ministry of Education, and it would create a Social Science Research Council (SSRC) to promote research and scholarship to meet some of Singapore's key challenges.

CONCLUSION

One of the key factors leading to the creation of a successful system of universities in Singapore has no doubt been the increased allocation of funding for research, and in part, the shift of a significant proportion of these resources to R&D carried out by the university scientists and research academics. But we hope that we have convinced you that its success required more than dollars and cents. The leaders of the government observed that most research and technology hubs in the world have grown in the vicinity of the top universities. While most of these earlier hubs were the result of organic growth, given the size of Singapore and its ability to attract foreign talent and MNCs, the government wanted to engineer the creation of such a hub. The other factors for building a strong research capability at the universities include:

- Strong and experienced leadership at the government and university levels;
- The creation of an environment that was favourable for R&D at the universities that included a community of top researchers who could groom the next generation of researchers. Attracting top performing researchers and the establishment of CREATE both inculcated this environment;
- A very open policy to attract foreign specialists who were willing and able to contribute to the development of the R&D landscape in Singapore;
- Changes in the university performance evaluation system, promotion and tenure processes, and the recognition and incentives for high-quality research;
- A resolute adoption of international research performance standards; and
- Careful management of public opinion in explaining the importance of R&D to the country's success and the need to attract foreign specialists.

As summarised aptly by President Lily Kong of SMU, "it was also about personalities, policies that drive behaviour and the politics of managing the public opinion".

BIBLIOGRAPHY

De Meyer, A., & Bhattacharya, L. (2020). *Johnson and Johnson's Choice of Regional Headquarters and Innovation Hub: Why Singapore?* SMU case no. 20-0002.
De Meyer, A., & Chan, C. W. (2020). *Schneider Electric: Optimising Business Opportunities from its Regional HQ in Singapore.* SMU case no. 20-0001.
Josey, A. (2012). *Lee Kuan Yew: The Crucial Years.* Singapore: Marshall Cavendish.
Khew, C. (2015). Mentor to a nation's science ambitions. *The Straits Times,* 25 September. [Online] Available at: www.straitstimes.com/singapore/mentor-to-a-nations-science-ambitions (Accessed: 20 December 2019).

Lee, K. Y. (2003). *Lee Kuan Yew at 80: 80 Quotes from a Life.* Singapore: Lianhe Zaobao. p. 90.

National Research Foundation (2020a). *2020 RIE Plan.* [Online] Available at: www.nrf.gov.sg/rie2020 (Accessed: 22 December 2020).

National Research Foundation (2020b). *Corporate Profile.* [Online] Available at: www.nrf.gov.sg/about-nrf/national-research-foundation-singapore/corporate-profile (Accessed: 20 December 2020).

Ng, R., Lim, S. Q. & Wong, P. (2018). *Singapore: 50 Years of Science and Technology.* [Online] Available at: https://lkyspp.nus.edu.sg/gia/article/singapore-50-years-of-science-and-technology (Accessed: 20 December 2019).

OECD (2019). *Main Science and Technology Indicators.* [Online] Available at: www.oecd.org/sti/msti.htm (Accessed: 22 December 2019).

Sharma, Y. (2017). The story of how Singapore became a research nation. *University World News,* December 15. [Online] Available at: www.universityworldnews.com/post.php?story=20171215122350628 (Accessed: 15 January 2020).

Singapore Statutes Online (2020). *Science Council of Singapore Bill.* [Online] Available at: https://sso.agc.gov.sg/Bills-Supp/9-1967/Published/19670527?DocDate=19670527 (Accessed: 22 March 2020).

Chapter 5

Governance
The autonomous university and its impact on diversity

All former and current leaders at Singapore's universities recognise the importance of the governance system of an autonomous university in building the system of universities. University autonomy is not unique to Singapore. It has been implemented elsewhere in East Asia as an application of the new public management system. While the concept of the autonomous university was well-designed, we argue that the way it was implemented in Singapore contributed to the success of the university system and we conclude that this governance system has stimulated diversity among the universities.

All the interviewees were unanimous that a third significant factor in the development of the successful higher education system was the change in governance and the successful implementation of the concept of the autonomous university in 2006. The autonomy in governance led to a more professional management of the universities and instilled a culture of ownership with the stakeholders of the universities. It also reinforced the differentiation between the universities.

Several of our interviewees, in particular the presidents and chairmen of the universities, emphasised that it was the implementation of the autonomous universities rather than the concept itself that made it a success. In this chapter, we will explain in short the concept of the autonomous university and then address the way it was implemented. We also show how the concept of the autonomous university has enabled the universities to enhance diverse and different models that cater to a variety of needs of the students and country.

GOVERNANCE THROUGH AUTONOMY

When SMU was created in 2000, it was given a new system of governance. Before 2006, both the existing universities, NUS and NTU, were run by statutory boards that were subsumed under the Ministry of Education and were subjected to the ensuing constraints in terms of decision-making, salary structure, performance evaluation, promotion, and budget allocation and expenditure.

During the process of formulating the plans to set up SMU, the incoming chairman of SMU Mr Ho Kwon Ping and DPM Dr Tony Tan were convinced that the new university should develop an innovative curriculum and compete with top-quality business schools and schools of applied economics worldwide. This meant that the SMU leadership was prepared to develop several "firsts" in the Singapore university landscape, including introducing a holistic and aptitude-based admissions approach for all its courses.

SMU needed more autonomy in its decision-making. Autonomy would enable the new university to ensure that talent management, in particular of the faculty, the organisation and administration of the university, and resource allocation within the university would be aligned to the objectives and the mission of SMU. While several of the initial faculty came from NUS and NTU, most of the faculty were hired on an international competitive basis to ensure that the standards of education and research would be world-class from the very beginning. The hiring, tenure and renumeration policies were aligned with practices in the United States, including the offering of competitive salary packages.

To implement the concept of an autonomous university in a practical way, SMU was established initially as a Company Limited by Guarantee[1] in December 1999. Subsequently, SMU was given the right to award degrees under certain conditions by an Act of the Singapore Parliament in April 2000. The function of SMU is described in the Act as:

> [...] the university company is to pursue, within the limits of the financial resources available to it, the objects provided by its constituent documents and, in particular, to confer and award degrees, diplomas and certificates, including honorary degrees and other distinctions.[2]

The conditions under which SMU could operate are described in the Act as:[3]

1   The university company shall comply with the accountability framework set out by way of any agreement in writing between the university company and the Minister or any person authorised by him.
2   The university company shall evaluate the performance of its activities in accordance with such quality assurance framework as the Minister may determine.
3   The university company shall participate in the evaluation of its activities by such external review panel as may be commissioned by the Minister from time to time.
4   The Minister may, in consultation with the university company, establish such policies on higher education in Singapore as the Minister thinks fit and may direct the university company to implement such policy.

5   The university company shall comply with any direction given by the
     Minister [...].

In practice, this Act created an interesting and workable balance between
the Minister for Education determining policy and the Ministry of
Education (MOE) providing enough funding on the one hand, and
providing the university with the leeway to organise itself if it lived up to
the agreements it signed with the Ministry on the other. Part of the governance meant that the university would be subjected to regular quality
controls. MOE would continue to set the policy parameters within which
the university could operate. This would include the disciplines organised
within the university, the programmes offered, the number of students
admitted each year into the undergraduate programmes, the percentage
of foreign students in the undergraduate programmes, the tuition fees,
and so on. Autonomy gave SMU a lot of flexibility in financial management, recruitment, performance appraisals and remuneration of faculty
and staff, and the prioritisation of its academic activities.

In parallel, DPM Dr Tony Tan set up a University Governance and Funding
Review (UGF) committee in 1999, chaired by MOE Permanent Secretary
Chiang Chie Foo to compare university governance and funding systems
in the United States, Canada, the United Kingdom and Hong Kong. The
conclusion of this review was that while top public universities were all
endowed with a significant level of autonomy, flexible and market-sensitive
appraisal and remuneration systems were essential to enhance the quality
of university leaders and academics (Ministry of Education, 2000). Following
the UGF Review in 2000, NUS and NTU were given considerable autonomy
in their operations, particularly in the areas of internal governance, financial
management, and staff remuneration and appraisal.

This evolution did not happen in a vacuum. Many governments in other
Asian countries started implementing autonomy and neo-liberal forms of
modernisation of the universities about three decades ago (Marginson,
2011). The systems of higher education were remodelled in East Asia as
quasi-markets and universities were transformed into quasi-firms while
central control was maintained. Thus, the familiar new public management
(NPM) reforms which had originated in the United Kingdom were rolled
out in East Asia and Singapore, such as the corporatisation of institutions
including the devolution of financial responsibilities to institutions and an
emphasis on entrepreneurship (Huang, 2006; Oba, 2007); and the use of
quality assurance, audit and accountability mechanisms to entrench performance cultures and steer activities in a more indirect fashion. Marginson
(2011) compared Asian approaches with the United Kingdom's version of
the NPM, and concluded that in East Asia there was less emphasis on
university executive autonomy and the devolution of policy responsibility.

SMU and its governance model showed promising results. It showed good
outcomes in terms of placement of its graduates, student satisfaction and

attraction of young high-performers into the faculty. Following the recommendations of the "Steering Committee to Review the University Autonomy, Governance and Funding", chaired by Permanent Secretary Lim Chuan Poh (Ministry of Education, 2005), and the success of SMU's pilot in demonstrating the university autonomy model, by 2006, the two other universities – NUS and NTU – were corporatised as well, and they started to operate as autonomous universities. Consequently, when SUTD, SIT and SUSS were created, these universities were given autonomous university status and were operated using the same governance system.

In implementing this framework of governance, the universities in practice had to sign two agreements with the Ministry that centred on a policy and a performance agreement to ensure that the "fit for purpose" objectives were addressed. The policy agreement, which describes the role of the university, enabled MOE to provide strategic direction and guidance for the university sector as a whole. It also demarcates the boundaries of the universities' autonomy. This meant that the universities needed to remain "neutral" and must ensure that its activities do not cause a breach of the peace; are not of an indecent, immoral, offensive, subversive or improper nature; do not cause unnecessary suffering or injury to any person or animal taking part in the activity or to any member of the audience; and are not contrary to public interest. A significant part of the section of the policy agreement stipulates that they need to act as vital national institutions while providing education and conducting research that is of high quality and of international standards.

The performance agreement was to be formulated by the university itself and had to be approved by MOE. It should establish what each university would want to achieve in the areas of teaching, research, service and organisational development, originally for a period of five years. The current agreements define the objectives and key performance indicators for which the performance of the universities will be assessed and judged. While on paper, these agreements appeared to give the universities full autonomy, in practice, MOE continued to play a much stronger role in determining the performance agreements than was intended originally.

The two agreements are to be reviewed regularly and the universities have to provide a formal report about their performance to MOE on an annual basis. These agreements allow MOE and the universities to work out a set of broad guidelines on the procedures to follow and consequences that would apply should there be divergence from the policy agreements.

MOE also created a quality assurance framework to ensure that the universities are managed "wisely in response to increasing pressure for accountability and efficiency. [...] The introduction of quality audit and control was aimed at ensuring improvement in the quality of teaching and research and distributing resources more rationally" (Lee and Gopinathan,

2008). In 2001, MOE developed the Quality Assurance Framework for Universities (QAFU) and set up a separate unit to oversee the quality assurance in government-funded post-secondary educational institutions (Ministry of Education, 2001). QAFU is meant to be a developmental tool for institutional self-learning and quality enhancement in the universities, and it involves a self-assessment against a set of institutional goals and self-selected performance indicators across the five areas of focus including governance, management, teaching, research and service.

An important element of this framework of autonomy is of course, the financing of the universities. Government funding remained the main source of funding for university education. But the universities were encouraged to generate other sources of income, for example, through donations and gifts, endowment income, continuing education and industry contributions. Government funding would come mainly in three groups: capitation or operating grants per subsidised student (mainly for undergraduate students and some postgraduate research students); a block grant for the operating, research and development infrastructure; and research funding on a competitive peer-reviewed basis.

The corporatisation of the universities led to an interesting combination of ample resources that came with autonomy and accountability and provided the universities with an opportunity to compete and differentiate amongst themselves.

BUILDING ENDOWMENT FUNDS

In the evolution towards more autonomy, the Singapore Government was already encouraging in the 1990s the universities to generate alternative sources of funding including cultivating relationships with industrial, individual and institutional donors to build their endowment funds as another strategy to support their missions and goals. This would help the universities to become financially more flexible and robust in the long term.

Following the successful endowment models in the United States, and the emerging attempts to build endowments in Europe, the government launched the Universities Endowment Fund (UEF) in 1991. The UEF was funded with an initial endowment of S$500 million that was provided by the government. Both NUS and NTU were encouraged to raise another S$250 million in total to acquire another S$250 million in matching funds. The two universities drew from the common UEF until the end of 1996, after which the UEF was dissolved to create separate fund-raising programmes at the individual universities.

In March 1997, DPM Dr Tony Tan announced that the government would match every dollar raised by another two dollars on top of the earlier dollar-for-dollar pledge for a limited time period. In 2010, the Government committed S$4 billion over the following 20 years to provide matching grants for tertiary institutions, of which S$2 billion was set aside in a Singapore Universities Trust so that matching grants could be provided regardless of economic circumstances. Even to this day, donating to the universities remains very attractive to potential donors. In principle, donations to the universities can be matched up to three times for the newer universities and up to one and a half times for other universities. And donors are given a generous tax advantage of 250 percent of tax deductions.

The early years of experimenting with building endowments saw the creation of the Advancement Offices in the universities to help the universities go through a steep learning curve with respect to advancement and fund raising. Consequently, the universities were able to build up sizeable endowments for bursaries and scholarships for the undergraduate and graduate students, talent acquisition of top-quality faculty and research stimulation. By April 2019, NUS had built an endowment of approximately S$5.9 billion, NTU's endowment amounted to S$1.9 billion, and SUTD had built S$1.1 billion in endowment. Next on the list of endowment amounts was Singapore Management University (SMU) with S$1 billion, followed by Singapore Institute of Technology (SIT) and Singapore University of Social Sciences (SUSS) at S$400 million respectively for the financial year that ended in March 2019 (Tan, 2019).

The universities also built up significant reserves as a consequence of accumulating operating surpluses over the past several years. These reserves are typically tied up in assets, for example, in buildings and/or long-term investments. When these reserves were discussed publicly and in Parliament, questions were raised whether the universities had become "fat cows" due to the head start provided by the government. Questions were also raised whether the universities are capable in managing university finances in a very efficient way.

Figure 5.1 shows the overall University Funding Framework that includes endowment as one component of the framework.

IMPLEMENTING AUTONOMY

Without any exception, the autonomous university status was mentioned in all the interviews as the single key factor that had enabled the individual universities to develop their own unique form of excellence. Several interviewees referred to a statement by Robert Brown, President of Boston University and former Provost of MIT. Brown has contributed in many ways to the development of Singapore's higher education system, in particular as a member of the International Academic Advisory Panel (IAAP) and chair of MOE's Academic Review Council. He was paraphrased to

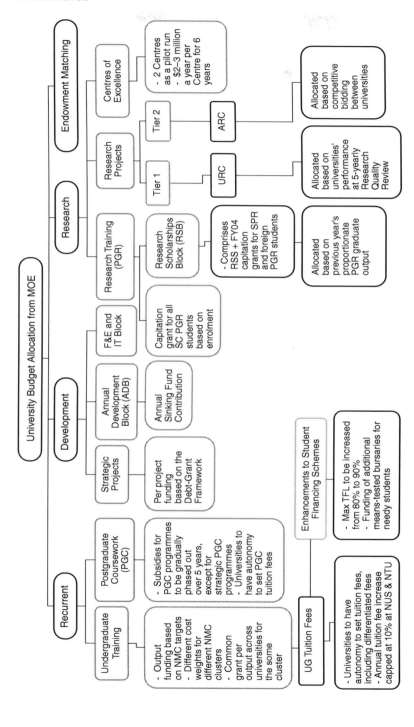

Figure 5.1 *University funding framework*

Source: Ministry of Education (2005)

have said: "Don't aim for only top universities but ensure that all institutions are top of the class in their segment" (International Academic Advisory Panel, 2007). The autonomous university governance system has allowed the universities to achieve this vision.

A well-defined policy framework for autonomy in the universities is not unique to Singapore. As we've mentioned previously, the move towards more autonomy and NPMs has been occurring worldwide, and in particular in East Asia. Both Korea and Japan have launched a similar policy, but in these countries, the concept has been less successful. For example, in Japan, the capacity of the institutional presidents to roll out strategic initiatives is limited (Newby et al., 2009; Oba, 2007; Yamamoto, 2007). In comparison to these countries, Singapore seems to have taken the concept of autonomy further.

The Japanese government initiated a series of reforms to render the national universities to be administratively more autonomous. The 2004 incorporation of the national universities became the hallmark of the government policy to allow the individual institutions to gain more control over their management. In 2017 the Japanese government introduced a policy reform aimed at improving the academic capacity, administrative efficiency and social contributions of the national universities. Funding schemes were tied to organisational restructuring including the closing of departments with low enrolments. On paper, it looked very similar to what happened in Singapore. However, it appeared that the institutions saw this series of reforms as another government directive which interfered with their internal decision-making. The reform clearly sent mixed messages and contributed to a political struggle between the government and the universities.

Unlike most Asian countries, the majority – about 85 percent – of the higher education institutions in Korea are private (Kim, 2008). Regardless of whether public or private, the Korean Ministry of Education has direct control over both types of institutions in the higher education sector. The Education Act calls for each institution to follow the Korean MOE charter despite having "autonomy". Until 1995, the government had strictly regulated the admission criteria and the number of students for each university. However, this changed in 1995 when the quota system was abolished, and the supply of university places started to exceed the demand. Furthermore, the Korean higher education reform has not kept up with the structural changes in the national economy, such as the demand for highly skilled knowledge workers. These factors led to an increase in the unemployment rate of university graduates.

In December 2004, the MOE and Human Resources Development (MOEHRD) announced a "University Restructuring Plan" to increase the competitiveness of Korean universities. Several initiatives were launched including the corporatisation of the national universities and the forming of the new university-industry links for economic development. However, in the process of higher education policy-making and execution, the Korean government regulations have remained as prescriptive as before; which is why the concept of the autonomous university is deemed to be less successful there. Despite the use of indirect NPM steering, the Korean Government continues to exercise detailed controls over the program contents, personnel management and research. East Asia is not alone in that "interference" from the government.

So, what created the success of the "autonomous university" in Singapore? This was a topic that received strong and passionate views from the presidents and chairmen of the universities. In fact, the answer can be summarised in one statement: "robust and professional implementation".

Based on the interviews, we learned the following characteristics for good implementation:

1   *Good preparation:* The government had laid a strong foundation for the implementation of university autonomy. The model that was rolled out was based on a thorough comparison of other successful systems in the United States. This model was also piloted successfully with SMU before its subsequent roll out in the other universities. The model was comprised of a good balance and combination of autonomy with accountability and short- and long-term quality control, and provided the support for alternative financial resources. One key factor in the preparation phase was the in-depth discussion in Parliament on the Act on Autonomous Universities, which provided a broad platform of support for the new organisation of universities.

2   *Selecting the appropriate trustees and chairmen of the Boards:* Autonomy required both managerial and governance experience. Trustees were selected by the government and appointed for their experience in running corporate boards or companies operating in a competitive environment, leading audit committees, and so on. In this context, it is noticeable that all chairmen of the six university boards are business people with experience in leading and managing companies. This ensures that they can combine their capabilities in running corporatised institutions with a deep understanding of the special characteristics of academic institutions. The chairmen of the boards of trustees are also appointed for long terms.

3   *A commitment to real autonomy:* Several interviewees indicated that originally there was some apprehension whether MOE was really prepared to "let go" of control of the universities, given the significant budget allocations. While they did not doubt the willingness of the senior management and leaders at MOE to implement autonomy, they feared that the middle management might not want to give up control. They also mentioned that both the management and the

boards experienced a steep learning curve. Before the autonomy, the boards acted more as advisory boards. However, after the corporatisation of the universities, the boards had a real governance role and were perceived to have strong fiduciary responsibilities – which was why audit committees were created with the support of external auditors to review how the institutions are managed. Autonomy entailed real risks and public scrutiny, especially if processes and rules were not well-implemented. Upon reflections on how autonomy has been executed, the presidents and the chairmen of the boards all confirmed that MOE has adopted a hands-off approach where the management of the universities is concerned but MOE has continued to play a role in determining the critical policies for the higher education sector. Ng Yat Chung, chairman of SIT mentioned: "Once you live up to the KPIs, it is actually a quite 'free' system. And therefore, you get the individual universities to be managed in a very different way".

4   *A growing trust at MOE that the universities can run their business well:* A key element in the successful implementation of university autonomy was affirmed when MOE realised that the university management and the boards took their responsibility very seriously and ran the universities in a proper and business-like way. It was evident that there was a culture of ownership and commitment that permeated right through the whole university from the Board of Trustees to the university leadership and key administrative staff and involved faculty. This created an atmosphere of mutual trust between MOE and the university leadership and board.

5   *Policies were perceived to be reasonable:* While university presidents would naturally prefer to have even more autonomy, especially on issues like fees, the creation of new disciplines or the percentage of foreign students in undergraduate programmes, the policies issued by the MOE were generally seen to be quite reasonable. One of the areas where MOE has kept strong control is in the creation of new programmes or disciplines. For competitive reasons, the university presidents may have liked to have more freedom in determining the programmes or disciplines to organise and launch. However, several of them felt it was reasonable for MOE to determine the portfolio of programmes offered by the different universities to avoid unnecessary and expensive overlap and redundancy in the higher education system of a small country.

Of course, not everything that was implemented went smoothly. MOE and the universities had to search for an optimal division of tasks. Tan Ching Yee, who was Permanent Secretary of MOE from 2007 until 2012, gave a few comments on this:

A merit-based admissions system was a clear policy directive, and you're not expected or be allowed to deviate from that. But how you determine merit, what tests you use, it is up to the university. But there was one area where we decided to take back the autonomy, and that was the fees setting. Originally, the Policy Agreement stated that fees were determined by the universities, and MOE had to be informed a few months ahead of the change. But when the fees go up, the Minister gets the hit, not the university president, not the chairman of the Board of Trustees. So, we decided that it was not enough just to keep MOE informed. The universities had to seek MOE's approval for their fee proposals. [...]

Another issue was administration, which is not typically a university's strong suit. Even if MOE has good ideas or practices that can be adopted or adapted by the universities, or have IT systems that can be shared, autonomy means that each university can say "no". With autonomy, MOE had some difficulties in dealing with this.

DIFFERENTIATION AND DIVERSITY

As we have mentioned in Chapter 3 on "fit for purpose", one of the objectives of the higher education system was to respond to the aspirations and expectations of young Singaporeans and their parents. Young Singaporeans vary in their expectations about their field of study, the learning mode or how their study would integrate with the rest of their lives. Some students prefer to work alone and study from textbooks and papers while others prefer to learn through groups and projects. Some are more theoretical and conceptual; others prefer to combine theory with practice through internships or work-study arrangements. Some like to do their studies full-time and in the shortest time possible. Others like to study part-time and combine their studies with a full- or part-time job. To address these variegated needs, a well-performing higher education system needs to respond to such expectations.

To meet this "fit for purpose" need, MOE could have adopted a central planning approach and determine a clearly differentiated role and design for each of the six universities. To some extent this happened. For example, MOE defined the scope and the modus operandi of SMU and SUTD for them to remain as specialised and research focused universities. But there are limits to such central planning. As discussed in Chapter 2, the original intent for SUTD was to be closer to what SIT is today – which was to provide a pathway for good polytechnic graduates who wanted to get a university degree. However, along the course of planning for SUTD, there was some mission drift, resulting in SUTD becoming less of an applied university and more research-oriented focusing on technology and design.

Autonomy led the universities to reflect on their specific role and this contributed to more diversification in the higher education landscape. MOE was flexible in allowing for an evolution in the mission and design of the universities. Let us discuss the interaction between autonomy and central planning in more detail.

During the 1990s and early 2000s, there were some reflections and discussions on whether Singapore should expand the two established and existing universities – NUS and NTU – or create new universities to address the emerging variegated needs of the population and to meet the economic requirements of the country. In a comprehensive review for the restructuring of the universities commissioned by MOE in 2003 (Ministry of Education, 2003), it was envisaged that by 2010, the university sector would be comprised of SMU as a specialised university and two large comprehensive universities – NUS with a main campus located in Kent Ridge and two niche campuses located in Outram and Buona Vista, and NTU in Jurong. According to this review, the NUS Kent Ridge campus would retain its "general purpose" focus on the existing spread of disciplines; NUS Buona Vista was envisaged to be a more research-intensive campus, offering programmes to undergraduates with an interest in engineering, information communications and technology, and sciences; and NUS Outram would focus on specialised medical and health education at both the undergraduate and graduate levels. This plan envisaged and positioned NUS as a very large university. However, as we know today, while some of the recommendations of the review have been implemented – as seen in the establishment of Duke-NUS graduate medical school at Outram to address the shortage of medical clinician researchers – rather than growing NUS into a massive university, the government opted to create different and diverse types of autonomous universities with the subsequent launches of SUTD, SIT and SUSS from 2009 onwards. The decision-makers recognised that there was no need or intention to grow NUS into a massive university. Neither was there a need to create clones of NUS to meet the needs of the society and country.

The fact that the university landscape looks very different today than it was envisaged in 2003 indicates the flexibility with which the government implemented its plan to increase the cohort participation rate and supports the fact that the current portfolio of universities was not the consequence of a grand master plan conceived 20 years ago. We will come back to this flexible evolution of Singapore's higher education system in Chapter 7.

Having different autonomous universities also allows for further differentiation. Diversity among the universities was significantly enhanced by having boards and university management that could pursue their own concept of what their respective university education should focus on while making the appropriate investments in order to achieve their goals. Former President Bertil Andersson mentioned that it was the autonomy that helped NTU in selecting Imperial College as a partner to set up a medical school while developing it in close collaboration with Engineering, thus, focusing more on the interface between Medicine and Technology.[4] With autonomy in operational decision-making, SMU and SUTD have been able to allocate their resources differently from NUS and NTU, thereby implementing different pedagogical methods. SIT has been able to implement an innovative integrated work-study programme, which is to some extent inspired by the experience and success of similar programmes in Germany and Switzerland. Many such different and innovative approaches were also initiated, facilitated or supported by MOE.

CONCLUSION

The change in governance, which was first experimented with in SMU, and later rolled out in NUS, NTU and the new universities created after 2006, was mentioned by all of our interviewees as a factor of success in building the universities. Singapore was clearly not alone in moving towards autonomy with accountability. New public management systems have been implemented all over the industrialised world. Several countries in East Asia experimented with similar approaches but were less successful in transforming their higher education systems. Thus, the real factor contributing to the success is not so much the concept of the corporatised university itself, but the way this governance system was implemented. Good preparation, a good choice of the office bearers who have had experience with autonomy, and a real commitment by MOE to "honour" autonomy have no doubt contributed to a successful roll out of the autonomous universities.

NOTES

1 A Singapore public company limited by guarantee is one which carries out non-profit making activities that have some basis of national or public interest, for example, promoting art or charity. Advantages of a public company limited by guarantee include a separate legal status and limited liability for its members, and no share capital. When the company is wound up, each member is only liable to pay the amount guaranteed by them per the memorandum of association of the company. This amount can be as little as S$1.
2 Section 3 of the SMU Act: [Online] Available at: https://sso.agc.gov.sg/Act/SMUA2000 (Accessed: 23 December 2019).
3 Section 3A and 3B of the SMU Act. [Online] Available at: https://sso.agc.gov.sg/Act/SMUA2000 (Accessed: 23 December 2019).
4 In Chapter 7, we will describe how the partnerships between NTU and Imperial College emerged. The original proposal from NTU was to have a graduate school with possibly an Australian partner. But under the guidance of Minister Ng Eng Heng, NTU finally moved to an undergraduate medical school with Imperial College as a partner.

BIBLIOGRAPHY

Huang, F. (2006). Incorporation and university governance: A comparative perspective from China and Japan. *Higher Education Management and Policy*, 18(2), p. 35–49.

International Academic Advisory Panel (IAAP) (2007). *Report on the 6th Meeting of the International Academic Advisory Panel (IAAP) 8–12 January 2007.* Singapore: Ministry of Education.

Kim, T. (2008). Higher education reforms in South Korea: Public–private problems in internationalising and incorporating universities. *Policy Futures in Education,* 6(5), p. 558–568.

Lee M. H., & Gopinathan, S. (2008). University restructuring in Singapore: Amazing or a maze? *Policy Futures in Education,* 6(5), p. 569–588.

Marginson, S. (2011). Higher education in East Asia and Singapore. *Higher Education,* 61, p. 587–611.

Ministry of Education (2000). *Fostering Autonomy and Accountability in Universities: A Review of Public University and Governance in Singapore.* Singapore: Ministry of Education.

Ministry of Education (2001). *Quality Assurance for the Singaporean Universities (QAFU) Final Report.* Singapore: Ministry of Education.

Ministry of Education (2003). *Restructuring the University Sector-More Opportunities, Better Quality.* Singapore: Ministry of Education.

Ministry of Education (2005). *Report of the Steering Committee to Review University Autonomy, Governance and Funding.* Singapore: Ministry of Education.

Newby, H., Weko, T., Breneman, D., Johanneson, T., & Maassen, P. (2009). *OECD Reviews of Tertiary Education: Japan.* Paris: OECD.

Oba, J. (2007). Incorporation of National Universities in Japan. *Asia Pacific Journal of Education,* 27(3), p. 291–303.

Tan, T. (2019). Parliament: NUS has largest endowment fund of $5.9 billion, followed by NTU with $1.9 billion. *The Straits Times,* 3 September. [Online] Available at: www.straitstimes.com/politics/parliament-nus-has-largest-endowment-fund-of-59-billion-followed-by-ntu-with-19-billion (Accessed: 23 December 2019).

Yamamoto, S. (2007). The Incorporation of National Universities and its impact on higher education in Japan. *Higher Education Forum,* p. 79–85.

Chapter 6

Active and adaptive learning from partners

The universities in Singapore were not developed in a vacuum or independent from one another. In creating the new institutions or new activities within the existing institutions, there were many partnerships that were fostered to help in their development. Through some case studies of collaboration, we learned that the learning often went two ways: learning was transferred from the overseas partners and key individuals, and new learning was acquired in Singapore by the overseas partners. We label this as active and adaptive learning.

The openness to learn actively from the experience from other countries, institutions and key individuals is a fourth factor contributing to the success of Singapore's higher education system. As we have already mentioned, many study tours to the United States, the United Kingdom and Continental Europe were organised to learn from the leading public and private institutions there. Consequently, most of the newer Singapore institutions were created in partnership with the leading overseas universities. The learning was not simply copying what was implemented elsewhere. It was *active and adaptive* learning: the models of higher education developed elsewhere were not adopted wholesale, rather they were adapted to the Singapore context and improved to meet the needs of country and society.

As described in Chapter 2, virtually all the newer institutions were created in partnerships: SMU with the Wharton School of Business of the University of Pennsylvania, SUTD with MIT and Zhejiang University, and SIT has a diverse portfolio of collaborators. We also see the partnership approach being adopted by the two incumbent universities – NUS and NTU. NUS had a partnership with Peabody College for its Conservatory of Music and it still works with Yale University for its Liberal Arts College and Duke University for its graduate medical school. NTU created its own medical school in collaboration with London-based Imperial College.[1]

The learning was not only one-directional from the overseas partner to the Singapore institutions. In fact, several overseas partners shared that they were able to apply creative thinking and innovation to both education and research. They could experiment with new pedagogical approaches with minimal resistance in Singapore, otherwise not possible on their home campuses due to inherent processes, bureaucracy and administrative heritage. Thus, they could learn from their experiences in Singapore.

While this chapter focuses on institutional learning, you would have read in Chapter 2 and will see in Chapter 7 that there was a lot of learning from key individual players who brought their experiences and insights from overseas to Singapore.

Let's review some of these collaborations. The summaries below are not detailed accounts of the collaborations. Our intent in writing these summaries is to highlight some of the success factors and discuss some of the challenges that were raised in our interviews.

SINGAPORE MANAGEMENT UNIVERSITY (SMU)

Singapore Management University was the first in the wave of new initiatives to establish institutions of higher education in the late 1990s. In Tan's *Daringly Different* (2015) account of SMU's history, the key players of the university deliberated on the model to develop SMU. Dr Tony Tan, who was then Deputy Prime Minister (DPM), was the initiator of SMU. Dr Tan strongly believed that the new university should be different from the two existing universities, hence, it should have a different starting point (Tan, 2015):

> By the late 1990s, it was quite clear that we needed another institution at the university level ... My view at the time was that rather than simply establishing another university, we should take the opportunity to further develop our university sector; provide differentiation, provide variety, provide new directions. NTU was different from NUS; so, I felt that the third university should be different from NUS and NTU. And that followed many years of discussion in the public, among the ministry officials, members of parliament about what type of university would be suitable. It had to be something that's relevant to Singapore, something that meets the needs of Singaporeans. Eventually we narrowed it down to a university that would be focused on management, on economics, on business which we thought would be complementary to NUS and NTU.

The architects of SMU were given a blank slate to establish SMU. SMU's first and incumbent chairman Ho Kwon Ping recalled (Tan, 2015):

> The government didn't even really have an idea as to what kind of university they wanted. We went through so many permutations, from a comprehensive

university with 25,000 people to a Business School; and to a Business School alone which would be the monopoly Business School for all of Singapore and all the other universities [would have to] shut down their business schools. [...] Tony Tan only had an idea in his mind; he didn't have a real direction. We were, sort of winging it together with him. He had aspirations, and we were working together to achieve those aspirations. That to me was an exciting period because we actually had a role to play. It wasn't as if this is what it's going to be, KP you take over. It was like, this is what I'd like to do, introduce more flexibility to the university system, autonomy and so on and so forth.

Under the leadership of Cham Tao Soon, the founding President of NTU and the Chairman of SMU-in-the-making's Academic Board, and Tan Teck Meng, the Chairman of the Working Committee comprising a team of academics who were mostly from NTU with two academics from NUS, the team started working on the original idea of creating an offshoot from the Singapore Institute of Management (SIM). In 1997, Tan Teck Meng and SIM Executive Director John Yip visited several business schools in Europe and the United States, such as the Haas School of Business at the University of California, Berkeley; the Wharton Business School at the University of Pennsylvania; the London School of Economics and Political Science; and the London Business School. They visited these institutions to understand how a specialist finance and business institution might feasibly function. Among the business schools visited, Tan Teck Meng was particularly impressed by the Wharton School of Business. He felt that Wharton's model worked best for the new university in Singapore since it was one of the few schools offering an undergraduate degree. Furthermore, the leadership at Wharton were particularly welcoming and open in sharing (Tan, 2015).

In parallel, in his efforts to find a suitable partner for SMU, DPM Dr Tony Tan visited several business schools and universities in the United States to meet with the faculty and administrators. He too found support and enthusiasm from the Wharton School. Dr Tan recalled his reception at Wharton (Tan, 2011):

I visited a number of universities to discuss with them, to find out whether any of them might be interested in partnering with the Singapore Government in establishing a university in Singapore. The University of Pennsylvania and its Wharton School were extremely enthusiastic about the possibility. Recognising the growth of Asia, the Wharton School was trying to find the means of increasing its footprint in Asia and they felt that they needed to have a base here. But as usual, they were not quite sure how to proceed. And partnering with the Singapore Government to form a Management University in Singapore seemed to be ideal to meet its Asian objectives. From the Singapore Government's point of view, we would be in partnership with a very prestigious and well-known School of Management in the US, the Wharton School. We had the full backing of the university establishment including its President. [...] It was very important to have complementary interests and it will provide a new model for business education in Singapore, so we were able to agree on a joint venture fairly quickly including the terms; what would Wharton do, who would come and so on.

This led to the signing of a memorandum of understanding (MOU) at Wharton in January 1998.

Shortly after the signing of the MOU, in January 1998, Ho Kwon Ping told the press that the "new" SIM – which later was to be called SMU – was on track to achieve university status in seven or eight years. This new university would eventually be established in a prime urban site, in the vicinity of the central business district. It would start to operate from the year 2000, admitting 1,400 students in a four-year programme leading up to a Bachelor of Business Management degree to be awarded initially by NTU. He also told the public that the Wharton School of the University of Pennsylvania would provide consultancy services for a five-year term to help establish this new university.

Around that time, the Wharton School was approached by another organisation in Singapore – the Economic Development Board (EDB). EDB was cultivating relationships with foreign universities to establish satellite campuses in Singapore under the Global Schoolhouse initiative, which was formally launched in 2002. One high-profile target institution under this scheme was, obviously, the prestigious Wharton School. EDB had contacted the Wharton School to discuss the possibility of establishing a campus in Singapore and running an MBA program. It was also a time when Wharton was looking to expand its footprint and research activities in Asia, and was looking for a partner institution to further that project. Wharton was not interested in EDB's proposal, but it had continued to explore the possibility of some kind of collaboration so that Wharton faculty could have a place where they could do research and learn much more about the economy and culture of the different parts of Asia (Bellace, 2010).

In March 1998, Ho Kwon Ping invited Janice Bellace, then Deputy Dean of Wharton and the prime mover in the Wharton-SMU collaboration, to serve initially as a Special Advisor to the Chairman of the board and later to be the Founding President of the university. Bellace's appointment as SMU's first President was for a period of two years. When she came on board as president, she critically re-examined SMU's strategic plan and was quick to conclude that the idea of starting up a large university with a projected student population of 15,000 was not "going to fly". Neither was the idea for NTU to confer degrees to SMU students a good one. She said (Tan, 2015):

You have to stand on what you produce very quickly; your reputation will be formed. And I came to realise that although this was a change for Singapore because that was not what had been done originally with NTU, they were willing to try it out. And that was what happened. They said they would accept that and then, we had the Act in January 2000.

In June 1999, SMU announced that it would be granting its own degrees. Its first intake of students, scheduled for the 2000–2001 academic year, would only admit 300 students instead of the projected 1,200.

There have been lots of arguments about how strongly Wharton influenced SMU's curriculum. Even though SMU adopted many ideas from Wharton, it came up with an academic programme on its own. Giving students a broad-based education was central to SMU's unique and new curriculum. As Low Aik Meng, one of the pioneers of the SMU team explained (Tan, 2015):

> [It was natural to use Wharton school's curriculum] as a starting block for the design of [ours]. However, we made various changes and additions to make the SMU curriculum more unique. For instance, we decided to implement a compulsory internship component to ensure that our students graduate with some work experience, making them more employable. Another compulsory requirement was community service. We wanted to inculcate in the students the spirit of giving back to society and to nurture students with a heart. Another addition was a course module named Business Study Mission which we had implemented successfully in the Nanyang MBA program. We saw the importance of developing in students a global mindset.

Up to this day, the Wharton footprint can be recognised in SMU's management practices, faculty handbook, the standards for tenure and promotion, and the commitment to research. An example is how Wharton's philosophy, encapsulated in "Academic Freedom with Responsibility", is translated into article 59 of SMU's Articles of Association:

> It is the policy of the university to maintain and encourage freedom of enquiry, discourse, teaching, research and publication. At the same time, the university expects its faculty members to exercise their freedom responsibly, within the realms of law and ethics, and bearing in mind the good name of the university.

The research orientation led to the establishment of the Wharton-SMU research centre. Janice Bellace remained a trustee of the university until 2014. She chaired the Board's Academic Advisory Committee for more than 10 years. She was able to ensure that SMU applied strict standards for promotion and tenure of the faculty and this is being practised until today.

The original agreement with Wharton was not renewed after five years given that SMU was able to quickly establish itself as a university. The first cohort of graduates were able to successfully find jobs. Chairman Ho Kwon

Ping often mentioned that one of the most important decisions taken by the Board of Trustees was that the degree would be an SMU degree, not some kind of joint or dual degree with Wharton. That signalled SMU's intention to be independent from its partner as soon as it made sense. The joint research centre with Wharton existed until 2012. A small student exchange programme continued until 2019. Despite the cessation of formal collaborations with Wharton, there still remain good personal relationships between the faculty members of both institutions and some joint programme activities still continue.

SINGAPORE UNIVERSITY FOR TECHNOLOGY AND DESIGN (SUTD)

In the "2008 Committee on the Expansion of the University Sector" report, led by then Senior Minister for State Lui Tuck Yew, it was proposed that a new publicly funded university be created to meet the continuing rise in cohort participation rate. It was mentioned that:

> [t]his new university will aim to provide a differentiated education, increase choice and diversity in the university landscape, and help supply the additional capacity to provide more students with a publicly-funded university education. It could cater to an annual intake of about 2,000 to 2,500 students at steady state.
>
> (Ministry of Education, 2008)

The report also mentioned that the new university should distinguish itself through an inter-disciplinary approach to education. Such an inter-disciplinary approach would be achieved by (1) organising inter-disciplinary courses where there would be significant integration from the outset between areas such as engineering, design and business; (2) having students work in inter-disciplinary teams focusing on projects that encourage the synthesis and application of knowledge; and (3) having inter-disciplinary research centres. There was also a strong emphasis on practice: the new university should "provide its students with extensive real-world experience to better equip them with the knowledge and attributes required to make an immediate impact when they enter the workforce" and it should stimulate entrepreneurship as part of the curriculum. The focus of this new university was very clear. Following consultation with the industry and government, the committee proposed for the new university to offer disciplines in: (1) Design and Architecture; (2) Engineering and Applied Sciences; and (3) Business and Information Technology. The new university was also expected to forge a strategic alliance with a high-quality overseas university at both the institutional and faculty levels. This would help the new university leverage the experience of this partner to develop a world-class curriculum and recruit experienced faculty. Such an alliance would also benefit the students of the university by offering them opportunities for exchange programmes to gain overseas exposure and giving some students the possibility of obtaining joint or double degrees in collaboration with the partner university.

A pro-tem committee for the establishment of the new university was created to kick-start this process. In the search for an international partner, the committee looked at some institutions in Australia, but soon focused on the top institutions in the United States like Stanford and MIT. After some exploration, the final choice for a partner was between Carnegie Mellon University (CMU) and MIT. While many members of the committee favoured CMU, the final choice by the Ministry of Education was MIT. The decision to partner with MIT was probably based on historical experience as there had been excellent research collaboration in the Singapore-MIT Alliance for Research and Technology or SMART initiative. The collaboration contract with MIT was initially for seven years for education and ten years for research.

MIT's Professor Thomas Magnanti, who had considerable experience in Singapore through his leadership role in the SMART initiative, and who had been a former Dean of the Engineering School at MIT, became the first President of SUTD. In his speech at the inauguration of SUTD and the convocation of the first batch of students in May 2012, Magnanti (2012) stated:

> SUTD will be a truly global university. With significant collaborations with Zhejiang University, Singapore Management University, as well as MIT, and with the benefit of being in Singapore, SUTD is beautifully positioned to bring together the very best of the East and the West. Through these collaborations and various programmatic initiatives, its engagement with the world, and more importantly, the creation of an open, empowering culture, SUTD also aims to become an innovation zone, a glowing hotbed of intrapreneurship and innovative design. Like our partners – MIT and Zhejiang University, and all the world's great universities, SUTD will be research-intensive. We have already launched the SUTD-MIT International Design Centre. It focuses on cutting edge design methodology and concepts with applications of important practical significance.

Our conversation with President Chong Tow Chong, SUTD's current president, also confirmed that SUTD benefited strongly from the collaboration with MIT to design its curriculum. Unlike other engineering courses offered in the early 2010s, one key distinguishing feature of SUTD's course included a foundation year in the first year of study; specialisation was only introduced in the later years of the course. Even though students can express their interest in a specialisation when applying, they need only select a major by the end of Year 1, and can change until right before the senior year of study. SUTD also learned about the integrated approach to education from MIT.

The second major support from MIT was in faculty development. SUTD was able to send a large number of its faculty to Cambridge, Massachusetts for a year. On average, SUTD sent seven to eight faculty members a year for a period of seven years. In the seven-year contractual period, SUTD sent approximately 60 faculty members to MIT. While this was resource-intensive and appeared to look like an early sabbatical for the junior faculty, the outcomes were promising. Research contacts between the faculties from the two institutions were established, curricula were transferred, and a pedagogical approach was developed.

The third benefit from the MIT collaboration was the exchange programme for the undergraduate students. Each year, SUTD could send up to 30 students for exchange. This number was obviously not enough to meet the student demand despite a lower intake of about 400–450 students per year, as compared to the original intention of 2,000–2,500 students. It was quickly realised that other partners were needed to meet the student demand for exchange.

From an international and holistic perspective, it made sense for SUTD to collaborate with a partner from mainland China to create a "syncretic fusion of East and West". During a visit by then Minister for Education Ng Eng Hen to China, a few universities were evaluated. There was a positive response from Zhejiang University in Hangzhou to collaborate with SUTD. Zhejiang is also an institution with a strong engineering and entrepreneurship orientation. There also existed good personal connections between Zhejiang and MIT. The two-way partnership quickly became a three-way partnership comprising SUTD, MIT and Zhejiang (Magnanti, 2012).

After seven years, the education partnership with MIT came to an end. By that time, SUTD could develop its curriculum and coursework on its own and had the credibility to do so, having been recognised in a study by MIT in March 2018 as one of the best emerging engineering education programmes in the world (Graham, 2018). This partly substantiates why SUTD has argued that it had "graduated" from MIT in terms of education. In the last three years of the seven-year agreement, most of the new courses proposed were developed by SUTD faculty members themselves. Some of our interviewees were of the opinion that SUTD had actually become better at design-oriented courses than MIT itself.

From MIT's side, there was a perception that they did not want to be a "service provider" to SUTD for a longer period of time. MIT's interest was first and foremost in research relevant to Asia, which could still continue through the International Design Centre. From MIT's point of view the collaboration always had to be a win-win for both parties. Indeed, for a top-level institution like MIT, there is no point in going all the way around the world for activities that can be done in Massachusetts. It only makes sense if one can perform activities in Singapore that need local presence.

The learning from the SUTD-MIT collaboration was again not unidirectional. In fact, several of the people we interviewed mentioned that MIT was able to design and implement in Singapore some pedagogical innovations, e.g. the integrated cross-disciplinary courses, that it wanted to implement in Cambridge (Massachusetts) but could not because of faculty resistance or administrative heritage.

NTU'S MEDICAL SCHOOL IN COLLABORATION WITH IMPERIAL COLLEGE

A third example of collaboration is the Medical School at NTU. This is different from the two previous examples as it was a new development within an existing established institution.

The Singapore Government had considered the setting up of a second medical school in the late nineties. As illustrated by the insufficient number of locally graduated doctors and the number of medical doctors with an overseas degree in Singapore, the demand was clearly there. Even as late as 2015, there were about 21 medical doctors in Singapore per 10,000 capita, as compared to 34 doctors per 10,000 capita in the United States and the United Kingdom. Also in that year, one in four medical doctors in Singapore's public health sector had received their degree overseas (Salma, 2015).

NTU had been approached earlier to start a medical school. But in the period 1999–2000, both the Board of Trustees and the leadership of NTU felt that NTU was not ready to start such a school. At that time, NTU did not even offer sufficient basic sciences courses in disciplines such as Chemistry and Biology. However, in the period 2000–2010, these basic disciplines had been created and strengthened. This period also saw the move towards the development of medical technology and social sciences related to health and medical care. By 2010, there were over 130 projects at NTU that had some relevance to medicine and healthcare. At that time, NTU appeared to be more ready to take on the significant project of starting a new medical school.

Initially NTU considered a graduate programme in collaboration with an Australian University. Minister Ng Eng Hen, then Minister for Education and a surgeon himself, believed that it would take a long time to develop a new school if NTU were to develop the school by itself. Furthermore, there was the risk that it could turn out to be a second-rate school in comparison with NUS' medical school – which was why NTU looked for a strong partner to establish the school. He suggested exploring collaboration with Imperial College. As then President Bertil Andersson commented:

> We considered Sydney University as they had a strong medical school with a focus on technology. Another potential partner was Warwick University, that

had recently set up a medical school in Coventry. NTU also had discussions with the Swedish Karolinska Institute. I had also connections with Imperial College in the UK, where I had been visiting. Imperial appeared to be an excellent choice, not in the least as it was well known in Singapore and it had many of its alumni working here. One of the factors favouring Imperial College was that it was also a strong engineering university like NTU.

The Imperial College's Medical School, even though it was only created in 1988, had become bigger than its Engineering School by 2010. Given the engineering heritage, Imperial College and NTU appeared to be logical partners. There were also strong personal connections between Imperial College and NTU. Both Presidents of Imperial College who were involved in the early decision and implementation, Roy Anderson and Keith O'Nions, knew Singapore well and had personal friendships with some of the decision-makers including DPM Dr Tony Tan.

In the implementation of the NTU-Imperial College Medical School, which was later renamed Lee Kong Chian School of Medicine (LKCSM), it was decided that the development would be different from NUS' medical school which had 100 years of experience in teaching and research. LKCSM resolutely opted for group and team-based learning. It incorporated and applied the most recent advances in educational technology to enhance student learning. It also mixed the conceptual and academic learning from the first year of the course with practice in the hospital environments. This new pedagogical approach was partially what Imperial College had attempted to do on its campus in South Kensington, London. But the College had run into resistance from some faculty members who did not want to change their way of teaching. When Imperial College came to Singapore to help NTU set up its medical school, they were given a green-field site and they could try out and implement some of these pedagogical innovations. Consequently, LKCSM has become an important learning platform for Imperial College in London.

In order to be successful and improve its international standing, LKCSM also focused on building its research capability. Andersson mentioned:

> That was not so easy as NUS had been dominating the research landscape for so many years and had a strong representation in most committees and decision-making bodies. But the specific focus on the interface between Medicine and Technology, a strength for both Imperial College and NTU, helped them to establish themselves rather quickly in research and obtain significant grants.

DUKE-NUS MEDICAL SCHOOL

The Duke-NUS initiative was born out of the initiative in the early 2000s to invest in research in biosciences, which we mentioned in Chapter 4. In order to be successful with this investment, it was important to enrich the environmental ecosystem and groom more clinician scientists who could manage the long process of translating early research results into clinical practice. As NUS President, Tan Eng Chye mentioned:

> When you invest in biomedical sciences, you must be very mindful of the time between when you have a research outcome, and when you actually use it on the patient. It can be a very long time, sometimes close to 20 years. And in the entire process, you need different expertise. When we looked at the Singapore research translation ecosystem, one group of expertise was missing: clinician scientists. [...] At that time, the Yong Loo Lin School of Medicine produced a lot of clinicians, but they didn't produce enough clinicians with a yearning to do research. There was a need to train a strong pipeline of research-oriented clinicians. At that time, about 200 clinician scientists were what we needed in Singapore. DPM Dr Tony Tan had the idea that we should set up a new school. [...] We went around, and we looked at many universities in US, where the medical degree is a graduate degree. If you look at their four-year curriculum, the first 2 years are usually basic science and didactics. Then years 3 and 4 are for clinical rotations. We noticed that Duke had a very special curriculum. The first 2 years are put into one year. So, they do basic science in just year 1. Year 2 and year 4 are for rotations. Year 3 is a special year where they call it the research year. Here, the students can do on top of some clinical rotations a research project with a university or hospital or research institute. It was also very clear to us that amongst all the universities in US, Duke produced the most clinician scientists, typically about 15%. That's the reason why we went to Duke to get them to collaborate with us. Then President Tan Chorh Chuan was personally involved in the initiative with Duke.

Former President of NUS, Tan Chorh Chuan also commented about the importance of creating a new and differentiated medical school with Duke. According to him, this could be achieved in two ways:

> One is that we would not want to just import the Duke model here, but we wanted to work with Duke to create something which does not or did not exist before in educational terms. And I think we succeeded in the end – that was actually a major attraction for Duke. And the second was in research to see how focusing on the Asian phenotype and Asian diseases could allow us to differentiate the work done in Singapore. And of course, that was of interest to Duke as well.

Tan Eng Chye continued to explain how Duke-NUS was able to establish itself quickly:

> I think we were lucky that the first Dean was actually Robert Sanders "Sandy" Williams. He was also the Dean of the Duke School of Medicine. Sandy had to step in in Duke-NUS because the person whom we identified, checked out at the last minute. He double-hatted. Because he managed both schools, Duke-NUS as well as the Duke School of Medicine, it facilitated that collaboration. That's the best sort of thing that can happen. If you have two

different Deans, that may be a different story altogether. Having Sandy Williams as the founding Dean was the best thing that happened for Duke-NUS. He did such a great job.

In line with Tan Chorh Chuan's thinking, Tan Eng Chye emphasised the intention to differentiate the medical school from the existing medical school in the United States:

And so we said, let's try to create something which you would like to do at Duke but couldn't do. Here in Singapore, Duke can have a greenfield. So that's how actually we came up with this idea of having blended learning at a time when not that many people were talking about blended learning. In 2007, we experimented with blended learning. Students didn't have to go for lectures. In those days, the lectures were put on a CD ROM. They only would go for "tutorials". It was a system that was specifically designed for Duke-NUS. There were some faculty members who felt that this was something which they'd like to do.

Unlike the other collaborations that we've highlighted so far in this chapter, one unique difference is that a joint degree bearing the crests of Duke and NUS would be offered. It was a significant achievement as NUS was still relatively unknown then. Tan Eng Chye commented:

At that time, I guess, NUS didn't have the international stature yet. And for you to actually say, "Okay, we will have a joint degree of Duke and NUS", it was a big deal for us. In 2011, we awarded our first joint degree. And now, we just graduated our eighth batch. So far, I think they have done very well. One key indicator is that our students have been doing extremely well in their basic science exam, which they have to pass before going for rotations in the US. They do better than the new students who are among the best in the universities in US. So, it shows that well, we have a pretty effective way of sharing the knowledge with our students.

YALE-NUS LIBERAL ARTS COLLEGE

The 2008 report by the "Committee on the Expansion of the University Sector" also highlighted the need to introduce liberal arts education in Singapore. It mentioned that "the introduction of liberal arts education will help [Singapore] offer an intellectually invigorating environment and an additional avenue to develop independent and critical thinkers who can go on to become leaders in the economic, social and political fields". Even though several institutions had been approached to create this degree, it was NUS that submitted a proposal to set up such a liberal arts college in Singapore. The committee supported this proposal but indicated that the NUS' proposed liberal arts college would need to partner with an established foreign liberal arts college to be better able to attract good students and faculty.

The suggestion to create a liberal arts college was first mooted by G. Leonard Baker Jr., a member of the IAAP, in response to a question on what was lacking in Singapore's higher education system. After receiving the call from MOE, a small taskforce was set up at NUS, principally with members from the Faculty of Arts and Social Sciences and the Faculty of Science. Similar to the other new initiatives, the team first gathered information from overseas and visited the Liberal Arts Colleges in the United States, from Pomona in California to Williams and Amherst in Massachusetts, to Swarthmore in Pennsylvania, and so on. The team came back with the insight that Liberal Arts Education is a form of education that had some resemblance to the two faculties involved but with a different ethos. For example, the two existing faculties at NUS have grown to be very large, and you could almost "get lost in a maze". In contrast, liberal arts programmes tend to be rather small, and have a very strong and specific culture. The NUS team had a big debate on whether they could create a liberal arts programme on their own or if they should work with a partner. There were pros and cons both ways. Hosting the programme in-house within the university meant that some of the resources of the larger university could be leveraged. But the danger of this setup could come from the influence of the larger university which could potentially curtail the development of this programme, especially when a very different model of education was to be introduced. There were supporters and detractors of working with partners. The detractors argued that "Singapore had come of age, and we don't always have to rely on someone else. There are enough people in our system who have been to Liberal Arts Colleges and who know how to do it. Must we always rely on somebody else?" But a representative from MOE on the task force said: "We really haven't done this before. Let's do it with people who know how to do it". As Professor Lily Kong, then NUS' Vice Provost for Education and chair of the taskforce, remembered: "therefore we did the usual Singapore way: if we don't know how to do something and we've never done it before, let's do it in partnership with someone else".

She continued:

> We did an analysis of possible partners, and we started a conversation with the Claremont Consortium. Roughly every 20 years, the Claremont Consortium has started a new Liberal Arts College. It was about 20 years since the last one, and perhaps time to start another one in their scheme of things. And they thought there could be an opportunity to start a sixth undergraduate college, but perhaps not in California. This was the age of universities going overseas. The timing was such that both sides saw the possibility of doing something together. So, we tangoed for maybe almost a year, there were visits both ways, and deep conversations. In the end, we agreed to disagree, because the model

that they were thinking of was different from what NUS really wanted. Thus, there was a need to find another partner. Joseph Mullinix who was then NUS' Deputy President for Administration, and previously Vice President for Finance and Administration of Yale University, suggested that we contact Yale. And I remember looking at him and asking, "Hey, where's that coming from?" We were thinking liberal arts colleges, not universities with undergraduate colleges located within them. And he said, "I know that's not the model we've been thinking about. But it's worth a try". We thought; "Well, that's quite an interesting departure. We'll explore it". And it was in January of that particular year, during the [World Economic Forum at] Davos meeting that year, Joe helped to set up a conversation between NUS President Tan Chorh Chuan and Yale President Richard Levin. It was a good starting conversation, and very soon, Yale got in touch and said it was something that they would want to have more conversations about. Literally, within 10 days, the Vice President of Yale came to visit at NUS.

In hindsight, the NUS-Yale collaboration helped to enhance NUS' strategic positioning as a global university that is centred in Asia. As commented by former NUS President Tan Chorh Chuan:

I was very much driven by the question of strategic positioning and differentiation for NUS. We had many favourable factors. The question was, what is NUS' strategic positioning? What is our differentiation? Our strategic positioning was to be a global university centred in Asia. I felt it was very important, to continually drill down and ask ourselves: What does it mean to be global? What does it mean to be centred in Asia? And why does it matter? Why should people care? [...] Yale-NUS was something which I strongly believed in. At that time, there was interest in the government in liberal arts education. But as you may know, the initial partner we engaged wasn't really the right one as they wanted to export their model. I was looking for a partner which was going to create something new, not export something to us. And so, we worked with Yale, they wanted to create something new, they wanted to leave a legacy. And therefore, we were really able to take this "Global University Centred in Asia" idea a lot further, quite like what we did with the Duke-NUS collaboration.

Lily Kong continued to elaborate about her experiences in establishing Yale-NUS Liberal Arts College and shared the long journey that it entailed:

We thought that Yale's Liberal Arts programme was an interesting model, because it was a liberal arts college within the university, which would be what NUS would have. [...] But it was a very intense journey of learning to work between two institutions. [...] There were many issues to be addressed. The major one was that some faculty in Yale felt that a liberal arts education cannot take root in what they described as a non-liberal democracy with issues of freedom of speech, freedom of action, LGBT issues, and so forth. We had several sessions with groups of faculty that were convened by Yale to explain how things worked in Singapore. What on paper may look very draconian, like section 377A, in practice, differed, including on campus, where LGBT students would be admitted on the same basis as other students, and they could have their own interest groups. We also put together publications of colleagues who were critical of the Singapore system and showed that they had gained tenure despite this.

She also recalled a specific problem that almost stopped the project from going ahead:

I remember being on the phone with Linda [Linda Koch Lorimer from Yale] having one of our conversations when I received a WhatsApp message from MOE saying; "By the way, have you alerted Yale that when international students get scholarships, they are obliged to work in Singapore for three years after graduation?" This service obligation which we call "the bond" was something we had assumed Yale would know. But of course, they did not. To Yale, it sounded like bondage. And so, I remember, this was in November, we were headed for signatures already, the legal document was almost done. [...] Then we had to really pause. We had to think about how to reconcile this. So, we took a 10-day moratorium, which was a long time in the scheme of things because we were on the phone three times per day, so a 10-day moratorium was like, what's happening? Linda and I had long conversations about whether we should proceed or call it off. [...] I credit Chorh Chuan for having the staying power. [...] So, our division of labour was that I would work on it further with Yale while he would deal with the local equity issues. The long and short of it was that we would not "bond" students but would provide them with a "service opportunity" if they wished. If they didn't, they could take a loan – we created a loan scheme without using any government or taxpayer's money – a revolving loan that students could take. And that's a summary of it. But that took another month of working. And finally, it got sorted out. We picked an auspicious date for the signature. I think it was March 28.

One of the significant differences between this collaboration and the SMU or SUTD examples is again that the Yale-NUS collaboration offers a joint degree programme. The contract that was signed is an open-ended contract with some limits to the financial arrangements and some exclusivity conditions. NUS entered this agreement with a view that this collaboration is meant to last. As to whether it will be discontinued or not depends probably more on cultural than contractual factors.

The question whether Yale-NUS has been able to produce graduates who are independent and critical thinkers, and can progress to becoming leaders in the economic, social and political fields, remains unanswered. It is still too early to make that call. The college clearly attracts the right students who have been able to get good jobs. For example, in 2019, 95% of Yale-NUS College's graduates found employment within six months of completing their final examinations.

SINGAPORE INSTITUTE OF TECHNOLOGY (SIT)

In this list of examples of collaborations, SIT presents quite a special and interesting case. When it was established in 2009, it was first and foremost a portfolio of collaborations with overseas universities. In this case, there had been less of an intention of learning how to create a new institution. The intention was to create a series of high-quality programmes aimed at graduates from the polytechnics who wanted to complement their diplomas with university degrees that were delivered by overseas institutions. But following the 2011 report by the "Committee on the University Expanded Pathways", led by Minister Lawrence Wong, then Minister of State for Education, and Minister Heng Swee Keat, decided to transform SIT into an applied university, with the status of an autonomous university.

When SIT was established, the issue at hand was whether to continue the transactional collaborations that the polytechnics had signed under the Polytechnic-Foreign Specialised Institution (Poly-FSI) degree programmes. Some of these collaborations were kept for practical reasons. In the beginning of 2020, SIT still mentioned nine university partners on its website. President Tan Thiam Soon commented:

> One of the very first decisions we had to make as an autonomous university was: "What do we do with our overseas university partners?" One of the critical decisions was, of course, to inform them that SIT would become a university in its own right. But within 3–5 years, would these partnerships with overseas universities cease or would we continue to proceed? So that was one of the very major decisions. But after lots and lots of debate, we decided to keep them. In fact, I had to terminate a couple of them for a variety of different reasons. And I sent a message that there is a certain profile of university we are looking for. We only want institutions who are prepared to be truly a partner.

SIT also wanted to focus on applied skills as a key differentiation for its graduates. However, applied skills and expertise are areas that were lacking within Singapore, which is why working with overseas partners was a good strategy for SIT. President Tan Thiam Soon emphasised that:

> When you teach subjects that are very applied and very skill based, instantly, you face quite a number of very daunting tasks. There is expertise that we need, but we don't have. [...] We very quickly realised that as a small university, in an even smaller country, we also deal with a full range of needs like any big country. It is probably a good strategy to have a group of universities to partner with you, so that SIT can have an extended ecosystem. As long as one of my partner universities has the expertise, I probably will be able to launch a degree much faster than any other university. In a typical university, when you decide you want a new degree, you would get a professor to be the lead professor. The professor has to go out and recruit another 3 or

4 staff to form a small team to start shaping the curriculum, and check with the industry. The first graduates will come out 7–8 years later. In the scheme of things, for applied courses, the application you prepare students for may become irrelevant in 7–8 years. So how do you quickly start something? We decided then that learning on how to work with other universities would be one way to allow adjusting very quickly.

President Tan continued with a few examples:

We wanted to start a degree in food technology. Because in the "Future of the Economy Committee",[2] it was very clear that the government saw food as a very major opportunity for Singapore. In the present context, given our reputation of being safe, our reputation of being multicultural – Indian food, Chinese, Malay, nobody would question the quality if food is manufactured in Singapore. We went to Massey University to find the expertise. And we were able to launch – from the time I went there to the launch of the degree, in one year. Similarly, for the nursing degree we decided not to continue with University of Manchester. So, I turned to Glasgow. Again, from the time I placed the call to launching the degree, it was one year. Working with partners gives you a lot of flexibility.

LESSONS FROM THESE COLLABORATIONS

None of our descriptions of these collaborations above give full credit to the amount of investment in work, time and effort, and the commitment required from the people who have championed these partnerships. However, they show how Singapore has been able to build a system of higher education that is based on a wide and diversified range of collaborations with well-selected, fit-for-purpose and overseas partners of high quality. While all examples are by nature idiosyncratic, we see at least four major commonalities among these collaborations.

Choice of partner

The choice of partner was a decision that combined: (1) the clarity of vision about the type of partner that was needed; (2) opportunism, as the partner needed to be willing to collaborate; (3) coincidence; and finally (4) personal relations for building trust and ease of partnership management. Given that the higher education sector was critical for producing the necessary skilled workers for the nation, there was always the ambition to go for the best partners possible. In selecting the optimal partner for collaboration, the quality of the partner institution on a world scale in their specific market segment was deemed as the first and necessary condition for exploring collaboration.

In the search for high-quality partners, the Singapore brand may have helped in two ways. The first was the fast-growing interest of European and North American institutions to set up overseas branches or significant education and research collaborations in Asia in the early 2000s. Secondly, Singapore was seen by many, not limited to educational institutions, as an attractive place to "set up shop", develop intellectual property (IP), and relocate international experts and management. Singapore was also perceived to be corruption-free unlike many of the other Asian countries. Consequently, it became easier to convince leading and sophisticated educational institutions to pay attention to the overtures made by the Singapore Government and the key individuals helming the different collaborations.

Openness to new ideas, but transforming them to fit needs

As we have seen in almost all our examples, especially in how the new institutions were established, Singapore was not interested in just importing overseas models. SMU did not copy Wharton's curriculum, NUS developed with Duke and Yale new models that fit its strategy of being a "Global University in Asia". NTU and SUTD, each in their own ways, became a testing ground for new pedagogical concepts for Imperial College and MIT respectively. We used the expression of active learning as the title of this chapter because it was evident that there was a significant transformation and reshaping of the contributions from the overseas partners. The learning was bi-directional. Not only was learning transferred from the overseas partners to the local institutions, the overseas partners themselves also benefitted from the significant learning developed through the collaborations.

More than an institutional partnership, but individual commitments

Janice Bellace at SMU, Thomas Magnanti at SUTD and Sandy Williams at Duke-NUS are examples of transfer of knowledge through key leaders. In any technology transfer, there is the explicit knowledge to be transferred. But there is the vast amount of tacit organisational knowledge that needs also to be transferred. The easiest way of doing this is through the transfer of people, which is what we saw in the examples of these key individual players. Their commitment to the success of their respective institutions was not limited to a short timeframe. Magnanti stayed for seven years. Bellace stepped down as President of SMU after less than two years, but she remained in a very critical leadership position as chair of the Academic Advisory Committee of the Board of Trustees, from where she influenced and developed the standards for tenure and promotion for more than ten years.

A collaboration limited in time or open-ended?

Collaborations and alliances usually have a declining return on investment over time. When learning happens, new developments replace the original programmes and structures. At some point in time, collaborations need to be reviewed and revised. In robust existing institutions, it is probably easier to continue with a more open-ended approach as shown in the Duke-NUS and Yale-NUS collaborations. But in new institutions such as SMU, SUTD or SIT, there comes a time when these institutions need to mature and establish their own reputation. While the duration of the collaborations was handled differently in each of these institutions, it has become clear that this "coming of age" process was handled well by SMU, SUTD and SIT.

CONCLUSION

In the rapid development of its universities, Singapore learned a lot from high-quality overseas partners. These partners were carefully chosen so that they could bring the best to Singapore. But it was not a one-way knowledge transfer process. The collaboration with the overseas partners was in many cases an intellectual win-win situation. The overseas models were developed and shaped to fit the local requirements. In that process of active learning, the partner also benefited from the creation of new intellectual property.

NOTES

1 Like almost all universities in the world, the six Singapore universities have of course, many agreements, alliances and partnerships for research and education. In this chapter, we focus on the partnerships that helped in the creation of new universities or the development of major new initiatives at incumbent universities.
2 The Future of the Economy Committee implemented some of the conclusions of an earlier high-level reflection in 2017 on how Singapore should transform its economy to prepare for the future. It approved a number of transformation maps for different industrial sectors, including the skills development that would be required.

BIBLIOGRAPHY

Bellace, J. (2010). *Oral History Interview,* Singapore Management University, Li Ka Shing Library, 27 April.

Graham, R. (2018). *The Global State of the Art in Engineering Education.* Massachusetts Institute of Technology. [Online] Available at: http://neet.mit.edu/wp-content/uploads/2018/03/MIT_NEET_GlobalStateEngineeringEducation2018.pdf (Accessed: 7 February 2020).

Magnanti, T. (2012). *Speech by SUTD President.* [Online] Available at: www.sutd.edu.sg/About-Us/News-and-Events/Press-Releases/2012/5/Speech-by-SUTD-President,-Professor-Thomas-Magnant (Accessed: 8 January 2020).

Ministry of Education (2008). *Report of the Committee on the Expansion of the Education Sector, Greater Choice, More Room to Excel.* Singapore: Ministry of Education.

Ministry of Education (2011). *Report of the Committee on the University Expanded Pathways.* Singapore: Ministry of Education. [Online] Available at: https://planipolis.iiep.unesco.org/sites/default/files/ressources/singapore_cuep.pdf (Accessed: 24 May 2021).

Salma, S. T. (2015). Number of foreign doctors rising in Singapore public hospitals and polyclinics. *The Straits Times,* 23 November. [Online] Available at: www.straitstimes.com/singapore/health/number-of-foreign-doctors-rising-in-singapore-public-hospitals-and-polyclinics (Accessed: 10 January 2020).

Tan, K. Y. L. (2015). *Daringly Different: The Making of the Singapore Management University.* Singapore: Singapore Management University.

Tan, T. (2011). *Oral History Interview.* Singapore Management University, Li Ka Shing Library, 20 May.

Chapter 7

Flexibility and quality in implementation

Success in building a system of higher education may result from good planning, well-designed governance systems and ample funding. But the quality and flexibility in the implementation of such plans and intentions is equally important. Through two case studies, we show the flexibility and pragmatism with which the Singapore leaders reviewed and implemented their plans to build the system of higher education. We also highlight that successful implementation requires capable and visionary leaders.

In the previous four chapters, we described the four major factors that have contributed to the success in building the system of higher education in Singapore: "fit for purpose" to meet the needs of the country and Singaporeans, the significant investment in R&D at the universities, the governance concept of the autonomous university and active learning from overseas partners. As we've already alluded to in these chapters, the success was the consequence of both having a good concept, as well as very good and focused implementation. In our opinion, the way plans were implemented is the fifth factor of success. The flexibility with which plans were adjusted when necessary and the quality of some of the leaders who led the implementation contributed to the ultimate success of the higher education system in Singapore.

In each of the interviews, we asked two standard questions. The first question was to ascertain whether there existed a grand master plan that guided the development of the system of higher education in Singapore. In many of our interviews, we explained that the combination of two comprehensive research universities, two specialised research universities and two applied universities catering to different target audiences looked like an almost ideal portfolio for an industrialised country of 5.6 million people. Had this portfolio been created by design? Or did it evolve organically? The second question was centred on whether there had been mistakes in the design or the implementation of the system of higher education, and whether some initiatives were shelved. Underlying these two questions was really the broader question of whether the system, successful as it is today, had been planned and implemented top down or whether it had grown organically.

FLEXIBILITY IN IMPLEMENTATION

The typical answer we received to the first question from the top decision makers was something like: "We had a rough terrain map. But along the way, the map evolved and was adjusted". Others said:

> The system was never static. We were constantly looking and planning ahead, thinking how to adjust and improve the system to meet both the individual as well as the economic needs. We had a constant review of our institutions and our system, and then, we think how we can improve on it.

Dr Tony Tan, whom many quoted to be the original architect of the system said:

> The system grew organically and developed gradually. At the very start, there was one university, the University of Malaya. The system of higher education evolved as the economy developed and the societal needs changed. We always had a pragmatic view of higher education as the future is hard to predict. The Singapore Government was always prepared to take risks and prepared to put significant investments in higher education. Our economy has evolved from a labour intensive to a knowledge economy, and now a digital economy. At each stage, the cabinet was prepared to take risks and re-look at the system of higher education. Our system is a hybrid system of education: it is inspired by the US while it has its original roots in the British system.

CONSTANT REVIEW AND REVISION OF THE DESIGN

From these and similar quotes, you can infer that the guiding roadmap was the "fit for purpose" concept that we introduced in Chapter 3. There were a series of committees and working parties that constantly re-examined the existing system and adjusted the plans. We have referred to the reports of some of these committees in the previous chapters, but in Table 7.1, you will see a summary of the most important reports that have been written since the year 2000. Each of these reports was prepared by a committee including representatives from the Ministry of Education, the universities and the corporate sector. The reports were presented to the International Academic Advisory Panels (IAAP), as well as other stake-holders, for input and comments. From the reports and the comments, it

Table 7.1 *The review committees 2000–2014*

Name of committee	Title of report	Date of report	Chair of committee	Some salient inputs
Committee to review upgrading opportunities at degree level		February 2002	Peter Chen, Senior Minister of State (Education and Trade and Industry) (till 23 November 2001)	Visits to: • Drexel University and Worchester Polytechnic Institute (USA) • Esslingen and Aalen Fachhochshule (Germany) • UMIST and Sheffield University (UK)
Committee to review the university sector and graduate manpower planning	Restructuring the University Sector: More Opportunities, Better Quality	May 2003	Dr Ng Eng Hen, Minister of State for Education	• Focus groups with representatives from industry, private education providers, universities and polytechnics
Steering committee to review university autonomy, governance and funding	Autonomous Universities: Towards Peaks of Excellence	April 2005	Lim Chuan Poh, Permanent Secretary (Education)	Visits to: • MIT • University of Virginia • University of Michigan at Ann Arbor
Committee on the expansion of the university sector	Greater Choice, More Room to Excel	August 2008	Lui Tuck Yew, Senior Minister of State for Education	Visits to: • Delft University of Technology • University of Applied Sciences of Eastern Switzerland • Cooper Union for the Advancement of Science and Art • Northeastern University (Boston, USA) • Franklin W. Olin College of Engineering (Ohio, USA) • Several Liberal Arts Colleges (Amherst, Harvey Mudd, Pomona and Swarthmore)
Committee on University education pathways beyond 2015 (CUEP)	Greater Diversity, More Opportunities	August 2012	Lawrence Wong, Senior Minister of State for Education and Information, Communication and the Arts	• Townhall and focus group discussions with 400 and 120 participants, resp. • Study trips to Canada, Finland, France, Germany, Hong Kong and the USA

became increasingly clear to us that there were no hesitations by the key players of the higher education system to adjust the plans when the context changed. We will illustrate this gradual and flexible development with two case studies, one on the fourth university, and the second on the Global Schoolhouse initiative that we mentioned in the Introduction.

THE DEVELOPMENT OF THE FOURTH UNIVERSITY

In this case study, we re-examine some of the materials about SUTD and SIT that we already introduced in the previous chapters, but we will look at them from a different perspective.

As early as in the 2002 report of the "Committee to Review Upgrading Opportunities at Degree Level", chaired by Senior Minister of State for Education and Trade and Industry Peter Chen, there was a proposal to set up a fourth university with a mission and a role that was different from NUS, NTU and the recently created SMU (Ministry of Education, 2002). Remember, SMU had only been conceptualised in 1997; its first intake of students took place in August 2000. The strategic mission of the proposed fourth university was described as a "teaching-focused university with some applied research activity, offering degrees with a technological bias and practice-oriented curriculum, that emphasises innovative technopreneur-ship which maintains strong links with industry". The total student popula-tion was expected to be 9,000 or an intake of about 3,000 students per year. Some of the features mentioned in the report that would characterise this new university were the inclusion of credit-bearing industry immersion and a flexible admission strategy, allowing for "different learning paths for students with a diversity of prior educational preparation and work experience including students with 'A' level qualifications, polytechnic diplomas, working adults and foreign students". Based on the list of over-seas universities that were visited in the United States, the United Kingdom and Germany, it is quite evident that the committee was looking for examples of practice-oriented universities that could provide a degree path for the polytechnic diploma holders. The concept of the proposed univer-sity was quite similar to what later became SIT, when it was established as an autonomous university in 2012. It was felt that by 2002 the existing three universities were quite selective and academic in their admissions. Singapore also needed access for more practically oriented students. There was a very large demand from students who wanted to study management and an expanding SMU was a solution for that. But there was also a need for a solution for students who wanted to pursue applied STEM subjects.

Yet in the report of the next "Committee to Review the University Sector", chaired by Dr Ng Eng Hen, Minister of State for Education and Manpower, only one year later, a more ambitious and radical plan was proposed and supported by the IAAP (Ministry of Education, 2003). It was proposed to transform NUS into a multi-campus university with three autonomous universities, each led by a president. The current Kent Ridge campus would remain a comprehensive university with an enrolment of 23,900 students, and two new "niche" campuses would be created. "NUS at Buona Vista" would be a research-intensive university with 4,000 postgraduates and 2,000–4,000 undergraduates with a research inclination. This would represent an undergraduate intake of 500–1,000 students a year. "NUS at Outram" would be a small, specialised campus providing medical and possibly allied health science education.[1] The committee envisaged that in the longer term, there might be scope to start a small undergraduate health sciences programme. The report also recommended for NTU to expand into a full-fledged comprehensive university with a steady state undergraduate enrolment of 22,300 students. SMU would continue as it was in its role of being a quality university offering business and management education with an enrolment of 6,200 students. The IAAP that discussed these proposals in 2003 noted the shift away from the proposed fourth university in 2002, though it understood that the commitment to expand the CPR remained. This panel and other commentators observed that a fourth university was a risky proposition as it might be difficult for a brand-new institution starting from scratch to quickly establish its reputation and attract students and faculty. There were significant risks involved in expanding too rapidly including the difficulty in attracting faculty and students, or remaining too small and not having sufficient economies of scale. While this was not explicitly mentioned in the report and commentary, you can safely assume that the success of SMU was not yet clear in 2003 and establishing a second "start-up" university would be considered risky. Therefore, the IAAP advised that with this new portfolio, the best polytechnic graduates would be able to pursue university studies locally. The panel also pointed out the potential confusion between NUS Kent Ridge and NUS Buona Vista, and that the second campus should not be to the detriment of the quality of the first. With the benefit of hindsight, we now know that NUS Buona Vista was never created and NUS Outram has led to the Duke-NUS programme.

Fast-forward to 2005, the report of the "Steering Committee to Review the University Autonomy, Governance and Funding", led by Lim Chuan Poh, Permanent Secretary for the Ministry of Education, did not mention the expansion of universities or new institutions. As we discussed in Chapter 5, the report focused on strengthening the existing universities through improved governance, accountability and quality control. In its introductory description of the university landscape, it reiterated the creation of a multi-campus structure for NUS, the development of NTU as a comprehensive university and the planned expansion for SMU. This report also added that the CPR should reach 25 percent by 2010. It made reference to the Global Schoolhouse initiative that the Economic Development Board (EDB) was chartered to develop. EDB was targeting foreign universities to establish branch campuses in Singapore, to drive more competition for NUS, NTU and SMU, and to attract the best faculty and students. We will go into more detail about this in the second case study below.

The report of the "Committee on the Expansion of the University Sector", chaired by Lui Tuck Yew, Senior Minister of State for Education, emphasised again an ambitious programme for the introduction of new institutions (Ministry of Education, 2008). This report pointed out that the higher education sector financed by the government was comprised of the three autonomous universities and other initiatives that were financially supported by the government, including the partnerships of some polytechnics with foreign specialised institutions (FSIs) to offer degrees in niche programmes and some support for the part-time degree programmes at the autonomous universities and SIM University. As we have mentioned in previous chapters, this particular committee proposed the creation of liberal arts education, and encouraged NUS to pursue this. It also proposed the creation of a fourth university, but with a somewhat smaller intake of 2,000 to 2,500 students per year compared to the original proposal from 2002. Some of the characteristics of the university proposed in 2002 were kept, for example the incorporation of extensive real-world experience, the inter-disciplinary approach in teaching and the practical component encompassing structured internships and programmes organised in collaboration with industry. By 2008, the term "technopreneurship" had lost a bit of its glamour, thus it was proposed that all students be equipped with "entrepreneurship skills to enable them to better grasp opportunities and create value in a rapidly changing world". While it was not explicitly stated, you get the impression that the aim was to create an applied university. This was confirmed in the interviews with some members of this committee. The IAAP reacted to these proposals by arguing that the new university should uphold the current (as in 2008) high quality of education in the university sector in Singapore, and achieve comparable standards to NUS, NTU and SMU. The result led to the creation of SUTD as a specialised research university.

On top of the five subsidised FSI programmes which provided places for about 200 students per year in 2008, the committee believed that there could be room for at least ten such programmes with an estimated intake of 460 students by the academic year of 2010. They recommended the polytechnics to establish more partnerships with FSIs. But rather than pursuing this very decentralised approach, it was decided that a new institution, SIT, be created in 2009 to coordinate these partnerships with the foreign institutions. As one of our interviewees mentioned: "we spent a lot of time 'papering' over differences among the polys and between the

FSIs. It was a crazy patchwork. Finally, we bit the bullet and we decided to champion all the Poly-FSI investments".

SIT started with 500 students in ten degree programmes, without its own campus. Its programmes were housed in the polytechnic campuses where the original FSI degree programmes had started. The 2010 IAAP commended the construction of the new university on the strong foundations of the polytechnic system (International Academic Advisory Panel, 2010), "allowing Singapore to preserve the polytechnics' strength while growing the upgrading pathways for polytechnic graduates to obtain industry-relevant degrees". The new model of a federation of degrees offered by foreign institutions on the premises of existing polytechnics seemed to work well. As the polytechnics were at full capacity, plans were made and resources were provided for the construction of new buildings for SIT on the premises of the polytechnics.

But by 2011, the context had changed. Prime Minister Lee Hsien Loong announced in his National Day Rally speech in August 2011[2] that there was a need to further expand the university sector. It was subsequently announced in his National Day Rally speech in August 2012 that the university cohort participation rate (CPR) would be significantly increased to 40 percent by 2020. The portfolio of existing institutions and programmes did not seem sufficient to achieve that goal. In 2012, the "Committee on University Education Pathways Beyond 2015", chaired by Lawrence Wong, Minister of State for Education and Information, Communication and the Arts, recommended transforming SIT into a fifth autonomous university (Ministry of Education, 2012). The recommendation reads as follows:

> established in 2009 primarily for polytechnic upgrades to obtain industry-relevant degrees, SIT, in partnership with overseas universities, currently offers a number of programmes with a strong applied element. [...] When SIT becomes an autonomous university, it should start to award degrees in its own name. In highly specialised areas, such as culinary arts and digital animation, however, SIT may continue to tap on the overseas universities for their established name and expertise.

Thus, it was envisaged that SIT would adopt a hybrid model that offered degrees on its own, but also joint and dual degrees. The original expectation to have a very applied programme with strong industry collaboration was re-emphasised through the offering of a cooperative education programme. SIT became the fifth autonomous university in 2014, and it will have its own new campus in Punggol by 2023. The buildings on the campuses of the polytechnics that had been originally constructed for use by SIT will be repurposed.

In 2015, the IAAP commented that with the combination of six universities, five polytechnics and the Institute of Technical Education, Singapore's post-secondary landscape had matured into a strong integrated system, and could be at the forefront of innovating and experimenting with newer education models: "Singapore stood at an inflection point, and [the IAAP] looked forward to how Singapore could build further on the success achieved since [the last] IAAP".

Our purpose in describing the evolving views on the fourth university was to show that:

1   The plan changed and evolved multiple times over the span of 12 years. While a fourth university was proposed, it was subsequently considered to be too risky; then the focus changed from an applied university into a more research-oriented university that led to the creation of SUTD. Applied degrees were first offered in collaboration with foreign partners, but later, the committee led by then Minister of State Lawrence Wong, realised that SIT should confer its own degrees as an autonomous university. The objectives for increasing the CPR to 40 percent and opening alternative pathways for polytechnic diploma holders were kept intact. But the implementation of the plan went through several iterations and was more organic in nature. There was perhaps some mission drift during the creation of SUTD as the fourth university, thus, a fifth autonomous university was needed to meet the original objectives and the CPR target.

2   There were some expensive initiatives that needed to be adjusted significantly, for example the buildings, campus and infrastructure for SIT, but these adjustments were made quickly. As one of our interviewees mentioned: "We did not make mistakes in the development of the system of higher education because Singapore has a system that detects quickly that something is not going in the right direction. We did however have some false starts".

THE GLOBAL SCHOOLHOUSE INITIATIVE

Another example of the flexible adjustment to the higher education plan was the evolution of the Global Schoolhouse initiative, which was rolled out as an economic strategy, not as an initiative of the Ministry of Education. The Global Schoolhouse initiative was initially proposed by the subcommittee on the "Services Industry of the 2002 Economic Review Committee".[3] The expenditure on education was until then, mainly seen as a cost for the benefit of Singapore society. The subcommittee's report suggested that it could also be a source of revenue and a significant contributor to GDP. This led the subcommittee to propose the broadening of outlook for the whole education sector. Singapore should aim to become a cluster (in the sense of Michael Porter's clusters) or a hub for education. Targets were set to raise the contribution of education from 1.9 percent to 5 percent of GDP, and to increase the number of foreign students to 150,000, especially full fee-paying foreign students. In summary, the project had three main goals:

- Through the increase of the number of students, the education sector could fuel economic growth. Then Minister for Trade and Industry, George Yeo, said in 2003 (Ng & Tan, 2010):

  This will be a growth market for us. If we can double or triple the number of international students in Singapore to 100,000 or 150,000, there will be all kinds of spin-offs for our economy. Our shops, restaurants and housing rental market will all benefit. More than that, these students when they return home will expand our international network.

- Foreign students and faculty would contribute to the human capital needed for the knowledge-based activities. It was believed that the existing institutions would not be able to ramp up fast enough to "produce" the number of graduates needed, and that the local pool of talent was not big enough to cope with the knowledge-based needs of the industry. It was clear that more foreign talent was needed. For example, when INSEAD's Asia Campus was created, EDB expressed the hope that the graduates from its MBA programme would stay on to work or create companies in Singapore.
- A significant number of young Singapore citizens were leaving the country to study overseas, with many of them opting to stay abroad at the completion of their studies. This outflow of local talent was negative to the economy and needed to be halted. Thus, offering more options for higher education through the creation of campuses of foreign institutions could discourage young Singaporeans from going overseas to pursue their education.

The Global Schoolhouse initiative was also an interesting attempt to develop an economic strategy that mixed public and private supply and collaboration on education and research. The EDB developed a three-tiered model. The first tier was one for world-class institutions to set up campuses in Singapore. They would be encouraged with loans, subsidies and attractive financial conditions, fairly similar to what other investors in Singapore could count on. The second tier was composed of the existing "bedrock" local institutions – NUS, NTU and SMU. They would provide the majority of university places for Singapore citizens. The third tier of the model would consist of a large group of private providers of education, offering places for up to 100,000 students, with the majority being international students who would be attracted by the quality of Singapore's higher education.

From our own notes on the negotiations about the establishment of INSEAD in Singapore, we saw that some expected that bringing in foreign institutions could improve the overall learning environment in Singapore. One of the ambitions of the Global Schoolhouse project was to inculcate the attributes of risk-taking, creativity and entrepreneurialism in Singapore.

This project was not created in a vacuum. NUS, NTU and SMU were rapidly developing their reputation. EDB had already attracted some top-level institutions including the European business school INSEAD and the Chicago Booth School of Business to offer MBA programmes. Additionally, EDB cultivated relationships with pure research organisations, for example, Johns Hopkins University and MIT through the Singapore-MIT Alliance. The latter collaboration would later be transformed into the Singapore-MIT Alliance for Research and Technology (SMART) and housed in the CREATE building together with nine other research projects with top universities. There were a number of existing institutions in the third tier. But the scale of the project was much more ambitious than what transpired.

Initially, the project appeared to work well and quite a few international institutions signed up. But fairly quickly, the Global Schoolhouse initiative ran into some difficulties. First, some of the universities that initially signed up withdrew for a variety of reasons. Johns Hopkins announced in 2006 that it would terminate its operations in Singapore, partially because it could not deliver on its promises in attracting doctoral students or produce the desired research outcomes. The most spectacular withdrawal was that of the University of New South Wales (UNSW). UNSW initially announced to establish a full-fledged university in 2004, as opposed to the postgraduate management programmes that INSEAD and Chicago Booth offered. But only three months after its launch in March 2007, UNSW decided to stop its activities because it could not meet the student intake numbers predicted in its business plan (Ng & Tan, 2010). Chicago Booth decided to move its successful EMBA programme to Hong Kong in 2014, to be closer to its main market in mainland China. New York University's Tisch School of the Arts closed down in 2015 after five years of losses.

Second, there was a challenge of quality assurance. While this issue did not apply to the first or second tiers of the education providers in EDB's conceptual design, this issue was apparent with the third-tier private education providers. Even though the subcommittee on the development of services indicated in 2002 that a system of quality assurance and control would be needed, it took seven years before Parliament passed the Private Education Act.

Third, many of the graduates from the private institutions had expectations to stay and work in Singapore after the completion of their studies. While this was originally congruent with the expectations of the Singapore

Government, there was a backlash against a liberal immigration policy, in particular in the period after the Global Financial Crisis in 2008–2009 and the period leading up to the 2011 general election.

Fourth, there was tension between the intention to engineer a market economy for tertiary education and the ambition to contain higher education within the parameters defined by the government. Sidhu et al. (2016) argued that perhaps the unintended consequence of the Global Schoolhouse initiative was to re-engineer the institution of citizenship, transforming it into a transient, self-sufficient, innovative, entrepreneurial identity and committed to self-betterment. But this created tensions within Singapore society especially when the competition for jobs became more intense during and after the Global Financial Crisis.

Fifth, the local bedrock institutions did not support this initiative when they were relegated to the role of second tier institutions. The three research-based universities all had the ambition to be at the top of their league worldwide, and had reservations in the manner that they had been positioned vis-à-vis other institutions under the Global Schoolhouse initiative.

Given these challenges, the government decided to adjust its plans. The target of 150,000 full fee-paying students was never reached. In early 2020, there were less than 75,000 foreigners studying in Singapore. It is still a significant proportion given the total student population in Singapore. Singapore remains relatively open to foreign students. In order to allay the concerns of Singapore citizens, the government decided to impose stricter quotas on foreign undergraduate students. In response to a parliamentary question then Minister for Trade and Industry, Lim Hng Kiang answered in 2012 (Lim, 2012):

> The Global Schoolhouse initiative was launched in 2002 to develop Singapore into an education hub offering a diverse mix of quality education services to the world. Three key thrusts were identified under the Global Schoolhouse initiative – first, for the education sector to be an engine of economic growth; second, to build industry-relevant manpower capabilities for the economy; and third, to help attract, develop and retain talent for the economy.
>
> The Global Schoolhouse initiative has helped to grow the scope and diversity of our education landscape. For instance, the Economic Development Board or EDB has attracted leading institutions such as French business school INSEAD and the Technical University of Munich or TUM to set up and grow their presence in Singapore. The Global Schoolhouse initiative also saw collaborations between foreign and local universities to offer joint academic programmes, such as the joint Executive MBA between Shanghai Jiao Tong University and the Nanyang Business School, as well as the Waseda-Nanyang double MBA. The presence of these Global Schoolhouse institutions in Singapore has helped to build Singapore's brand name in education.
>
> As at July 2012, there were approximately 84,000 student pass holders in Singapore. The majority of these students, or about 68%, are in tertiary

institutions, with the remaining 32% in pre-tertiary institutions. The break-
down of enrolment in public and private institutions is fairly even, with about
48% in private education institutions and 52% in public institutions. In terms
of the economic contributions of the sector, as at December 2011, the education sector contributed 3.2% to our GDP, and its share of total employment
was 2.7%, equal to 86,000 jobs. The private education sector has seen significant consolidation after the establishment of the new regulatory regime
under the Private Education Act in 2009. However, while the number of
private education institutions has fallen by half since 2009, international
student enrolment in the sector has decreased only by about 11%. The
industry consolidation, coupled with more stringent regulatory standards,
has generally benefitted students as well as the education sector as it has
ensured that baseline standards are achieved across the industry.

Since 2009, the Global Schoolhouse initiative shifted its focus towards
building industry-relevant manpower capabilities and helping to attract,
develop and retain talent for our economy as global competition for talent
has intensified. EDB has therefore encouraged the introduction of
programmes which are relevant to our economy, such as TUM's Master of
Science in Transport and Logistics and its joint Master of Science in Aerospace
Engineering with NTU. [...] Going forward, while the education sector
remains an important part of our economy, the Global Schoolhouse initiative
will emphasise quality of education and relevance to the economy, and not
student numbers or GDP share. [...]

As it regularly happens in Singapore, when a programme does not meet
the expectations, the concept of the Global Schoolhouse was quietly
dropped. The goal of attracting overseas institutions to set up base in
Singapore moved from having a volume target towards a quality target.
The Global Schoolhouse Initiative has created an environment in which
foreign institutions can flourish and where new initiatives are still welcome.

By early 2020, many foreign institutions have stayed and grown. INSEAD's
Asia Campus is thriving. The French business schools, for example, ESSEC
and EDHEC, are very active, and have developed new activities and other
focus areas including executive education in their portfolio of offerings.
The overseas campuses of Australian universities, James Cook University
and Curtin University, and Swiss hospitality and leisure management school
École Hôtelière de Lausanne (EHL) are examples of some successful
newcomers. The research arrangements with the nine international partners at CREATE have been renewed and created a pool of researchers
who are committed to working in Singapore and collaborating with teams
from NUS and NTU. It is of course an open question at the time we write
this book whether all of these campuses and institutions will survive the
consequences of the COVID-19 pandemic.

This case study suggests the flexibility with which the government has
adjusted its concept of higher education. The value of the Global
Schoolhouse initiative resulted in a conceptual framework to integrate
public and private, including non-profit and profit-oriented, institutions

for both education and research. But the champions of this project did not fully anticipate the significant number of foreign students who wanted to stay and work in Singapore, and the tension and discontent this would create for Singaporeans. Without doubt, some of the international partners had also counted on the continuation of the financial support beyond the initial five years as their proposed business plans were not robust enough to survive after the initial start-up period. It is interesting to note that INSEAD, one of the more successful foreign educational ventures in Singapore, had developed a business plan that was financially sound to break-even regardless of financial or other support from the government. Nevertheless, the support from the government was instrumental in accelerating the development of its Asia Campus while helping to initiate activities such as a PhD programme that otherwise may not have been set up in Singapore.

One of our interviewees observed that there had been insufficient coordination between the objectives of EDB and the Ministry of Trade and Industry and the Ministry of Education in the Global Schoolhouse initiative. With the passing of the Private Education Act, and later on, the reorganisation of Continuing Education and SkillsFutures under the Ministry of Education, the oversight of the system of higher education, including the role of the private education, was finally subsumed under the responsibility of one ministry.

IMPLEMENTATION REQUIRES PEOPLE

This chapter started with the observation that the quality with which the evolving vision for higher education was implemented was one of the reasons for its success. But good implementation requires good people. It is without doubt that the development of Singapore's system of higher education was significantly enhanced by the continuity of visionary leaders in the government, as well as the quality and international experience of the leaders at the universities.

First, virtually all the interviewees identified Dr Tony Tan as the real architect and driver of the system. Dr Tan had been an academic before joining the private sector. He has a Master of Science from MIT and a PhD from the University of Adelaide. He was the first Vice-Chancellor of the unified National University of Singapore in 1980–1981, and served as Minister for Education from 1980 until 1981, and again from 1985 until 1991. He had intimate knowledge of the higher education sector. He knew the sector of higher education both as an insider and as a policymaker, and he understood the challenges of instilling change in an academic environment. He is a strong believer and proponent of instilling competition to drive excellence in the higher education sector. Dr Tan was Deputy Prime Minister from 1995 until 2005. Even though he was the visionary force behind the creation of SMU, he gave Chairman Ho Kwon Ping sufficient freedom to shape SMU, and introduce innovations as the first autonomous university developed from "scratch" with an international partner institution – Wharton. After his retirement from the cabinet in 2005, Dr Tan became the Chairman of the National Research Foundation and Deputy Chairman of the Research, Innovation and Enterprise Council. In these positions, he steered significant investment towards R&D while supporting the transformation of NUS and NTU into research universities, as we have described in Chapter 4. With more than 25 years in key positions in the government and research institutions, Dr Tan had a significant and consistent influence on the development of higher education and research in Singapore and was in many cases, the decision-maker.

Similarly, other key decision-makers, for example, Senior Minister (SM) Tharman or Deputy Prime Minister (DPM) Heng Swee Keat, had long-standing involvements in the higher education sector. SM Tharman was Minister for Education and Trade and Industry from 2001 until 2003 and he became Minister for Education from 2003 until 2008. But in our interview, he remarked with some pride that he had served in the Ministry of Education as a Senior Deputy Secretary for Policy in the early 1990s, where he had created the first unit for higher education. DPM Heng was Minister for Education from 2011 until 2015. He also served as Director for Higher Education in the Ministry of Education in 1997, during the time when the initial discussions on the creation of SMU were held. He mentioned to us that he was the one who contacted Ho Kwon Ping to assume the role of founding chairman of SMU.

The involvement of these key leaders indicates the continuity in policy-making for higher education. These policy-makers had the big-picture view and understood the basic philosophy and principles of what Singapore wanted to achieve for its higher education. To this end, these key leaders could optimally act both as implementers and decision-makers.

The university leaders who managed the transition of NUS and NTU, or created SMU and SUTD, were experienced leaders, often with a deep understanding of Singapore while possessing rich experience from overseas. Professor Shih Choon Fong has been credited for leading the first true transformation of a Singapore university. He is a Harvard-trained scientist with an outstanding career in both industry and academia, having worked extensively for GE and as an academic at Brown University in the United States. He joined NUS in 1997 and became its President in 2000. His successor, Professor Tan Chorh Chuan was equally distinguished in his leadership. During his tenure, he projected NUS onto the world stage with the many alliances and collaborations, some of which were described in Chapter 6. As a medical specialist, he was also ideally positioned to lead the development of research in life sciences, as well as establish Duke-NUS as the first graduate medical school in Singapore.

The same happened at NTU. Professor Su Guaning, who was NTU President from 2003 until 2011, had significant experience working in Canada and the United States. He appointed Bertil Andersson as NTU Provost in 2007. Professor Andersson became its President in 2011, and held this position until 2018. He brought with him the experience of being the Rector (President) at Linkoping University in Sweden from 1999 until 2004. He also led the European Science Foundation in Strasbourg as its Chief Executive from 2004 to 2007.

In its initial ten years, SMU was led by three US citizens, again with extensive academic management experience. Janice Bellace brought the Wharton experience where she had been Associate Dean. Both Ronald Frank and Howard Hunter had experience as Deans at Emory University. Howard Hunter had also been the interim Provost at Emory. Arnoud De Meyer brought the experience as the founding Dean of the Asia campus of INSEAD. He also held the directorship at the Judge Business School at the University of Cambridge.

The first President of SUTD, Professor Thomas Magnanti, had been the Dean of the School of Engineering at MIT. In that capacity, he had a lot of interactions with Singapore through the Singapore-MIT Alliance. He became SUTD's first President from 2009 until his retirement in 2017.

You can easily find details of their curricula vitae by "googling" these prominent leaders. Suffice to say – all of these university leaders have credibility as scholars; they possess extensive academic management experiences, often from top institutions in the world, and all of them had a clear mandate to transform and shape their respective institutions. They were also fully committed to making a difference and elevating their respective institutions.

Perhaps it is interesting to come back here to an excerpt from the inaugural speech by President Shih when he started his first term at NUS in June 2000. While we have referred to this speech in Chapter 2, to recap, President Shih outlined his ambitions for NUS as: "[having the] goal of transforming the National University of Singapore into a Global Knowledge Enterprise". He elaborated further: "first change the mindsets of staff, making room for the entrepreneurial spirit, shutting out the bureaucratic mindset, and becoming resourceful, innovative and pioneering. Second, build borderless departments and faculties, in effect, establish a borderless knowledge community". He called out Life Sciences as the disciplines that would present significant intellectual challenges which required the strategic expertise of Medicine, Dentistry, Science, Engineering and Computing. These disciplines were singled out for their potential to contribute to Singapore's nascent pharmaceutical and biotechnology industries. NUS' Social Sciences, Law, and Humanities faculties were recognised to be well-placed to contribute to Singapore's development by providing critical analysis and indigenous insights into Asian economics, policy and society. Third, he wanted NUS to produce "citizens of the world, versatile and alert to global, as well as local opportunities, willing participants in lifelong learning, with a sense of personal responsibility and moral obligation to contribute to society". It was probably the first time that such an ambition for a public university was publicly acknowledged, and this was later adopted by his successors at NUS. No doubt, this set the foundation for the future direction for all the university presidents in Singapore for the next 20 years.

CONCLUSION

In this chapter, we wanted to show that beyond a vision and resources, the successful implementation of the higher education system in Singapore was also the consequence of the quality and flexibility in implementation. The quality was partially determined by the experience of the university leaders, and the long-term involvement, investment and commitment of the political decision-makers. The other important point worth mentioning is the long view and tenure of these involved and committed leaders.

That said, there were difficulties that arose during the execution of the plans. There was a mission drift for the fourth university. Some unintended consequences, for example, the number of foreign students wanting to stay on in Singapore to work, were not well estimated. There was misalignment among the different government departments in the execution of the Global Schoolhouse initiative.

While the context of the conditions changed, the "speed to adjust" was highly commendable. The deviations were quickly corrected. Existing plans were quickly changed; committees were formed with a variety of stakeholders holding key positions in the government, academia and business; information was sought from the top institutions in the United States and Europe to learn about what worked and what should be avoided; and the proposals were checked with the IAAP – a panel comprising international specialists. Thus, arguably, the success of the higher education system was partially the consequence of this flexibility in implementation.

NOTES

1 Kent Ridge is the location of the current campus of NUS. Buona Vista and Outram are two locations respectively about four and eight kilometres from the main NUS campus.

2 The National Day Rally is an annual address that the Prime Minister of Singapore makes to the entire nation, on the first or second Sunday after National Day on 9 August.
3 For the sake of transparency, Arnoud De Meyer was a member of this subcommittee. He was also the founding dean of INSEAD's Asia Campus and thus, was closely involved in the negotiations with EDB, and he led the establishment of INSEAD in Singapore.

BIBLIOGRAPHY

International Academic Advisory Panel (2010). *Report on the 8th Meeting of the International Academic Advisory Panel (IAAP) 8–12 November.* Singapore: Ministry of Education.

Lim, H. K. (2012). *Minister Lim Hng Kiang's Written Reply to Parliament Questions on EDB's Global Schoolhouse Initiative.* [Online] Available at: www.mti.gov.sg/Newsroom/Parliamentary-Replies/2012/10/Minister-Lim-Hng-Kiangs-written-reply-to-Parliament-Questions-on-EDBs-Global-Schoolhouse-initiative (Accessed: 4 February 2020).

Ministry of Education (2002). *Report of the Committee to Review Upgrading Opportunities at Degree Level.* Singapore: Ministry of Education.

Ministry of Education (2003). *Restructuring the University Sector – More Opportunities, Better Quality.* Singapore: Ministry of Education.

Ministry of Education (2008). *Report of the Committee on the Expansion of the University Sector.* Singapore: Ministry of Education.

Ministry of Education (2012). *Report of the Committee on University Education, Pathways beyond 2015 (CUEP).* Singapore: Ministry of Education.

Ng, P. T. & Tan, C. (2010). The Singapore Global Schoolhouse: An analysis of the development of the tertiary education landscape in Singapore. *International Journal of Educational Management,* 4(3), p. 178–188.

Shih, C. F. (2000). *NUS – A Global Knowledge Entreprise,* Inaugural address by the Vice-Chancellor of the National University of Singapore, 1 June.

Sidhu R., Ho, K. C., & Yeoh, B. (2016). The Global Schoolhouse: Governing Singapore's knowledge economy aspirations. In S. Marginson, S. Kaur & E. Sawir (eds), *Higher Education in the Asia-Pacific.* Berlin: Springer Verlag. p. 255–271.

PART III

THE FUTURE

Chapter 8

The changing context and how universities can respond

In this first chapter on the future challenges facing the university system in Singapore, we focus on four of them: the capacity adjustment that may be needed when the size of cohorts starts shrinking; the degree to which a university needs to have a core group of Singapore citizens in its faculty; the role of technology and its influence on education and research; and the changing needs of the world economy.

In the previous parts, we gave an overview of the development of the system of higher education in Singapore, and the creation and development of the six universities. We also described what we consider to have been the main drivers of the success of the higher education system and highlighted some of the adjustments that were made in the development and evolution of the six universities. In this third section, we reflect on what can be done in the short to medium term to ensure that the university system evolves and remains aligned to the needs of the country and society.

A system of higher education will always need to evolve in line with changes in society. We will address four such changes in this chapter. Some of them are specific to Singapore, such as the consequences of demographic trends, characteristics that are related to the evolution from an emerging to a highly developed economy, and what it means to be a Singapore university. Other changes are more universal such as the distinctive ways in how the millennials and Generation Z students learn, the influence and adoption of technology in the delivery of education, and the changing needs of post-industrial societies worldwide. It is a fair question to ask whether the consequences of the COVID-19 pandemic will trigger other changes. We have learned from previous crises that they mainly accelerate some of the existing trends that could already be observed before the pandemic started and we will thus focus on those.

In the next chapter, we will examine the trends and evolution in continuous and lifelong learning. In Chapter 10, we will address the need to move from R&D to innovation and what this entails for multi-disciplinary education, in particular, the role that arts and design can play in this.

CHANGING DEMOGRAPHICS: THE REDUCTION IN BIRTH RATE

As we've already alluded to in Chapter 2, one of the chilling statistics about Singapore is the declining birth rate, measured by the number of live births per 1,000 residents. The total population of Singapore has been growing since independence, but since the late 1990s the key contributor to this has been immigration. As you can see in Table 8.1, the number of babies born per year started to decline significantly in the early 2000s. The total fertility rate oscillated between 1.60 and 1.95 per woman until the mid-1990s. Then it started to decline, and the birth rate stabilised around 1.20 per woman in the early 2000s.

The birth rate measured by the number of births per year per 1,000 residents was in the higher tens until the mid-1990s. This figure dropped to below 10 after 2010. In terms of the absolute number of babies born, the number of births per year grew to around 50,000 in the middle of the 1990s; then it dropped to less than 40,000 by the early 2000s. We have chosen to table the total number of babies born in the country, as opposed to the number of Singapore babies. This averaged around 33,000 per year between 2014 and 2018, as compared to 31,400 and 32,000 in the two five-year periods before this.

Table 8.1 *Birth and fertility data for Singapore for 1978–2018*

Year	Total live births	Birth rate per 1,000 residents	Total fertility rate
1978	39,441	16.8	1.79
1983	40,585	16.3	1.61
1988	52,957	19.8	1.96
1993	50,225	16.8	1.74
1998	43,664	13.1	1.48
2003	37,485	10.5	1.27
2008	39,826	10.2	1.28
2013	39,720	9.3	1.19
2018	39,039	8.8	1.14

Source: Department of Statistics, Singapore

Given the stability of the number of babies born over the last 15 years, it is safe to assume that there is not going to be a marked change in birth rate, fertility and number of newly born babies in Singapore in the coming ten years, notwithstanding the efforts of the government to increase the birth rate and encourage marriages.[1]

This has of course, a significant impact on the enrolment rate at the universities. One can predict the number of places required for undergraduate education, with its customary adjustments and limitations on the number of foreign students, reasonably well over a time horizon of 18 to 20 years if you know the total live births.[2]

Let us first analyse the recent evolution of university intake. As you can see from Table 8.2, the number of students in Singapore universities has risen significantly from 11,232 students commencing their first year of tertiary education in the year 2000 to over 20,000 students by 2018. Correspondingly, the cohort participation rate (Lim, 2013) has risen from around 20 percent in 2000 to close to 40 percent in 2018 (Ministry of Education, 2019). By this time, there was also a doubling of the number of tertiary institutions from three to six universities. In Figure 8.1, you can see the number of students entering primary one. It would take

Table 8.2 *Total intake of students in undergraduate programmes for the six universities 2000–2018*

Year	NUS	NTU	SMU	SUTD	SIT	SUSS	Total
2000	6421	4506	305	–	–	–	11,232
2001	6479	4156	509	–	–	–	11,144
2002	6019	4411	607	–	–	–	11,037
2003	6245	4350	824	–	–	–	11,419
2004	5722	5377	1095	–	–	–	12,194
2005	6095	5206	1207	–	–	–	12,508
2006	6631	5746	1356	–	–	–	13,733
2007	6554	6196	1603	–	–	–	14,353
2008	6432	6033	1670	–	–	–	14,135
2009	6775	6719	1770	–	–	–	15,264
2010	6568	6132	1686	523	–	–	14,909
2011	6724	6177	1729	936	–	–	15,566
2012	6733	5905	1930	1304	327	–	16,199
2013	6892	6660	1924	1510	265	–	17,251
2014	7108	6480	1912	1836	317	217	17,870
2015	6935	6525	1944	2076	362	284	18,126
2016	7011	6138	1961	2559	460	423	18,552
2017	7121	5955	2004	2589	424	575	18,668
2018	7856	6160	2161	2660	437	767	20,041

Source: www.data.gov.sg

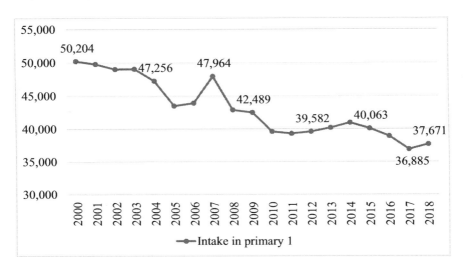

Figure 8.1 *Student intake in primary one from 2000 to 2018*
Source: www.data.gov.sg

approximately 12 or 13 years for the young women and 14 to 16 years for the young men before they can enter the universities.[3] This graph shows the significant impact of the declining birth rate on the school system. The same impact would have been felt on the higher education system if not for the government's goal to increase the cohort participation rate.[4]

It is a reasonable hypothesis to assume that the total number of university students in Singapore would remain relatively stable in the near term. However, in the mid to long term, we expect the decline in birth rate to be a key factor in determining the number of university students. In Figure 8.2, we have attempted to project the total number of students in the next ten years assuming that there are no significant changes in the cohort participation rate, no policy changes pertaining to the proportion of foreign students, and no significant changes in the immigration policies. This is a very rough forecast calculated based on the past and current number of students in primary one. *Ceteris paribus,* the intake is likely to shrink from about 20,000 students in 2020 to around 17,000 in 2030.

A key challenge is how the universities will cope with the potential surplus capacity that has been built over the last twenty years. There are many solutions that could address this key issue. University presidents have made suggestions to remove the cap and limitation on the number of foreign full-fee-paying students. However, this remains a politically sensitive issue, even more so in the aftermath of the COVID-19 pandemic.

There are other options to address this problem. The larger comprehensive universities could be asked to reduce their undergraduate intake and shift the balance between undergraduate and graduate intakes to

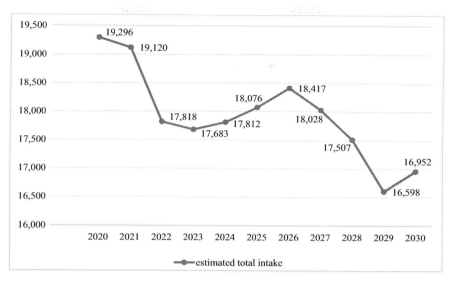

Figure 8.2 *Estimated university intake*
Source: Author's own calculations

move towards the latter. Another option is to rationalise and optimise similar courses offered by different universities, either by merging some departments or reducing some programmes within the existing universities. Several of our interviewees suggested, for example, a closer investigation into the programme portfolio of engineering education. According to them, Singapore needs more engineers, and it needs a portfolio of different types of engineers. The country needs applied and practice-oriented engineers who can build and maintain different types of infrastructure such as railroads, telecommunication networks, and so on. But it also needs a smaller group of high-end conceptual thinkers and technologists who can help the country's industry to transform and innovate. While both types of education now exist in the universities with high-end engineering at SUTD, NUS and NTU, and applied practice-oriented education at SIT and to some extent NTU, many of the interviewees argued that there is a need to evaluate the higher education system for engineering as a whole so that the total capacity at the different universities can be optimised to meet the needs of the country and society.

Another approach is to further increase the cohort participation rate. This would mean more opportunities for Singapore citizens, especially to give a chance to the diploma holders from the polytechnics and students from the junior colleges who currently could not pass the admissions criteria. Without doubt, this would require a change in the admissions criteria, as well as a greater emphasis on the programmes that are skills-based and practice-oriented. The two applied universities, SIT and SUSS, may be well-suited for this approach, but it would not solve the potential overcapacity problem in the four research-intensive universities, which might want to keep their current admissions standards.

The coronavirus pandemic that started spreading far and wide from January 2020 onwards has provided an interesting twist to this situation. The restrictions imposed by governments worldwide have driven universities in Singapore and across the world to hold online-only classes until the end of the academic year 2019/20 and beyond. This has led some young Singaporeans to reconsider their plans of either commencing or continuing their studies abroad. Some polytechnic diploma holders have also opted to further their studies rather than join the weak job market. Given this unexpected demand for more university places locally, the MOE announced in early July 2020, an additional 2,000 places across the six autonomous universities or a 2 percent increase in cohort participation rate from the original 40 percent target (CNA, 2020).

But in long term, there is potentially a capacity surplus. In order to address this challenge and come up with an optimal solution, a reflection on the long-term capacity evolution of the system as a whole and the allocation of that capacity to the different universities will be required. The challenge to address this capacity issue is compounded by the changing demands for the type of graduates and the disciplines in which they graduate, as well as the potential changes in the pathways that the future students may want to pursue. The society may require different types of graduates, for example, with a stronger grounding in digitalisation, artificial intelligence and data management. Students may also prefer to spread out their studies over a longer period, perhaps interspersed with projects and work experience. We will discuss this as the fourth challenge later in this chapter.

The capacity adjustment will have an impact on the faculty teaching and research capabilities. The number of faculty members at a university to a large extent, correlates to the teaching needs and the number of students. Universities all over the world may apply different student to teacher ratios. Different disciplines may also require different student to teacher ratios. But within any given system and discipline, you can always calculate approximately the number of employed faculty based on the number of students at the universities. With changing demographics and changing needs for specific disciplines, there will be a change in the demand for faculty in these disciplines. Some groups of academics may need to be redeployed, and learn new skills and knowledge to address the understaffed disciplines for teaching or be consolidated with the other disciplines that lack critical mass to produce good research output.

CHANGING DEMOGRAPHICS: AN AGEING POPULATION

Let us start this section with the good news. Singaporeans are getting older and healthier. Life expectancy has been rising steadily and has reached 83.66 years in 2020; this is one of the longest in the world (Macrotrends, 2020). Combining this higher life expectancy with the low birth rate, the Singapore population is rapidly ageing. It is expected that by 2030, the percentage of the population above 65 years old will be 27.0 percent (UOB, 2018), higher than in any other country today including Japan, where the population above 65 years old is currently 26.6 percent. Thus, in ten years, Singapore will be in a position similar to Japan's in 2020. For the economy, this has many implications. The dependency ratio, that is, the number of working adults supporting seniors above 65 years old, will drop from 7.4:1 in 2010 to 2.6:1 by 2030. As this rapid drop in dependency ratio has a lot of implications for the economy, you can expect the retirement age to keep rising, as it was already announced by the Prime Minister in the 2019 National Day Rally speech (Lee, 2019).

What does this imply for the universities and the university system? The first consequence is, without doubt, a much higher demand for high-quality and innovative continuing education. People will work longer and will have several different jobs during their career. On-the-job training will be insufficient to cope with the changing demands of the workplace. Thus, a relevant education will become a regular part of a long working career which could span from forty to fifty years or even longer. We will discuss the future role of continuing education in more detail in the next chapter.

A second and indirect consequence may well be the need to improve productivity at the universities. An ageing population will require more resources to support eldercare and provide improved healthcare. The multibillion-dollar pioneer and merdeka packages that have been launched since 2015 provide significant support to senior Singaporeans for outpatient care, disability assistance and hospitalisation, and provide some sort of financial assistance and insurance for future expenses that come with ageing. With a reduced number of young people in Singapore resulting in a decreasing demand for the number of places in the universities, it is anticipated that a part of the budget that is allocated for education will be allocated towards this growing group of the population.

In Figure 8.3, you will see the budget trend for tertiary education in Singapore from 2009 until 2018. Notwithstanding a significant dip in 2012 amounting to S$420 million, and some smaller reductions in 2014 and 2017, the moving average of the budget allocation for tertiary education has been rising slightly. These moving average budget increases have existed since 1985 (Table 2.1). Given the ageing population, it is fair to expect that the budget for tertiary education would stabilise or even decline in the future. A former university President mentioned that "we have benefitted

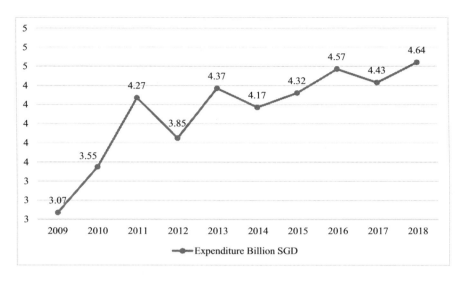

Figure 8.3 *Government expenditure on tertiary education in Singapore from 2009 to 2018 (in billions of Singapore dollars)*

Source: www.data.gov.sg

from large increases in resources; our successors may have to tighten the university belts". He implied that this was going to be the case for both the operating grants from the Ministry of Education (MOE) and the resources available for fundamental research. Should such resource constraints be imposed onto the autonomous universities, the follow-on implications could result in a focus on productivity improvements and rationalisation in the management and operations of the universities. While the transformation of existing comprehensive universities and the creation of the newer universities as autonomous universities may have given them the quasi status of a private company, the administrative and management systems may not have transformed fully as the government remained the biggest provider of the budget and financial resources for teaching, research and management. There is room for productivity improvement at Singapore's universities. Another interviewee mentioned: "Our universities are overstaffed. Due to the autonomy, the ability of the Ministry of Education to force through the improvement of fossilised systems is very limited".

BUILDING THE SINGAPORE CORE UNIVERSITY: HOW "SINGAPOREAN" SHOULD A SINGAPORE UNIVERSITY BE?

In Chapter 6, we discussed how the Singapore universities have developed through active learning from overseas partners. Even though the collaboration was at the organisational level, the quality of research and education was also enhanced by many key foreign individuals who have committed themselves to working for Singapore institutions. They were attracted by the favourable research environment and working conditions, the reputation of the institutions and the quality of life in Singapore. The generous grants that the National Research Foundation (NRF) offers for early career scientists, regardless of their nationalities, through its highly competitive NRF Fellowship programme have attracted some of the best minds from all over the world to Singapore.

For the three larger research-oriented universities (NUS, NTU and SMU), the proportion of foreigners (permanent residents and employee pass holders) among the tenure-track faculty is close to 60 percent. This number could be higher for the combined PhD students, post-doctoral (post-doc) researchers and junior faculty members. The universities have grown their talent pool by partially relying on foreign talent. There is no doubt that many of these men and women have committed themselves to their institutions and to living in Singapore. Some of them have become Singapore citizens. Others have adopted a more transient perspective for their careers and saw their contract in Singapore as a stepping stone towards building their international career.[5] Many of the doctoral students and post-doc researchers are overseas citizens and it is quite possible that many of them may return to their home countries after obtaining their PhD or when another career advancement opportunity becomes available at the universities in their home countries or elsewhere in the world. The quality of the research in Singapore and the high rankings of Singapore universities make this talent visible – which is why they are potential targets for many overseas institutions and companies.

It is common for top-ranked quality universities to have a high proportion of foreign talent and a high turnover. As we have mentioned earlier in a footnote, the number of foreign graduate students at the University of Cambridge, for example, was 62 percent in 2019. Some turnover is normal and even healthy in an academic environment for the renewal and refresh of talent. But it raises two questions: whether there should be a local core among the academic staff and how large this local core proportion should be. These questions are not exclusive to Singapore. They are relevant to all universities across the world. However, the smaller the country, the more pressing these questions become. We are personally convinced that such a local core is needed, especially when one of the roles of the universities is nation building, as is the mission for all government-supported universities in Singapore.

In August 2019, then Minister for Education Ong Ye Kung mentioned that "[…] around 50 per cent of tenured faculty members at local universities are Singaporeans. But the pre-tenure pipeline is not as strong and needs to be built up" (Teh, 2019). One can assume that, all other things being equal, local citizens will on the average have a higher commitment to their local institutions – which is why such a local core group is needed. The challenge, of course, is in the expression "all other things being equal".

It assumes that this group of local academics are at a similar level as the foreign academics who have helped to build the universities in teaching and research. While there is a lot of talent in Singapore, there is a lack of interest in and an insufficient number of young Singaporeans choosing to pursue an academic career. Consequently, the pool from where to build such a core faculty has remained far too small.

The government and the university leaders have been fully aware of this shortage of talent. They have invested significantly through the universities and NRF to fund doctoral education for Singapore citizens. They have also ventured overseas to convince Singapore talent working in foreign universities to return to Singapore by providing them attractive packages to return. In 2015, in collaboration with NUS, NTU, SMU and SUTD, MOE created the Singapore Teaching and Academic Research Talent scheme (START) to encourage young Singaporeans to pursue an academic career. The financial support can start at various times in their careers, even at the undergraduate and postgraduate levels. They are also provided with development opportunities, including academic mentorship from their respective universities to introduce and prepare them for a career in academia. One example is the MOE-AU Scholarship which provides sponsorship for their undergraduate studies. Upon graduation from the undergraduate studies, the scholar will be expected to apply for the START PhD scholarship from the university that the scholar is paired with. Upon graduation with a PhD, the scholar would be required to serve a bond of four to six years in the paired university as an academic staff member. Recognising that many undergraduate students may not have discovered their interests in their first year of studies, the scholarships offer flexibility in terms of their commencement date, either at the beginning or during the course of the undergraduate programme.

MOE also provides the universities participating in START, the flexibility to adapt the START scheme for their unique differentiation. For example, SMU describes its programme as prestigious scholarships that aim "to attract and encourage talented young Singaporeans to embark on an academic career by providing financial support for an overseas PhD/terminal degree programme, as well as academic guidance and mentorship" (SMU, 2020). The scholarships may be awarded to applicants who have completed a Bachelor's degree or a Master's degree, working professionals or those who are currently enrolled in a PhD programme overseas. Upon completion of the PhD/terminal degree programme, the scholar will be considered to join SMU's faculty as an assistant professor on the tenure track. The START scheme also provides the possibility for Singaporean PhD graduates from a local university to obtain international research exposure as overseas post-doctoral fellows. Under the same START scheme, in August 2019, MOE announced that returning Singaporean pre-tenure assistant professors could get a grant of S$200,000 spread over four years for their research.

From the examples above, you can see that flexibility is the key to meeting the goal of enriching the pool of Singaporean academics to join the autonomous universities. The START scheme and the corresponding scholarships are by definition long-term programmes. As to whether they would be successful in creating a significantly larger pool of Singaporean academics who would be prepared to work at the Singapore universities, the verdict will only come in ten years' time. That said, these programmes are essential for building the Singapore core, which many of the interviewees believe will enhance the long-term development of higher education in Singapore.

MOE is not the only organisation that is introducing such schemes to build the local core pool of "brain" talent. The National Research Foundation (NRF) also has a programme for returning Singapore scientists. The programme seeks to attract outstanding overseas-based Singaporean research leaders back to the country to take up leadership positions in Singapore's autonomous universities and publicly funded research institutes. On its website, NRF mentions five outstanding researchers who have benefited from the scheme (NRF, 2020). One of them is Ho Teck Hua, the current Senior Deputy President and Provost at NUS.

The general question we raised in this section of the chapter is whether a university needs to have a minimum number or proportion of local faculty who would be committed to building the institutions. We believe so. However, additional research would be required to determine the minimum optimal number or proportion of local faculty. In order to have a credible local core, we believe that the universities would need to groom and build it from a large enough pool of academics. The ongoing challenge for Singapore is to have a strong and continuous pipeline of Singaporean PhD graduates and researchers who excel to make up such a core. While the government has kick-started this process with the START and NRF programmes, close monitoring and adaptation of the programmes will be required to deliver the desired results and expectations.

THE INFLUENCE OF TECHNOLOGY: CHANGING THE WAY YOUTH LEARN AND CONDUCT RESEARCH

The millennials and Generation Z are the current and incoming generational groups of students and researchers who grew up with technology at their fingertips. These two generational groups have different learning and research approaches to the Baby Boomers, and Generations X and Y. The fundamental difference between the millennials and Generation Z and the earlier generations is their relationship to technology. Many of the current university students get their information from massive databases. They have ready access to multiple devices to access information and they consume information in many forms, be it written, verbal (podcast) or visual (videos). And during the pandemic crisis we all have gotten used to online meetings, project work and courses. This shift in how information is consumed and how we communicate has a profound impact on the way these students learn and conduct research. We have written elsewhere about the impact of technology on education and research (De Meyer, 2016). Without going into all the details, we quote five major trends for university education. And these trends will no doubt be accelerated as a consequence of the rapid roll out of technological solutions for online learning and interacting that we saw during 2020.

First, we are moving from a teacher-centred paradigm towards a student-centred learning paradigm. We come from an era where universities had some quasi-monopolies: they were the only institutions that could grant degrees; university academics were a major source of knowledge and university libraries had a quasi-monopoly on information. Universities were bound by their physical location and their primary task as educators was to provide knowledge to the students. We have heard remarks from students who have mentioned in jest that a professor acted as a "sage on the stage". Nowadays, geographical location and distances have become almost irrelevant. Due to the ubiquitousness of the internet and high-speed internet access, knowledge has become readily accessible and often relatively free across geographical and organisational boundaries. In many cases, the educator does not know much more than the students who have easy access to the vast wealth of databases that the libraries have made available, or the open access resources that are available free or almost free on the internet. Therefore, the role of an educator evolves more to that of a mentor and a facilitator: as a mentor, the educator provides guidance to students on how to see the difference between "the good, the bad and the ugly" information and shows the students how to apply that information; as a facilitator, the educator helps to make sense out of the information overload that is available at our fingertips. This is why curriculum design is shifting from the academic as a supplier to the student as user and a purveyor of information. It is likely that we will evolve towards a world where students attend courses in different institutions, in person or online, and are given the opportunity to "assemble" micro-credentials that lead to a degree at the end of the study period. Students can and are able to attend classes at a US or UK university from their homes in Singapore. Some students mentioned to us that in 2020 they went for a virtual exchange programme with an overseas university. The learning experience at the university could be alternated with hands-on kinesthetic learning in the workplace to provide both theory and practice aspects of the course.

President Tan Eng Chye from NUS commented on this:

> If you look at it, the half-life of many skill sets is now less than five years. If you look at the current conditions, a graduate is likely to work 45 to 50

years, developing his or her career. They are likely to go through at least ten job changes. And these can be very drastic job changes. The paradigm for universities is going to change. The way I see it is that we will have to go back to basics and strengthen the foundations, rather than to focus on specialized disciplines. [...] One clear disruption is that the line between work and education is going to be blurred. There is a strong likelihood that many jobs will require students to stop their education, go and work, and then come back and complete. Maybe a degree may not make any sense. Maybe it will be a collection of certificates and not a degree. The way we organise credentialing will be disrupted.

Chairman Ng Yat Chung from SIT commented:

For me personally, the traditional university model is broken. The idea that you can spend 2 to 4 years at university when you reach 18, and that you know what is needed for the next 30 to 40 years, that model is broken. It has been broken for decades but the traditional universities continue to offer that model. [...] It is very clear to me that when you start with your undergraduate programme, you need to find a way to have stackable modules that people like. [...] You need to structure your modules so that you can stack them up in different ways and at no additional cost. And you need to have modules that depend on what the industry needs. Our priority is to show that we can produce good quality undergraduate programmes that are acceptable to the employers.

Second, the new learning paradigm will no doubt be more experience-based. Project-based learning as a subcategory of experience-based learning is not new. It was a hallmark of a lot of engineering education. The simple idea of project-based learning is to start from a real problem as opposed to a stylised problem, and to ensure that the students learn from the experience they gain in solving these problems and applying them to other disciplines. SUTD has made project-based learning as one of its differentiators. SMU has invested heavily in SMU-X, where the X stands for experience-based learning,[6] to provide students with real-life problem-solving skills and application in the business context.

Third, related to this, is the concept of the flipped classroom where the students learn the conceptual frameworks outside the classroom, thus, freeing up time in the classroom to apply the concepts by solving problems, debating applications, and so on (The Economist, 2011). This concept may not sound revolutionary to the educators who teach using the case study method, a pedagogical method that was popularised by Harvard University. Similar to the other pedagogical methods, the focus of the classroom shifts from listening to lectures to the application of concepts and theories. This flipped classroom change is no doubt aligned to the learning possibilities now readily made available through rich media, social networking and video-conferencing platforms. It was interesting to observe that during the lockdown period when students could attend classes only online, many of them would ask for recorded lectures that they then would view at their own initiative, and preferred the synchronous online sessions to be about application of the concepts.

Fourth, "going to the classroom" will become less identified with spending time in a well-defined and constrained physical location. The classroom has become virtual, boundaryless and may exist everywhere and at all times of the day. Students can collaborate and communicate over multiple networks and applications during class hours and outside these specific times. They can work with colleagues sitting next to them in the library via online tools and social media, or with friends and colleagues who are located elsewhere in the world. Geographical and organisational boundaries have become less and less meaningful and important. Student interactions will move increasingly from one to one (as in tutoring), or one to many (as in a lecture) to many to many interactions (as in social networking). The opportunity to use different pedagogical approaches based on the intelligent use of technology seems limitless. You should be careful not to fall victim to the hype that is often created around some technological solutions and online learning.[7]

Fifth, educators will have to spend much more effort and creativity on learning analytics (Greller and Drachsler, 2012). We don't want to go into a detailed description of learning analytics here. Generally, it is about the use of learner data and analytics to predict and prescribe student learning. While we may always have had some data and support systems to advise the students, in this technological dependent environment, it is important to recognise that the responsibility for the design of the learning is shifting from the educator to the student. Hence, educators need to provide much more information about the progress of learning to guide the student.

Technology may also create more potential for inter-disciplinary education and research on pressing societal issues. As an example, many countries in the world are confronted with the challenges and opportunities created by an ageing population. Understanding how we can get productive and age gracefully requires research in areas as diverse as medicine, mechanical engineering, finance and economics, sociology, ethics, sensors, data processing, and many more. We also know that grasping the real opportunities of an ageing population will require complex interactions among all these different disciplines. Technology may help us to bridge these differences. NUS president Tan Eng Chye commented on this:

> I think there will be a need for us to teach our students how to integrate different skills and disciplines. Currently when you look at our universities, we teach and research according to disciplines. You transfer knowledge and skills according to disciplines. There is a need for our students to understand and combine knowledge and skills from different disciplines. We don't teach our students this integration, not in a broad manner. The smart students,

the top five percent, we don't have to teach them this because they know how to integrate the disciplines. But the rest, you have to teach it to them.

His predecessor Tan Chorh Chuan supported this argument: "An important driver in the future will be the need to have more comprehensive research agendas, more comprehensive educational offerings that give people that rounded view of things".

Many universities have responded to this need for integration. With no traditional departments, SUTD's curriculum is organised around four initial pillars with fluid boundaries. Architecture and Sustainable Design is one of the four pillars, next to Engineering Product Development, Engineering Systems and Design, and Information Systems and Technology Design. A fifth pillar – Design and Artificial Intelligence, was introduced in 2020. The design of the SUTD campus also enables this seamless integration by seating the different pillars next to one another. For example, in their autonomous car project, you will find representatives of all five pillars seated together to work on the project. Recently, SMU launched bachelor programmes that combine the different disciplines. Examples of these programs include "Bachelor of Science in Smart City Management and Technology" and "Bachelor of Science in Computing and Law". Other new inter-disciplinary majors launched include "Health Economics and Management", and "Politics, Law and Economics".

In research, the changes engendered by technology can be equally important. A first change may well be the radical internationalisation of research. We envisage that future research will be more "networked" and collaborative than it used to be. The tools and platforms for communication and research support, which are free or almost free, have enhanced the productivity of internationally networked research. Research, design and engineering support systems, such as specialised social networks (for example, WhatsApp, Google Hangout), product lifecycle management (PLM) systems for design (Sketch, SolidWorks), cheap video communication systems (Zoom, Microsoft Teams, Jitsi Meet or WebEx) and retrieval and document management systems (Dropbox, Google Drive, OneDrive) have made huge improvements in how international research can be organised, and it has enabled a new generation of international research networks.

Secondly, big data and predictive analytics will make non-hypothesis-based inductive research more attractive. Both the way we ask questions and how we solve them will be adjusted and modified during the course of the research. Technology has enabled huge opportunities for this type of inductive research. We can now study phenomena that were out of our reach or study phenomena in situ. But there are some risks. Pattern recognition rarely addresses causality. While pattern recognition is effective in prediction, often, it does not explain why or addresses the causes driving the problem statement. "Fishing", a more colloquial word for data mining, is not yet fully accepted and it may become a real problem when the datasets are too small or when the sample is too weak to support any insights. You can foresee future battles between the promoters of big data and data science, and the traditional scientific and positivist approach to research. Some of these battles will occur at our universities.

A third trend, and corollary to the second, is the emergence of what some call "Social Technology", or the application of data science and big data to social problems. How many psychological and sociological experiments have been carried out with undergraduate students at the top universities in the United States? Or how many healthcare studies were limited to small samples of a few hundred subjects? In the social sciences, we are often limited by small sample sizes, prohibitive costs or difficult access to subjects for experiments. Apps on mobile devices have made it possible to transform healthcare studies to the study of tens of thousands of subjects easily. While the older studies that have been carried out have rigour, you cannot help but think that the samples were socially and culturally biased, thus, making generalisation difficult. The rapid diffusion of sensors to capture data on all aspects of life and society, and the creation of vast, varied and fast-evolving databases of user behaviour in social networks, online retailing, and so on, has opened up tremendous perspectives for rigorous, relevant and truly revealing social sciences research. This development is not without risks. There are concerns about security, privacy and ownership of personal data. Frankly speaking, we don't think university administrators or the committees of the Institutional Review Boards will be able to stop or prevent researchers from embarking on these newly accessible research opportunities. But university administrators will have to address the issues of cybersecurity and government legislation such as offshore information usage or data protection while creating a common and agreed international consensus on the working guidelines for big data researchers.

Our overview of the influence of technology on education and research is far from complete. But it is sufficient to predict that these changes will have a worldwide influence on the operating model of universities and their competitive environment. First, we will see the emergence of new competition. Most of the research universities are built on the combination of the Von Humboldt model of a research institution of early nineteenth-century Germany, combined with the teaching methods developed at the universities of Oxford and Cambridge, and refined at the top universities in the United States. It was and still is a strong and performing model that was partially based on a monopoly of awarding degrees, either granted to the universities by the government, or in very few cases, based on the sheer exclusivity and quality of the institution. But we know from other industries that disruptive innovations based on technology pose a risk for the incumbents, in particular, when and if a university degree becomes less valued or can be offered through means other than a government decree. Private universities have emerged all over the world, and have filled the voids that are unaddressed by the traditional universities. Alternative pathways to success in the professional world are pondered upon by the governments, for example, as suggested in the OECD report on Continuing Education (OECD, 2014). New education entrants such as Coursera[8] offer modules by very distinguished faculty from very recognised institutions, therefore making it difficult for other players to charge premium prices for sharing knowledge. The Lambda School,[9] a different technology school, positions itself as an investor in human beings. They require payment of the fees only when the graduate gets a job that pays more than US$50,000 per year. There is little doubt in our mind that the traditional top universities will easily overcome this new competition. But many of the other players in the academic sector will be forced to act more and more like a commercial operator. They may have to adjust some of their values that position the university as a "social good" for the citizens.

Big data and data analytics will allow us to radically redesign and customise courses for delivery either face-to-face or electronically. While this may result in significant economies in paper wastage, reduced teaching redundancy and lower administrative costs, as mentioned before, to some extent, there is a shift of the design of the curriculum from the faculty to the students. Will these savings be passed on to the students? It is likely, as the OECD (2014) suggests: "It is possible that there may be a growing prevalence in the universities adopting hybrid pricing structures using the fee premium from commercially viable sources as funding to provide education access for the underprivileged".

The change in learning methods and environment will have an impact on the physical assets of the universities. These changes are already evident in NUS, NTU and SMU. NUS built UTown to create a supportive friendly environment to cultivate "spirited" communities through social, educational and cultural interactions. NTU built the Hive as a learning hub to take learning beyond the classroom, and "SMU Connexion", a building designed for collaborative and experience-based learning, was completed in January 2020. SIT is building a new campus in the North of Singapore in Punggol, to create a learning-industry-community hub. The Punggol Digital District is expected to be completed in 2023, and is envisioned to be a "living lab" where the students and industry can test-bed and implement innovations. This campus will be closely integrated with an industrial complex built by Jurong Town Corporation (JTC).[10] There is a high possibility that with the increase in technology use in higher education and the shifting from the physical classroom to a virtual classroom, universities will be required to reconsider the optimal design and use of their physical assets. The experience with online learning during the COVID-19 pandemic will accelerate the need to rethink the use, type and size of the physical assets, similar to the changes that are now considered for office space.

As technology continues to enhance the possibilities for learning and scholarship by research universities, the expectations of the stakeholders will rise. Public donors and funders, especially the institutional donors of education, may soon expect greater accountability for the return and impact of their investments, and likely in more tangible and immediate terms. Another application of technology in research is the tracking of the diffusion of knowledge created through grant-funded research by the research agencies. Governments may adopt a more involved approach to research and require big data efforts to monitor the social and economic impact of research-informed policy interventions.

An observation common to all these trends is the significant move towards the corporatisation and commercialisation of higher education and the university. We know that this is not without risks. Derrick Bok (2004), a former president of Harvard University, argued that the commercialisation of universities may jeopardise their fundamental mission by accepting more and more compromises of basic academic values. The two significant risks that come to mind are: increasing commercialisation could lead to more secrecy in corporate-funded research; and there might be compromises in the rigour of the education due to the increased 'customer' orientation towards the needs of students and parents. In a rather passionate commentary, even as early as 2011, Marginson (2011a) wrote about the significant risk that a neo-liberal approach to academia could lead to a large part of university education being reframed as solely a private consumer good (Marginson, 2011b). He pleaded for the preservation of the social democratic notion to ensure that higher education is there "for social improvement, collective and individual", and that universities have an important role in "generating global public goods". These two concepts are quite close to the "fit for purpose" that we described in Chapter 3 and Singapore universities and MOE may have to reflect on the proper equilibrium between universities producing public goods for social improvement and education as a private consumer good.

How then should the Singapore system of higher education adapt to the changes engendered by technology without losing its contribution to nation building? The changes we described – how students would have more influence over the curriculum might change the traditional pathways to a pathway that is interspersed with education and work, the need for more integration, flipped classrooms, new forms of physical assets, and so on, are imminent and unavoidable. These trends will be accelerated by the consequences of the COVID-19 pandemic. The challenge for the universities is how to respond to these changes without reducing higher education to a private consumer good while keeping the social good or the original purpose of the university.

CHANGING NEEDS OF SOCIETY

A fourth and universal shift is associated with the changing needs of society. What skills would society, employers, government and NGOs need in the future? How would the universities address them? All over the world, the role of digitalisation and its influence on jobs will be amplified. As a small economy, Singapore will need to address these shifts as they are highly integrated within the world trade flows, while positioning itself as a key global player of trade.

The concept that jobs change because of technology and automation is a very old concept. The earliest industrialisation already had a profound impact on jobs and organisations. This led to significant resistance from those affected, often referred to as Luddites.[11] The dramatic impact that digitalisation can have on the redefinition of jobs was perhaps best crystallised by a study of Frey and Osborne (2013), two researchers at the University of Oxford. Their work received a lot of popular and worldwide attention because they calculated for a long list of jobs the probability that they would disappear with computerisation. The mainstream and broader press reported on this research and published that some very common jobs such as telemarketers, tellers, cargo and freight agents or accounts clerks would be more than 98% automated. That said, some jobs that require a lot of personal attention and care, such as recreational or occupational therapists, clergy, choreographers or human resources managers, will remain difficult to automate or replace. It was no doubt a wake-up call for many educators to reflect on how they are preparing and equipping the students for the critical skills needed for future jobs.

The study also received its fair share of criticism. Other studies (McKinsey's Global Institute, 2017) have since reappraised the findings. They suggest less the disappearance of jobs but rather, many if not all jobs will be affected by digitalisation. Some jobs will be partially automated, others may be enriched. This is why education must be adjusted to prepare graduates from all disciplines to work with the digitalised tools including data analytics, artificial intelligence, machine learning, robotics and so on. The six universities in Singapore have already adapted their curricula to include this important change. Now, you can find many programmes that include data analytics as a key part of the curriculum. But the transformation has just started in the universities.

Another task for Singapore universities is to widen the perspectives of students and inspire them to appreciate and know more about the region and the world. It appears that young Singaporeans do not know much about Southeast Asia and often have formed erroneous concepts about its development (Tang, 2018). This is probably a sweeping overstatement. But in our own casual observations, we noticed how little young Singaporeans know about the economic history and development of

Indonesia, Malaysia, Vietnam, or ASEAN (Association of Southeast Asian Nations) as a whole. Perhaps the education system is reinforcing the nanny state environment in which the government and the related institutions take care of its citizens "from cradle to grave". To address this conundrum, universities have introduced opportunities for undergraduate students to go overseas for exchange programmes or immersion activities. As a condition for graduation, SMU makes it mandatory for all its undergraduate students to have a meaningful overseas experience. NUS has built an impressive network of overseas colleges for student exchange in places like Beijing, Shenzhen, Nagoya, Ho Chi Minh City, Munich, New York, Israel and so on. But an open question remains as to how many of the graduates obtain a deep understanding of what it takes to operate internationally and in the region.

Finally, due to the changing needs of society as we have already suggested when we discussed the influence of technology on learning, the pathways for a university education may change. Students may want to spread out their educational experience over more than three to four years and intersperse study with work. In 2014, Stanford University engaged in an interesting "imagineering" exercise to envision the evolution of universities in our era to the year 2100. They came up with three interesting propositions which are the open loop university, paced education and purpose learning (Stanford 2025, 2020).

Open loop university means that students would learn over a lifetime with knowledge obtained from the classroom and practical settings, and adults would return to the university at the pivots in their career. The whole concept of alumni would disappear as a person would remain in some student relationship with the university over their lifetime. Some of the characteristics of the open loop university can be found in the design of the SIT curricula. These characteristics, and more specifically the SITizen concept, has been a unique differentiation for SIT. President Tan Thiam Soon mentioned in the conversation that:

> once a SITizen, always a SITizen. My ideal vision for SIT is that I don't have alumni anymore. I have only SITizens studying today or working outside tomorrow and waiting for their turn to come back. [...] You are always learning. There is no such thing anymore as having graduates.

Paced education is about removing the current pacing from freshmen to senior, and moving to a three-phase learning path of calibration, elevation and activation. Purpose learning is a proposal to replace majors with purpose and mission, and answers the most important question "not what I study is important, but why I study". This reflection at Stanford University is only one of the many imagineering exercises that are taking place across the world.

The rapid changes that are happening with digitalisation call for a significant rethinking of the organisation of universities. Some of these evolutions in society will require universities to adjust significantly to the new demands for better foundations in digitalisation, internationalisation and a reorganisation of the learning paths. All six universities have already taken some actions to adjust and change. We foresee that this pace of higher education learning will accelerate especially when technology is changing at an exponential rate. Universities must learn to be agile and address the fundamental question of "How are we meeting the changing needs of the country and society?" And they may have to adopt more of a "pracademic" approach as to how skills and knowledge are imparted while instilling a global mindset in the students.

SMU president Lily Kong mentioned in the interview that in the process of rapid innovation, there is a risk of the different universities copying good ideas one from another. This could lead to a homogenisation of what they offer to both the young and the more mature Singaporeans. She highlighted that this trend is partially evident in continuing education.

Since 2015, the MOE has strongly encouraged all six universities to support the SkillsFuture initiative. In response to the SkillsFuture initiative and the increasing demand for continuing education, all six universities established their Lifelong Learning Units. In reviewing the list of courses offered by these universities, we conclude that there is indeed quite a significant overlap in their offerings. Hopefully each university will over time, develop differentiated solutions and new niche areas to add value to their core areas. We will discuss this topic of continuing education in more detail in the next chapter.

RESULTING IMPORTANCE OF FACULTY DEVELOPMENT

One cannot but wonder whether faculty are ready for these rapid changes. Perhaps it will be good that some university faculty members embrace a "pracademic" approach to education, especially in the more applied disciplines such as Business or Engineering. We may need this at both the research intensive and the applied universities. A closer link to practice will help faculty to appreciate the rapid changes that are sweeping across the work environment and improve the way they educate students for the professional world. Reviewing performance appraisal, compensation and faculty development is therefore of high importance to the universities.

One idea that has been raised for the more applied disciplines such as business education is that of "externships" for faculty, or short spells of industry exposure to provide faculty with first-hand knowledge on what it takes to thrive in the professional world. Such externships are quite common in the industry and can take the form of job shadowing. Job shadowing can help faculty members gain new expertise and multi-dimensional problem-solving skills. A complementary approach is to favour more applied research projects in close collaboration with industry partners and to stimulate clinical research.

There are many benefits from such a focus on faculty development and applied and clinical research projects. Faculty may do a better job in preparing the young students for the professional world and the universities would become more agile in addressing societal needs.

CONCLUSION

In this chapter, we highlighted four major shifts that the higher education system in Singapore will have to respond to. We recommend a detailed analysis of the capacity in the higher education system, and how this needs to be adjusted in view of the demographic evolution and new societal requirements. We also expect the universities to have to tighten their belts and invest in productivity improvements relating to teaching, research and management.

We raised the question of how strong the core of Singapore citizens should be in the university. While this is a subject for further research and discussion, we are convinced that whatever the outcome, there is a need to significantly increase the pool of Singapore PhD graduates to build the critical mass of researchers and innovative thinkers.

It is without doubt that reorganisations will be needed to respond to the opportunities offered by technology both for education and research. Educational pathways will also change, driven by the employers, government and students.

Finally, all over the world, universities need to adjust their curricula to respond to the rapid digitalisation and the continuing globalisation of the professional world. The universities also need to focus on faculty development to ensure that they are in lockstep with the rapid changes that are happening in the workplace and affecting the future of work.

While the universities have already taken many initiatives to respond to these shifts, the urgency to align and adapt to the changes will increase, resulting in the acceleration of new innovations. The COVID-19 pandemic will no doubt accelerate these trends even further.

We hope that these innovations will not be to the detriment of the diversity that exists in the current system.

NOTES

1 While the total fertility rate has dropped, the number of children per family has remained relatively constant since the 1990s. However, young people are either marrying less or getting married at a later age.

2 It is generally accepted that most countries limit the number of foreign students in the undergraduate programmes, and that undergraduate students tend to study in their own country. Even the University of Cambridge, which is positioned as a global university, has 62 percent foreign postgraduate students compared to 25 percent foreign undergraduate students.

3 There is some variation in the number of years between primary one and the year of entry since there are different pathways; for example, students who may join the polytechnics after middle school and may take a year longer before they can enter the university. The difference between men and women is the consequence of the years that young men serve their national service (NS). In many cases, they cannot start NS immediately after finishing polytechnic or junior college. They often take two and a half to three years in between finishing secondary studies and starting university.

4 This reduction in number of pupils has already led to mergers of primary, secondary schools and junior colleges. For example, in 2019, four pairs of junior colleges merged.

5 From time to time, there are major stories about some of the top researchers who have been drawn to Singapore with large research grants, but return to their country of origin after a few years. One story that made some international news headlines was reported in *Nature*: www.nature.com/articles/468731a (Accessed: 20 February 2020).

6 https://x.smu.edu.sg/ (Accessed: 23 February 2020).

7 Arnoud De Meyer has been involved in four waves of technology-based and online learning: in the early 1990s with the use of videos, the first online courses developed during the internet bubble around 2000, the development of MOOCs after 2010, and now with the development of online courses using more blended learning. In the first three waves of technology, the expectations were never met, and universities often fell for the hype.

8 www.coursera.org/ (Accessed: 27 February 2020).

9 https://lambdaschool.com/ (Accessed: 27 February 2020).

10 JTC is a major developer of industrial buildings, owned by the Singapore Government.

11 Luddite has become a universal concept used to describe people who dislike new technology and its impact on jobs. Its origins date back to an early nineteenth-century textile labour movement that opposed mechanised manufacturing and how unskilled workers using machines undermined the jobs and livelihood of skilled craftsmen.

BIBLIOGRAPHY

Adam, S. (2013). Singapore laments the bygone era of the birthquake. *Sydney Morning Herald*, 23 January. [Online] Available at: www.smh.com.au/world/singapore-laments-the-bygone-era-of-the-birthquake-20130122-2d52c.html (Accessed: 15 February 2020).

BBC (2020). Cambridge University: All lectures to be online-only until summer of 2021. *BBC.com*, 19 May. [Online] Available at: www.bbc.com/news/education-52732814 (Accessed: 31 August 2020).

Bok, D. (2004). *Universities in the Marketplace: The Commercialization of Higher Education*. Princeton, NJ: Princeton University Press.

CNA (2020). Students whose overseas studies were disrupted by COVID-19 have options in local universities: MOE. *CNA*, 6 July. [Online] Available at: www.channel

newsasia.com/news/singapore/covid-19-university-students-overseas-studies-local-unis-moe-12905342 (Accessed: 31 August 2020).

De Meyer, A. (2016). Impact of technology on learning and scholarship and the new learning paradigm. In L. E. Weber and J. J. Duderstadt (eds). *University Priorities and Constraints.* Paris: Economica.

Frey, C. B., & Osborne, M. A. (2013). *The Future of Employment: How Susceptible Are Jobs to Computerisation?* Oxford Martin School, University of Oxford. [Online] Available at: www.oxfordmartin.ox.ac.uk/downloads/academic/The_Future_of_Employment.pdf, (Accessed: 20 February 2020).

Greller, W., & Drachsler, H. (2012). Translating learning into numbers: A generic framework for learning analytics. *Educational Technology & Society,* 15(3), p. 42–57.

History SG (1972). *National Family Planning Campaign Is Launched – 20 July 1972.* History SG. [Online] Available at: https://eresources.nlb.gov.sg/history/events/eea3d96d-93aa-455a-ac8a-1564d1b6d215 (Accessed: 15 February 2020).

Lee, H. S. (2019). *National Day Rally Speech.* [Online] Available at: www.pmo.gov.sg/Newsroom/National-Day-Rally-2019 (Accessed: 25 February 2020).

Lim, C. P. (2013). *The Evolution of Universities – A Singaporean Story* at the Times Higher Education World Academic Summit, Nanyang Technological University, 3 October. [Online] Available at: www.a-star.edu.sg/News-and-Events/News/Speeches/ID/1888 (Accessed: 15 November 2019).

Macrotrends (2020). *Singapore Life-Expectancy 1950–2020.* [Online] Available at: www.macrotrends.net/countries/SGP/singapore/life-expectancy (Accessed: 14 February 2020).

Marginson S. (2011a). Higher education in East Asia and Singapore: Rise of the Confucian Model. *Higher Education,* 61, p. 587–611.

Marginson S. (2011b). The public rational of the universities. *Dissent,* Spring: 26–31.

McKinsey's Global Institute (2017). *Jobs Lost, Jobs Gained: Workforce Transitions in a Time of Automation.* [Online] Available at: www.mckinsey.com/~/media/mckinsey/featured%20insights/Future%20of%20Organizations/What%20the%20future%20of%20work%20will%20mean%20for%20jobs%20skills%20and%20wages/MGI-Jobs-Lost-Jobs-Gained-Report-December-6-2017.ashx (Accessed: 20 February 2020).

Ministry of Education (2019). *Singapore's University Landscape.* 11 October. [Online] Available at: www.moe.gov.sg/news/committee-on-university-education-pathways-beyond-2015/singapore-university-landscape (Accessed: 15 February 2020).

NRF (2020). *Returning Singapore Scientist Scheme.* [Online] Available at: www.nrf.gov.sg/programmes/returning-singaporean-scientists-scheme (Accessed: 21 February 2020).

OECD (2014). *Skills Beyond School: Synthesis Report, OECD Reviews of Vocational Education and Training.* OECD Publishing. [Online] Available at: http://dx.doi.org/10.1787/9789264214682-en/ (Accessed: 25 February 2020).

SMU (2020). *Overseas Graduate Scholarships.* [Online] Available at: www.smu.edu.sg/moe-start/overseas-pg-scholarship. (Accessed: 21 February 2020).

Stanford 2025 (2020). *Learning and Living at Stanford. An Exploration of Undergraduate Experiences in the Future.* [Online] Available at: www.stanford2025.com/ (Accessed: 22 February 2020).

Tang, L. (2018). The Big Read: As ASEAN economies take off, young Singaporeans need to shed misperceptions about the region. *CNA*, 25 September. [Online] Available at: www.channelnewsasia.com/news/singapore/young-singaporeans-asean-southeast-asia-mentality-work-overseas-10751274 (Accessed: 15 February 2020).

Teh, C. (2019). $200,000 cash grant for Singaporeans looking to become NUS professors. *The Straits Times*, 7 August. [Online] Available at: www.straitstimes.com/singapore/200000-cash-grant-for-overseas-singaporeans-looking-to-become-nus-professors (Accessed: 21 February 2020).

The Economist (2011). *Flipping the Classroom*, 17 September. [Online] Available at: www.economist.com/united-states/2011/09/17/flipping-the-classroom (Accessed: 7 April 2021).

UOB (2018). Singapore focus: Reaching a critical demographic crossroad in 2018. *Quarterly Global Outlook.* [Online] Available at: www.uobgroup.com/assets/pdfs/research/SG-Focus_1q18.pdf (Accessed: 14 February 2020).

Chapter 9

The challenge of continuing education

Continuing education to support and upskill workers has been a focus for the Singapore Government since the late 1970s. Since the creation of the SkillsFuture movement in 2015, it has become an important element of the integrated education system. The universities have been called upon to help shape the future state of continuing education. While the universities have responded to this call, the leaders of the universities realise the significant challenges of continuing education, for example, the issue of andragogy, the capability of the faculty in teaching continuing education and the type of model for implementing university-level continuing education.

In the previous chapters, we have made only a few references to continuing education and training (CET) at the universities. There is a good reason for the paucity of our comments. With the exception of business education and executive development, most of the universities and polytechnics had limited activities related to CET until the middle of 2010s. Others had taken on that role. Starting from the early 80s to the mid-90s, the Economic Development Board (EDB) set up training institutes to help enhance Singapore's economic competitiveness through worker upskilling. In 2003, the Singapore Workforce Development Agency (WDA) under the Ministry of Manpower was established to oversee and continue CET to enhance the employability and competitiveness of the Singapore workforce and help develop the first CET Masterplan to prepare Singaporean workers for the future. Since 2011, MOE has been enhancing the delivery of CET programmes for greater accessibility, affordability and industry relevance, while responding to upgrading opportunities for working adults. In 2015, the national SkillsFuture movement was launched to provide Singaporeans with opportunities to develop themselves to their fullest potential throughout life regardless of their starting point. With the launch of SkillsFuture, CET came under the purview of the Ministry of Education

(MOE) as an integrated, "whole-of-government" approach to provide greater support for individuals to take ownership of their learning based on their strengths and interests. Strongly encouraged by MOE, the universities saw an opportunity in CET to compensate for the expected fall in undergraduate activities (see Chapter 8). But are the universities really prepared to capitalise on this opportunity? What should be the contribution of CET to the total education portfolio?

A BRIEF OVERVIEW OF THE EVOLUTION OF CET IN SINGAPORE

CET[1] is not new to Singapore. Companies and the Singapore Government have been investing in the upgrading of their workforce over the last few decades.[2] The government took an active role in it when it established the Skills Development Fund (SDF) in the late 1970s. In the early days, SDF focused primarily on the low wage employees. Employers had to contribute a percentage of the gross salaries for all employees up to a cap.[3] Employers could tap on the grants facilitated under the SDF to offset the training costs for their employees. The focus of the SDF was on the employers. They were encouraged to increase the skills content of the low-end jobs with an intent to eventually lead to the upgrading of the Singapore workforce. To a large extent, the system was quite successful in creating broad training activities that targeted basic numeracy and literacy skills (Ashton et al., 1999). But it was considered a relatively passive tool with the policy focusing on the employers to act. The employees could not take control of their own development.

After the economic difficulties engendered by the 1997 Asian Financial Crisis, the 2000 dotcom bubble bust, 9/11, the SARS crises and the rise of China as a low-cost manufacturing source, a radical change was proposed to support the upgrading of skills of the workforce. A lot of low-skilled workers were retrenched during these difficult economic times. However, they could not take advantage of the SDF initiative to reskill because the funds were disbursed to the employers. Recognising this issue, the government decided to support workers directly.

Following the recommendations of the 2003 Economic Review Committee, a new statutory board, the Singapore Workforce Development Agency (WDA) was created in September 2003. The WDA established a country-wide framework for skills development, implemented a quality assurance scheme, designed curricula, and stimulated the development of private training institutions. As the resources of the SDF were considered insufficient, the government created the Lifelong Learning Endowment Fund (LLEF). LLEF had been created in 2001 with an initial endowment of S$500 million, injected from the government's surpluses.

The LLEF complemented the SDF. As its objective was to promote and support lifelong learning in Singapore, it helped Singaporeans to meet the needs of a knowledge-based economy and cope with the threat of structural unemployment. Since then, another S$4.1 billion has been injected, bringing the total endowment capital to S$4.6 billion. In the financial year ending March 2018, the cumulative income generated from the fund was S$367 million, of which S$212 million was spent on training and education in that financial year.

In 2014, the MOE launched a committee to review the polytechnics and the Institutes for Technical Education under the ASPIRE (Applied Study in Polytechnics and ITE Review) initiative. While ASPIRE did not focus on CET, one of the key recommendations was to build more pathways allowing polytechnic and ITE graduates to progress in their careers by developing deeper skills. New Place-and-Train programmes, previously known as the Earn-and-Learn Programmes, were launched to provide polytechnic and ITE students with more opportunities to deepen their skills after graduation and better support their transition into the workforce. These programmes were designed in collaboration with industry to ensure their relevance. The universities, polytechnics and ITE and other training providers had also started to offer short, industry-relevant courses that individuals could take to build up their skills. This formed a deeper recognition that CET is more than a tool in economic development. It has been expanded to include the upskilling of workers to improve productivity, and grow and develop talent pipelines. Continuing education and training are important over the lifetime of an individual for her or him to stay relevant for continued employment. CET could potentially be an important contributor to social mobility for disadvantaged groups of the population.

In 2015, a further development totally transformed CET when SkillsFuture was created. SkillsFuture describes CET as follows on its website (SkillsFuture, 2020):

> SkillsFuture is a national movement to provide Singaporeans with the opportunities to develop their fullest potential throughout life, regardless of their starting points. Through this movement, the skills, passion and contributions of every individual will drive Singapore's next phase of development towards an advanced economy and inclusive society. No matter where you are in life – schooling years, early career, mid-career or silver years – you will find a variety of resources to help you attain mastery of skills. Skills mastery is more than having the right paper qualifications and being good at what you do currently; it is a mindset of continually striving towards greater excellence through knowledge, application and experience.

There are four key objectives of the SkillsFuture initiative. First, it is about helping individuals make well-informed choices for education, training and careers. Second, it aims to develop an integrated, high-quality system of education and training that responds to constantly evolving needs. Third, it promotes employer recognition and career development based on skills and mastery. Fourth, it fosters a culture that supports and celebrates lifelong learning (see also Yorozu, 2017).

The transformation of CET had two important implications. First, the initiative and responsibility of CET is at the level of individual Singaporeans, who are expected to upgrade themselves to contribute to Singapore's future development. The website continues to explain:

> Everyone is a part of Singapore's SkillsFuture journey. The choices you make or guide others to make in education, jobs or careers should lead to opportunities to maximise one's potential and develop a mastery of skills. To meet challenges and achieve success, chart your own paths through lifelong learning and skills mastery. Every Singaporean, every job, at every stage of life, counts.

This initiative was made very concrete when the government offered an opening credit of S$500 to all Singapore citizens aged 25 and above in 2015. An additional one-off, time-limited SkillsFuture Credit Top-up of S$500 was announced in Budget 2020 for every Singapore Citizen aged 25 years and above as of 31 December 2020. And a further one-off, time-limited SkillsFuture Credit (Mid-Career Support) was provided to Singapore citizens aged between 40 to 60 years old inclusive. This was on top of the S$500 SkillsFuture Credit Top-up for Singapore citizens aged 25 years and above. The messages that highlighted the initial credit and the top-up credit for SkillsFuture signalled the importance of lifelong learning and continuous upgrading of skills. As the credit can be spent on a wide and diverse variety of courses, it also signalled that it is the responsibility of the Singapore citizens to take continuing education into their own hands.

The second implication of CET is about education in general. Education is not only a tool for economic development, it is a must in a world where we are living and working longer, and where there will be continuous technological disruptions and changing economic context. This explains the logic for why CET came under the purview of the MOE. In October 2016, a new statutory board was formed under the MOE, SkillsFuture Singapore (SSG), to drive and coordinate the implementation of SkillsFuture. SSG took over many of the functions performed earlier on by the WDA.[4] The Minister for Education from 2015 until 2020, Ong Ye Kung stated: "What we really hope to bring about in the coming years is the concept that we don't have to frontload education and then backload work in our lives. For many people, you will intersperse work and learning". It is interesting to note that Minister Ong was Chief Executive of the WDA from 2005 until 2008, thus, he had a deep understanding of CET and its purpose. This is another example of the continuity in leadership we described in Chapter 7.

THE ROLE OF UNIVERSITIES IN CONTINUING EDUCATION

The universities have always played some role in continuing education. The business schools in NUS, NTU, SMU and the former UniSIM have been offering short executive development programmes for many years. You can argue that some of the part-time Master's programmes are a form of continuing education. Frankly speaking, most of these offerings were marginal to the core activity of most of the universities[5] except for SUSS, the former UniSIM, which was set up for part-time students. Continuing education was in fact the original mission of UniSIM.

From the early to mid-2010s, many of the other universities started getting interested in continuing education. After the creation of SSG, the universities were strongly encouraged by the MOE to increase their focus on CET. Many of them saw and still see CET as a new source of income that could compensate for the loss of operating grants driven by the shrinking number of undergraduate students. The universities also recognised that if they did not seize this opportunity, they would "lose" it to the private education providers.

But focusing on CET is more than a source of income for the universities. The universities can play a key role in shaping the Singapore-specific system of continuing education. Senior Minister Tharman Shanmugaratnam envisioned the evolution of the system of higher education in Singapore to be:

> about developing universities for life. It is really the broader re-envisioning of education, to provide for learning throughout life. Our publicly funded universities have to be anchors in this system, and have the high standards and credibility in the minds of the Singapore public that is needed to play such roles. They are taking this on as part of their core mission. We will need some flexibility in the system, so it's not about receiving a single shot of higher education that is counted on for a lifetime, or about each institution catering to only its own alumni. The new capability of higher education in Singapore must be to enable people to acquire knowledge and skills through a mix of programmes over time, coming in for short or extended periods each time. It is an important new approach, still being developed, and part of our future.

In response to this call, the polytechnics and universities developed many courses and created specialised institutes or academies to offer SkillsFuture and lifelong learning related courses. NUS created SCALE

(School of Continuing and Lifelong Education). Both SMU and SUTD launched their own Academies. NTU launched the Centre for Professional and Continuing Education (PACE). The Centre for Continuing and Professional Education (CCPE) at SUSS and SITLEARN at SIT are also responses to this call. In the interviews with the presidents and the chairmen of the six universities, we learned that all of them are committed and have strong views about continuing education. But they also raised several issues pertaining to it. These can be summarised in the following four categories:

1 *Andragogy*: Do we know enough about andragogy or how adults learn? Is there sufficient knowledge about how adults acquire skills and knowledge, as opposed to how 20-something-year-old students learn and acquire skills and knowledge? There are some interesting studies on adult learning (Jarvis & Griffin, 2003) that show that there is a negative correlation between ageing and the ability to learn in a traditional way, and that there are differences in crystallised and fluid intelligence between younger and older people. These studies inform us that in order to be successful in continuing education, education providers need to address multiple factors including the different methods of learning that are appropriate to the different ages and work experience, and the motivation of the older people to learn. The other implication of these studies is related to the admissions criteria, especially on the judging of past work experiences as a guide for admissions to the programmes for adults. It is recognised that a good framework to address adult learning is still lacking, specifically on the application in and adaptation to the Singapore context.

2 *Role of the research faculty:* The second issue that was raised in the interviews is how willing and prepared the faculty of a research-oriented university are to engage in adult learning. The universities in Singapore have a different mix of full-time tenure track faculty, practice and education track faculty, adjunct lecturers and facilitators. No doubt the practice faculty and adjunct lecturers are well-placed to work with adult learners who are in the workforce and have a lot of experience. But if and when continuing education becomes a core activity of the universities, the core tenure track faculty should be prepared to engage in it. In reviewing why some of the top graduate business schools like INSEAD, Harvard Business School, the Wharton Business School or London Business School have been successful in adult learning, especially in the executive development programmes, we conclude that this is partially due to the commitment of their best research faculty to these programmes. Motivating and grooming research faculty to take on this

new role at the Singapore universities is still a challenge for the university administration.

3   *Specialisation:* In the rush to launch programmes that are aligned to SkillsFuture, it is evident that all six universities have invested in a portfolio of quite similar programmes. One observer mentioned tongue-in-cheek that all programmes with data analytics in their title would sell well. Just like there is differentiation for the undergraduate programmes, there is a need for some differentiation and specialisation among the institutes of higher learning including the polytechnics and ITEs. The applied universities – SIT and SUSS – clearly have a bigger role to play. For a specialised research university like SMU, it makes a lot of sense to engage deeply into continuing education as high-quality continuing education can be the source of research problems and insights. But what is the role of continuing education for a research-based comprehensive university? For some of the more professional schools like the business schools, engineering schools or schools of public policy, it makes a lot of sense to commit to it. But the case is perhaps less attractive for the traditional science-based schools. Some of our interviewees suggested that perhaps MOE could take a role in organising a division of tasks. Ong Ye Kung, Minister for Education from 2015 to 2020, commented:

> When universities started to respond to SkillsFuture, they picked what participants wanted to do and they may have all gone for the fad of the day: digital marketing, artificial intelligence (AI), data sciences, bitcoin and distributed ledger. So, you saw the universities going for the same areas. But now I see the first signs of differentiation. Some of the institutions that focused on data sciences do well. Others focusing on robotics and advance manufacturing are doing quite well. SMU focusing on finance and fintech is doing well. SUTD has come to the realisation that design thinking is something that can define and distinguish them. The niches are emerging.

We would add that competition probably will help in the differentiation of these SkillsFuture courses.

4   *The business model for organising continuing education:* All the interviewees agreed that close and deep collaboration with employers is essential. The continuing education initiatives of the universities are driven by advisory councils that are populated with business people and corporate leaders. Many questions have been raised by these advisory councils. To what extent should employers have a say on the design of the programme curricula? Who should teach the programmes? When should the courses be organised? How should the credentialing of micro-credits be implemented? What is the ideal model – a retail model for open enrolment programmes or a business-to-business (B2B) model where the universities collaborate with large companies to

educate their workforce? How should the continuing education activities be scaled? Many of these questions are still unanswered and we see all the universities experimenting with different models and learning as they go on this journey.

It is also apparent that the university leaders of all the universities are committed to implementing continuing education as a core activity and not treating it merely as a commercial activity. Where it comes to continuing education, there still exist many concerns and unanswered questions. While there are some overseas examples and best practices that have been published by the OECD (2019), the universities in Singapore will have to develop their own idiosyncratic models that align to their value propositions and differentiating factors.

LEARNING FROM PRIVATE INITIATIVES? CORPORATE UNIVERSITIES AND COMMUNITY-BASED LEARNING

Universities can learn from the experience of corporate universities to improve their capabilities in continuing education. An often-quoted example of a successful corporate university was Motorola University. Unlike most learning and development departments, Motorola University was not just set up for employees, rather it was an educational ecosystem to educate customers including institutions, regulators, suppliers, as well as employees. In the 1990s, there were different colleges established, such as the College of Engineering, College of Sales and Marketing, and College of Leadership and Management. There was also a network of educational partners comprising universities and certification companies in different parts of the world to provide learning programmes that were relevant and cutting edge (Hartley, 2012).

One way for universities to enhance continuing education may be to adopt a reverse Motorola University model, that is, to partner with the multinationals from different sectors to jointly develop programmes that are aligned to changes in the industry. This could be the difference that is needed to bring academia and industry closer together. Partnering to deliver postgraduate programmes, especially at the Master's level, is not new for the universities. NUS has been partnering with Yale to offer the NUS MBA – Yale Master of Advanced Management double degree programme – and SMU has been partnering for many years with Spain's IE Business School to offer the IE-SMU MBA. But there are very few examples of partnering between the Singapore universities and large companies to jointly develop continuing education programmes. The collaboration with corporates tends to be one-directional where the university or select faculty members are commissioned to develop tailor-made programmes. But programmes where universities and corporations work as equals in developing curricula are still rare.

An interesting initiative is the collaboration between SMU and Google to offer an SMU-Google Squared Data and Analytics Programme to SMU's undergraduate students.

Adult learning benefits from peer learning. One quite interesting experiment is the altMBA[6] programme, a leadership and management programme that is based on a community learning model. The programme is completely delivered online and focuses on "learning by doing". Students have typically between five and eight years of work experience. The learning is enhanced through teamwork, personalised feedback, coaching, curated readings and the delivery of 13 projects in four weeks. Each session of the workshop is led by a group of coaches who help the students in their individual and group work. There are no assigned teachers or professors for the course, only coaches who play the role of nudging the students towards their goals. Students also get the nudging from their peers. They are expected to work in small groups and openly critique one another's work.

Many continuing education programmes that are offered by the executive development department of the business schools include some of these elements of peer- or community-based learning, but the use of this methodology could perhaps be intensified and diffused in other disciplines to reinforce personalised learning and community building.

FURTHER CHALLENGES CONFRONTING THE TRANSFORMATION OF CONTINUING EDUCATION

There are three other issues in the development of continuing education in Singapore that go beyond the universities: the relevance of the courses to the socio-economic development of Singapore, the required change in mindset among the Singapore citizens, and employer buy-in.

The ambition of SkillsFuture as expressed in its vision and mission is to get all Singapore citizens to upgrade themselves to prepare them for the future. In our interviews, we observed some differences of opinion. One group thought that a more liberal approach is needed so that every Singaporean can pursue her or his own interests as it is believed that this is the best approach to motivate the citizens to start learning. This group of interviewees seemed convinced that the market would sort out itself in the mid to long term. It is believed that after some time, Singaporeans would invest in the programmes that provide value for themselves and society. The other group thought that we should attempt to match the supply of education programmes with the future needs of the economy. For this group, continuing education is perceived as one of the tools to enable economic development and a tool for future proofing the citizens and Singapore against the disruptive changes that are sweeping across the world. They referred to the 23 industry transformation maps that were developed and approved by the Future of the Economy Committee (Ministry of Trade and Industry, 2020). Each of these maps contains detailed information about the future skills needed for each of the sectors. They saw these maps as excellent input to the design of the curricula of the different SkillsFuture programmes.

The second issue is the willingness and the mindset of Singapore citizens to invest in continuing education. This of course, includes the time needed to learn, as well as the willingness to spend the resources and effort on reskilling. It is without doubt that there exists an aspiration and a hunger for Singaporeans to obtain a degree, a diploma or a certificate. Singapore is a country made up of people who like credentialing. But continuing education is much more about learning than about obtaining paper certificates. The initial results of SkillsFuture at the five-year juncture after the launch showed encouraging signals. The 2019 report by SSG mentioned that:

> Since the launch of the SkillsFuture Credit in 2016, more than half a million Singaporeans have utilised their SkillsFuture Credit. The top three areas of training have been Information and Communications Technology (ICT), Food and Beverage, and Productivity and Innovation. About 124,000 individuals also tapped on the enhanced support in 2019, such as the Mid-Career Enhanced Subsidy and Enhanced Training Support for SMEs to support their training needs; an increase from about 114,000 individuals in 2018. In 2019, sign-ups for courses remained strong for priority and emerging skills in areas such as urban solutions, data analytics and advanced manufacturing. More than 37,000 individuals took courses under the SkillsFuture Series, up from over 28,000 in 2018.

Innovative schemes like SkillsFuture Credit need some time before the impact is shown. The uptake and impact of programmes typically follow an S-shaped curve. After a slow start, you could say that Singapore may soon be experiencing a quasi-exponential growth in the adoption phase of the curve.

The real issue confronting continuing education is how you would interest and engage potential learners in pursuing continuing education and lifelong learning. The European Union has developed an interesting overview of best practices to overcome what they describe as the structural, situational and psychological barriers to participate in continuing education (European Commission, 2012). Their matrix of actions to be taken by the different stakeholders including governments, employers, unions, education institutions and so on, contained 52 proposals. This large portfolio of proposals is an indication that there is not one simple solution to motivate and encourage adults in continuing education and lifelong learning.

The third issue raised is the need for collaboration and support from employers. Multinational corporations have a tradition of continuing education and training, with many of them having their own learning and development organisations. But small and medium enterprises (SMEs) lack the focus on training and development of their employees. What will it take to entice companies regardless of their size to invest in continuing education? How should companies create the space for their employees to invest in their own learning and development? The early literature on the varieties of capitalism (Hall and Soskice, 2001) made a rather crude distinction between liberal market economies, often associated with an Anglo-Saxon model of capitalism, and coordinated market economies that are typical for regions like Scandinavia or countries like Germany or Japan. As there is less job security in the liberal market economies, hence, a lot more job hopping, it is generally accepted that companies in these countries would be less inclined to invest in training and development. These companies prefer to link CET to individual performance appraisals and prefer to leave it to the government to organise more generalist vocational training. In the coordinated market economies where there is more job security, more loyalty from employees and longer tenure working for the same employer, it is evident that these employers are more prepared to invest in training for firm-specific skills. Employees working in coordinated market economies are also more ready to invest time and effort in developing these skills because of the possibility of moving up the organisational hierarchy within the company.

We estimate Singapore to be a bit of a mixed model. While it is a coordinated market economy, there is evidence of relatively high turnover and job hopping – which is why you would expect companies to be less inclined to invest in training and development. For employees working for the larger companies, this is perhaps mitigated by the fact that training and development is a part of the employment package that is used to retain workers. The Singapore Government has played a key role in providing financial support during downturns, for example, the 2008 Global Financial Crisis, or more recently, the Coronavirus pandemic, to help employees keep their jobs. The government is also playing a role convincing companies to show that investing in the skills upgrading of their employees is both a competitive advantage for the company and a tool for employee retention, as during a downturn companies do not want to lose organisational knowledge which results from individual learning.

More recent empirical work (Goergen et al., 2012) has shed some light on the differences between the coordinated market economies with respect to the investment in human capital. There appears to be some differences between countries like Germany and Japan on the one hand, and countries like the Netherlands, Denmark and to some extent Norway on the other hand. In the latter group, there is less legal job security but a high perceived job security, and they have high-quality vocational training systems (OECD, 2019). In these small and prosperous countries in Europe, high levels of foreign competition require them to develop a skilled work-force to remain competitive. As Goergen et al. (2012) have argued, in these countries:

> vocational training is provided in a cooperative manner at the industry and company levels. This is matched by high levels of state expenditure on labour market training programs aimed at supporting individuals throughout their working lives. For example, in the Netherlands, whilst vocational qualifications are normally gained in full-time schooling, voca-tional schools have a very high rate of attendance among post 16-year olds and the resultant qualifications are highly regarded by Dutch employers. The system has led to a strong emphasis on constant retraining. At the same time, centralisation and coordination encourage the clear definition and transferability of specific skills within the individual industries. Approaches to training at the workplace itself may not be all that much different from other coordinated market economies. [...] the role of employers in vocational training is institutionalised in these economies just as it is in high job protectionist coordinated market economies. In all these economies, employers can build on strong vocational training systems, allowing for focused and cost-effective workplace based continuous training to fill any gaps in needed organisation specific skills.

Perhaps Denmark, Norway and the Netherlands are interesting examples for Singapore on how to engage employers, both large and small. What is striking about the systems of these countries is the partnership and a well-developed division of tasks between the governments and the employers.

CONCLUSION

Singapore has gone through an interesting transformation of its overall system of continuing education. Under the influence of changing demo-graphics, disruptive innovation and a changing economic landscape, continuing education has moved from a tool to support economic devel-opment into an activity that is fully integrated in the concept of lifelong learning and education. Like other educational institutions, each of the universities can play a key role as a supplier of education, but also as a key anchor and a source of new insights on how adult learning should be organised for maximum impact for the individual and country. In the earlier cited 2019 OECD report, it is mentioned that: "no country is consistently amongst the top performers [for adult skills learning] across all the dimensions of future-readiness. Denmark and Norway perform well across most dimensions, yet each country still faces unique adult learning challenges". This is an area of education that still requires a lot of experimentation, research and learning. The universities in Singapore have an opportunity to contribute to developing the uniquely Singapore approach in order to preserve the competitive position of the country and provide thought leadership on adult education.

NOTES

1 In other countries like the United Kingdom, this is often referred to as VET for vocational education and training.
2 For a more detailed overview of the development of CET in Singapore, see for example Sung (2011).
3 When SDL was first set-up, the contribution rate was 4 percent of gross monthly remuneration, for employees earning up to S$750. Both the percentage and the salary caps used for calculating contributions changed over time.
4 It also absorbed the Committee for Private Education.
5 This may have been different in other countries. For example, in the United States of America, many universities have extension programs which are often as large as the full-time activities of the university.
6 https://altmba.com/info.

BIBLIOGRAPHY

Ashton, D., Green, F., James, D., & Sung, J. (1999). *Education and Training for Development in East Asia: The Political Economy of Skill Formation in Newly Industrialised Countries.* London: Routledge.

European Commission (2012). *Strategies for Improving Participation in and Awareness of Adult Learning.* Luxemburg: Publications Office of the European Union.

Goergen, M., Brewster, C., Wood, G., & Wilkinson, A. (2012). Varieties of capitalism and investment in human capital. *Industrial Relations,* 51(1), p. 501–527.

Hall, P. A., & Soskice, D. (eds) (2001). *Varieties of Capitalism.* Oxford: Oxford University Press.

Hartley, D. (2012). The learning and development pioneer: Bill Wiggenhorn. Chief Learning Officer, 15 August. Available at: www.chieflearningofficer.com/2012/08/15/the-learning-and-development-pioneer-bill-wiggenhorn/ (Accessed: 18 March 2020).

Jarvis, P., & Griffin, C. (2003). *Adult and Continuing Education.* London: Routledge.

Ministry of Education (2014). *Better Choices, Deeper Skills, Multiple Paths: Government Accepts ASPIRE Committee's Recommendations.* [Online] Available at: www.moe.gov.sg/news/press-releases/better-choices–deeper-skills–multiple-paths–government-accepts-aspire-committee-s-recommendations (Accessed: 7 March 2020).

Ministry of Trade and Industry (2020). *Overview: ITMs.* [Online] Available at: www.mti.gov.sg/ITMs/Overview (Accessed: 22 March 2020).

National Archives of Singapore (2019). *Lifelong Learning Endowment Fund – Annual Report.* [Online] Available at: www.nas.gov.sg/archivesonline/government_records/Flipviewer/grid_publish/8/8a00be47-c361-11e8-ab1b-001a4a5ba61b-S.383of2018/web/html5/index.html?launchlogo=tablet/GovernmentRecords_brandingLogo_.png&pn=3 (Accessed: 23 March 2020).

OECD (2019). *Getting Skills Right: Future-Ready Adult Learning Systems, Getting Skills Right.* Paris: OECD Publishing. [Online] Available at: https://doi.org/10.1787/9789264311756-en (Accessed: 7 March 2020).

SkillsFuture (2020). *What is SkillsFuture.* [Online] Available at: www.skillsfuture.sg/AboutSkillsFuture (Accessed: 22 March 2020).

Sung, J. (2011). *The Singapore Continuing Education and Training (CET) System.* Skills Development Scotland, Labour Market Research. [Online] Available at: www.researchgate.net/publication/258831168_The_Singapore_Continuing_Education_and_Training_CET_system, (Accessed: 7 March 7 2020).

Yorozu, R. (2017). *Lifelong Learning in Transformation: Promising Practices in Southeast Asia.* UNESCO Institute of Life Long Learning. Publication series no. 4, p. 50. [Online] Available at: https://unesdoc.unesco.org/ark:/48223/pf0000253603 (Accessed: 7 March 2020).

Chapter 10

From R&D to innovation

Singapore aspires to be an innovation-led economy. It is internationally recognised to be good at innovation input, but not yet as good in translating research output into innovation. The universities can contribute to this transformation. Improving the flow of the R&D results into the companies, helping start-ups to mature and "grow up" to medium-sized or larger companies, getting better at education and research in design, instilling a different culture for collaboration and innovation in the universities, and improving the linkage between STEM research and research in social sciences are some potential strategies to adopt.

Singapore wants to become more innovative. In a comment published in 2017 in the Straits Times, the main local newspaper, Dr Beh Swan Gin, chairman of Singapore's Economic Development Board, argued that Singapore was then able and ready to make the shift from a knowledge-led to an innovation-led economy (Beh, 2017). Three factors, specifically the rise of Asia as a market, the concentration of dynamic and diverse multi-national corporations (MNCs) in Singapore and the availability of private risk capital, put Singapore in an ideal position to become a significant driver of innovation. Furthermore, the strong scientific base, the growing vibrancy of the start-up ecosystem coupled with Singapore's traditional strengths as a trusted business location and attractiveness to talent and connectedness to the world should enhance Singapore's position as an innovation hub. Others have suggested that Singapore should shift its strategy to focus on deep technology, or technologies that drive fundamental breakthroughs in science and engineering, to have a more profound impact on industries and lives (Zen & Chua, 2019). Making this next move requires an evolution in the whole ecosystem for innovation including ensuring a favourable business environment, the continuing presence of risk-taking capital, a dynamic and evolving intellectual property (IP) regime, a vibrant start-up community and so on. It also requires the universities to play an important role in transforming successful research and development (R&D) into value-creating innovation that can be monetised, commercialised and sustained.

INVESTING IN INNOVATION

Many economic observers have argued for some bold adjustments in the Singapore economy to sustain its extraordinary economic performance over the last decades (Bhaskaran, 2018). These observers have challenged Singapore to become more innovative. In some of the world rankings, Singapore has scored well when it comes to innovation. For example, in the recent 2020 World Global Innovation Index (GII), published by the World Intellectual Property organisation (Cornell University et al., 2020), Singapore ranked eighth in the world for innovativeness. We know that such an overall score in itself is rarely insightful. The real information is in the details.[1] Singapore scored exceedingly high in terms of innovation input, where it is at the top of the world rankings, but it is 15th in terms of innovative output. Digging deeper into the components of this score, Singapore scored very high with respect to institutions (1st), human capital and research (8th), market sophistication (4th) and business sophistication (6th), but not as high in infrastructure (13th), knowledge and technology outputs (14th) or creative outputs (18th). Digging even deeper into the details of this composite ranking, we learn that Singapore's tertiary education, which is a component of human capital and research, is ranked first worldwide whereas the quality of research human capital is ranked 13th in the world.

In another innovation index, published by Bloomberg (2020), Singapore scored third behind Germany and South Korea. This index is also a composite of other factors. Singapore scored first in tertiary education efficiency which combined factors such as the cohort participation rate, the share of the labour force with an advanced level of education and the annual science and engineering graduates as a percentage of the total tertiary graduates. Singapore scored second in value-added manufacturing. Relatively speaking, it lagged in high-technological (hi-tech) density, defined as the number of domestically domiciled hi-tech companies, where its rank is 17th. As for R&D density and researcher concentration, it is ranked number 12 and 13 respectively. This index suggests a similar result as the GII index: despite being highly ranked for government-sponsored input and education, the creation and growth of domestic innovative companies in Singapore is still not yet at the level of the top performers.

Even with good rankings for innovativeness, why do economic observers remain critical of Singapore's capacity to innovate? The International

Monetary Fund (2017) identified several reasons for the weakness in innovation in 2017. Two of them stand out. The first reason is about culture. Singaporeans' known risk-averse culture could be holding them back from doing and achieving more in innovation. Another reason is the lack of economies of scale as Singapore companies only have access to a small domestic market unlike the companies in Silicon Valley. Silicon Valley innovators can achieve low unit costs fast through economies of scale that are available through the ready access to the large American consumer or business markets. Innovators in smaller European countries such as Sweden or Switzerland can also achieve economies of scale because of access to the single European market. Israel's entrepreneurs can leverage and access the North American market because of Israel's extensive links with the United States. Singapore's small domestic market poses challenges for scaling up. Of course, Singapore is strategically located at the hub of a Southeast Asian market with 650 million consumers. However, there is a consensus that young Singaporeans think global but not regional. They travel the world and feel comfortable in Paris, Tokyo, London, New York, Hong Kong or Shanghai. But as we have mentioned in Chapter 8, they have preconceived and often erroneous ideas about Southeast Asia and know little about the region – its culture and market (Tang, 2018). In fact, the weakness of having a small home market in Singapore may be related also to its culture and a lack of curiosity about the countries in the region.

Lim Chuan Poh was the Chairman of A*STAR until April 2019 and was closely involved in R&D and innovation in Singapore. In commenting about the results of the 2016 Global Innovation Index, Lim wrote that the challenge for Singapore is to enhance the private sector innovation capacity (Lim, 2016). He mentioned that:

> although public sector research has grown in intensity and excellence, that of enterprises, especially the local enterprises, has yet to grow at a corresponding rate. The MNCs, by and large, dominate in many R&D intensive industry clusters, such as electronics, pharmaceuticals and biomedical sciences. In comparison, local enterprises are still relatively modest in their research investments and capabilities although their growth rate appears to have picked up in the last 5 years or so.

He continued with the need to reach out to the local SMEs:

> Therefore, in recent years, government policymakers have placed greater emphasis on the technological upgrading of SMEs. A*STAR also carries out programmes that supported the transfer of technologies and expertise from its research institutes to SMEs. [...] In addition, Singapore is stepping up its efforts to develop its entrepreneurial ecosystem. [...] Singapore has some way to go in terms of cultivating a vibrant, R&D intensive private sector, but it is on the right trajectory.

Going from being first in innovation input to being a top performer in innovation output will require changes in many ways. Bhaskaran (2018) proposed that:

> to be successful in innovation, Singapore needs to address several areas. The education system needs to be less competitive and more tolerant of late bloomers. However, a reluctance to undertake a bold restructuring of education means the response has been tweaks (many of which are commendable). Others argue that a freer media and willingness to tolerate dissent is also important for creativity. Here, too, there has been a disappointing reluctance to change.

This calls for a whole new programme to transform the universities: more pathways, perhaps different credentialing as we have discussed in Chapter 8, an increased emphasis on creativity and critical thinking. Former NTU president Bertil Andersson commented about this: "We have a need in the future for people who can do more than accumulate facts; we need people who can show leadership, critical thinking, teamwork, and have a social and a cultural capability".

In an interview with University World News in 2017, Andersson added (Sharma, 2017):

> Today, the big success story in Singapore is research. Innovation has not come that far. Research has to come before innovation and the country has high ambitions to do that. Singapore is a small country, you cannot compare it with Germany, the United States or the UK. But you can compare Singapore with Sweden, Finland, Switzerland, Israel – these are what we call small, smart nations. Still, I don't think we have the same culture here in Singapore like Sweden, Switzerland or Israel. Singapore is much more risk averse, for example. In terms of innovation, I don't think things are going to be radically different in 2020 but maybe in 2025 and 2030. The question is – will the Singapore government, the Singapore taxpayers have the patience to wait for that?

That said, there have been some successes. Many MNCs have set up innovation centres in Singapore. Often cited examples are the Visa Innovation Centre, the Philips Health Continuum Space or P&G's Innovation Centre. Our extensive case studies on Schneider's Innovation Hub (De Meyer & Chan, 2020) or Johnson & Johnson's Design Lab (De Meyer & Bhattacharya, 2020) illustrate in detail why companies choose Singapore for their innovation hubs in Southeast Asia. The start-up landscape is also vibrant. On average, over 50,000 new companies are formed in Singapore each year. According to the Singapore Department of Statistics, the number of technology start-ups in the country has been rising from 2,800 in 2003 to 4,300 in 2016. In addition, a 2018 Bain & Co. study found that the number of recorded venture capital deals in Southeast Asia quadrupled and rose to

524 in six years from 2012, with many of these deals being executed in Singapore (Varma & Boulton, 2018). The universities have also set up successful incubators to support their students and alumni in starting new companies. Block 71, an initiative that was rolled out by NUS Enterprise, the Media Development Authority and SingTel Innov8, was described by The Economist (2014) as "the world's most tightly packed entrepreneurial ecosystem, and a perfect place to study the lengths to which a government can go to support start-up colonies". It is also important to note that five of the ten recorded "Unicorns" in Southeast Asia were headquartered in Singapore: Razer, Sea (formerly Garena), Lazada, Grab and Trax. This shows that there is a rapid growth and expansion of Singapore's innovation ecosystem.

Based on our discussions and interviews, we formulate five suggestions for what the universities can do better to contribute to the innovation ecosystem. First, there is a need to improve the collaboration between the universities and the industry, in particular with the small and medium enterprises (SMEs). The primary purpose of R&D investment in Singapore is not to create a global public good. Rather, it is to support economic and national development. Therefore, there is a need to improve the flow of the R&D results into the companies to drive innovation in the industry. Second, while there are many start-ups and budding entrepreneurs at the universities, there is a need to ensure that these start-ups mature and "grow up" to medium-sized or larger companies. Third, it is recognised that Singapore needs to get better at design. Thus, the universities need to invest in education and research for design. Fourth, there may be a need to instil a different culture for collaboration and innovation in universities. Finally, there is a need to improve the linkage between STEM (science, technology, engineering, and mathematics) research and research in social sciences.

ENHANCING THE FLOW OF R&D RESULTS FROM THE UNIVERSITIES TO THE INDUSTRY

In this section, we want to focus on two issues: matching the R&D effort with the absorptive capacity of the local industry and enhancing the physical proximity between academia and the industry. Before we dive deeper into this, we emphasise that there already exist some encouraging collaborations between the universities and the industry. The most visible are without doubt the Corporate Labs sponsored by the National Research Foundation. As we mentioned in Chapter 4, there exist many strong collaborations. They include the collaborations between Keppel and Sembcorp with NUS, the Urban Computing Lab at SMU that was set up in collaboration with A*STAR and Fujitsu, and ST Engineering has two collaborations with

SUTD – ST Engineering-SUTD Centre for Smart Systems and the ST Engineering Electronics-SUTD Cyber Security Laboratory. NTU has created corporate labs with Rolls Royce, Alibaba, BMW, Lockheed Martin and Johnson Matthey. Most of these labs have significant government funding and are required to demonstrate their long-term sustainability in turning R&D into innovations that can be applied to the industry.

Matching the R&D effort with the absorptive capacity of the local industry

When it comes to the relevance of R&D, one of the main differences between a small and a large country is the role of the absorptive capacity (Cohen & Levinthal, 1990). In practice, this means that in large industrialised countries like the United States, China, Germany or the United Kingdom, there will always be a company or an agency that can absorb the results of the R&D efforts at the universities. In such cases, the commercialisation of the R&D output can lead to local economic development and contribute significantly to the GDP. For smaller countries with less local (large) companies, there may be areas of research for which there is no user within the country.[2] While the consumer or user might exist elsewhere, or perhaps the R&D results could be monetised through licensing to a foreign partner, in such a case, the R&D outcomes would not contribute significantly to the economic development of the smaller country in the short to medium term. In spite of this, the technology push resulting from the outcomes from R&D could lead to the formation of a new company and these entrepreneurial initiatives could grow into larger companies in the long run. Or the budding local companies could be acquired by the large MNCs that can subsequently set up a local presence through the acquired innovator. The economic development for such cases might take a lot more time. In 2008, when we researched the evolution of the "Cambridge Cluster" around the University of Cambridge, we learned that the focus on R&D can and does lead to significant economic growth, but not necessarily to an equivalent growth in the number of jobs. And the time lag between the original positive research results, as measured for example by first publication, and commercialisation may take up to 20 years, in particular for applications that require significant investments in complementary capabilities or technologies to commercialise the core invention.

In the case of Singapore, after the massive shift to R&D in life sciences in the early 2000s, it has taken more time for this shift to lead to significant economic activity than perhaps the government had initially hoped. While there was a presence of large pharmaceutical companies in Singapore and many more that were drawn to Singapore through the efforts of the

Economic Development Board (EDB) over the last 20 years, it became evident that these companies did little original research in Singapore. The absorptive capacity of the research conducted in Singapore was also limited. Virtually no significant local companies were active in this area. Tan Chorh Chuan, former president of NUS, played a crucial role in the development of the research activities in life sciences. He was more positive and commented in our interview:

> I think in the last 5 years, there have been many green shoots. What has really changed in the last 5 years that has led to this? First, I think that the Singapore ecosystem has matured. Besides basic researchers, we now have many more clinician-researchers who are capable leaders, which is needed because a lot of applications of our research are really in the clinical space. The second change is the nature of drug discovery. You can develop more targeted therapies and test them on much smaller groups of patients than before when we typically needed much larger trials. This is particularly so for areas like cellular therapy. [This evolution is to our advantage in Singapore]. Therefore, if you look at Singapore in recent years, we have had about 80 biotech and 230 med-tech start-up companies and the indicators in terms of their quality and the stage of development are promising. We cannot declare success yet. All we can say is that after 20 years, we're seeing some very good developments. We hope that at least some of them will make it big. I am quite convinced today that some of them will succeed in a big way.

Other observers have noted that the effective response of Singapore to the 2020 COVID-19 pandemic, the low mortality rate and the successful vaccination campaign may have benefited from the learning and the extensive networks that Singapore researchers in the life sciences have built up over the last 20 years.

As a response to the lack of alignment between R&D spending and the absorptive capacity of Singapore institutions and companies, the 2020 Research, Innovation and Enterprise Plan (RIE 2020) prioritised funding for technology sectors for which Singapore already had some strengths and/or anticipated national needs. The sectors were Advanced Manufacturing and Engineering, Urban Solutions and Sustainability, Services and the Digital Economy and Health and Biomedical Sciences, the latter of which had been broadened to include health-centric R&D as opposed to focusing solely on biomedical research and life sciences.

We do not recommend an almost exclusive focus of R&D in the areas where Singapore institutions or companies already have a strong position or show a latent demand. There is a need to develop new expertise in other areas. However, a careful balancing between strengthening of what has been mastered and developing new areas of competitiveness through innovation will be needed in the development of the future RIE plans. The disruptions created by the COVID-19 pandemic will no doubt influence future choices, as new opportunities may arise.

Enhancing the flow of R&D results to commercial applications: The role of intermediaries

Improving the interaction between the university as a supplier of R&D results and the industry as the receiver of ideas is not a new problem or a challenge that is limited to Singapore. All over the world, governments in industrialised countries have struggled with overcoming two types of problems: industry and academia are not connected or have limited communication; and what is considered an advanced demonstration outcome in academia is rarely ready to be a laboratory prototype for the industry.

In order to overcome this cultural distance between these two important groups of stakeholders, quite a few countries have created some form of intermediary. In the United Kingdom, for example, the Engineering and Physical Sciences Research Council (EPSRC) has created Innovation and Knowledge Centres (IKC), which are considered to be:

> a key component of the UK's approach to the commercialisation of emerging technologies through creating early stage critical mass in an area of disruptive technology. They are able to achieve this through their international quality research capability and access to companion technologies needed to commercialise research. Based in a university, they are led by an expert entrepreneurial team. While continuing to advance the research agenda, they create impact by enhancing wealth generation of the businesses with which they work.
>
> (UKRI, 2020)

In Germany, the Fraunhofer institutes have a somewhat similar function to EPSRC with some of their other roles that are broadly similar to the roles of A*STAR research institutes; these institutes also perform applied research and development. In Belgium, the Interuniversity Microelectronics Centre (IMEC) is an independent applied research institute, located in Leuven and close to the well-known University of Louvain, which is financed partially by the regional Flemish government. It has built up a worldwide reputation for the translation of scientific results into practical technology solutions for companies in the field of electronics.[3]

All Singapore universities have some form of technology transfer offices. But we see the need to expand their roles, even transforming them into organisations similar to IKC or IMEC. The universities should continue to put their resources into producing high-level knowledge that very few other organisations in the economy are capable of generating. Their key source of competitive advantage resides in the development of advanced, cutting-edge theories and methods. It is probably not their biggest competitive advantage to invest in translation. Therefore, intermediaries can play an important role. But such intermediaries should not become a hurdle for academics to interact with the industry. They should focus on enabling academics to interact with the industry instead of attempting to regulate all the interactions between the academics and the participating companies.

Enhancing the flow of R&D results to commercial applications: Improving face-to-face communication

It is a well-known fact that effective technical and scientific communication is still very dependent on face-to-face contacts, even in these times of sophisticated electronic communication and social media (Sosa & Mihm, 2008).[4] This is particularly necessary for the exchange of tacit and non-codified knowledge that is characteristic for early R&D results or when the two groups of stakeholders representing the university and the industry are starting to interact with each other and initiate their collaboration. Physical proximity between the stakeholders from the university and industry would help them to meet, connect and get to know one another while strengthening their collaborative efforts. Therefore, the experiment with the future SIT campus that is to be located in Punggol is noteworthy. The campus will be integrated with a business park built by Jurong Town Corporation (JTC), called the Punggol Digital District (2020) to provide a "seamless transition" from the campus to the industrial park, and both groups representing academia and the industry will be given access to use one another's facilities.

Such similar clusters already exist in several parts of Singapore. NUS is close to the One-North ecosystem. Originally master planned and developed by JTC, One-North features a research and business park offering facilities for research, innovation and test-bedding. The 200-hectare development houses companies in sectors such as biomedical sciences, info-communications technology and media, and start-ups with capabilities in science and engineering. One-North aims to offer a work-live-play-learn environment that enables the integration of industrial developments with the residential communities providing lifestyle options and educational institutes to build an environment conducive to congregate, collaborate, and create (JTC, 2020). It also houses Biopolis where biotech companies and A*STAR biomedical research institutes are co-located.

SMU is close to the business district and the Supreme Court and many law firms. This enables a seamless interaction between the business-related schools and the law school, and their partners. NTU is located close to the engineering and industrial activities in Jurong.

SUTD, which is located close to Changi Airport, has developed close research ties with the aviation industry, as well as with Changi General Hospital. When we asked President Chong Tow Chong of SUTD about the challenges for the future, he mentioned that universities need to become better at stimulating innovation, and he gave three examples where SUTD benefited from close proximity:

> One of them is the aviation industry, because we are quite fortunate to be close to a world-class airport. How do we capitalise on this? The timing is just right. Singapore is building a fifth terminal and an integrated air-sea-land transport system to boost trade and connectivity.[5] Imagine! This is going to be quite different in terms of logistics, the supply chain, passenger experience and so on. Thus, we want to collaborate on air traffic management. [...] The other one is a long-term relationship with Changi General Hospital (CGH). We have adjunct faculty from CGH and some of our academics work there. The good thing is that we are just a couple of feet away from the hospital. The third area we look at is the Changi Business Park. We have a smart city development programme and that may be relevant to them. There are supply chain and finance companies that we may be able to help. Our long-term vision is to develop a vibrant innovation ecosystem in Changi for the future growth of Singapore.

In these clusters, there are exchanges between academia and the industry but there may not be real integration. In the case of SIT in Punggol, there is an expectation to go beyond just having different activities side by side. JTC will build a business park next to SIT and will share its facilities with SIT. Lawrence Wong, Minister of Finance and former Minister for National Development and Minister for Education, mentioned:

> We are quite good at clustering industries. [...] But now we are trying to go beyond that. We want to cluster business parks, education and residential and commercial all together. JTC has a business park next to SIT. Do companies in the business park need separate big auditoriums? Or can they start sharing facilities with each other? Can there be a higher porosity between institutions and their buildings, thus, obtain the full benefits of clustering? [...] There is also a theme to the district by focusing on IT, technology and digital media. Having such a theme lends itself to closer collaboration and integration. The students can make use of JTC's facilities as makerspaces where they can go to experiment or even to do their own start-ups. The JTC space can be an incubator or an accelerator space, to where the students can move from the university quite seamlessly.

These clusters may well become the driver of the future economic development of Singapore. As envisioned by Ong Ye Kung, former Minister for Education:

> We had an earlier phase in our development where EDB, STB were the ones driving and shaping the character of our economy and our city. Going forward, I think the six universities are going to play a huge role. A lot is about the kind of students you are developing, the post-grad students you

can bring in, the kind of research, the innovation, the prototyping, the experimentation, and the whole buzz you can create. Companies will be coming to Singapore because of the universities, because of the education, because of the talent pipeline you can offer, because of the upgrading opportunities that universities can offer to their staff. The role of the universities is rising both economically and socially.

This is why it is important to nurture and further the development of these clusters. The planned SIT-JTC cluster is an interesting development and is one that justifies close observation to ascertain how this physical seamless integration might lead to seamless integration for the commercialisation of research.

FROM START-UPS TO "GROWN UP" COMPANIES

All the universities have some form of incubators or accelerators within their premises to help their students and alumni in starting up companies. We have already discussed NUS Enterprise and its overseas colleges. NTU has created NTUitive, which offers several programmes for their students, faculty and alumni including the Lean LaunchPad (LLP)[6] programme to help its research scientists and engineers to turn their inventive technologies into commercially viable products and feasible business ventures. NTU also offers an Overseas Entrepreneurship Programme (OEP) to its undergraduate students. SMU has launched the Business Innovations Generator (BIG) programme under the Institute for Innovation and Entrepreneurship (SMU IIE). The BIG Incubation Programme is a nine-month programme that helps aspiring entrepreneurs to validate and refine their product and the start-up's value proposition. It helps early stage founders validate their product and prepare for seed investment. The beneficiaries of the programme can receive support for grant opportunities, get advice from mentors, learn from master classes, as well as use a joint working space in the heart of downtown Singapore. SMU's IIE programme also offers a three-month overseas internship programme for the entrepreneurs, called the Global Innovation Immersion programme. In partnership with some high-growth start-ups in multiple countries, especially in Southeast Asia in cities like Jakarta, Bangkok, Manila and Ho Chi Minh City, the Global Innovation Immersion programme aims to provide SMU students with the opportunity to develop entrepreneurial skills while experiencing a world outside of their "bubble" at the same time.[7]

Beyond these initiatives by the universities, there are many other incubators and accelerators, which are often created by MNCs or real estate developers. The government too has launched several programmes to support entrepreneurs while making it easy to get matching seed funding for a good business plan. Many organisations including ACE (Action Community for Entrepreneurship)[8] and SGInnovate[9] have been set up to drive and enhance the entrepreneurial activities in Singapore. As we have suggested at the beginning of this chapter, the results have been quite successful. The incubators have been operating in full swing. There are an increasing number of start-ups being created and entrepreneurship has become culturally more accepted in Singapore.[10] The real challenge for these start-ups is scaling up. All too often, young entrepreneurs prefer to cash out when they receive a good offer from a larger company, rather than growing their company. This phenomenon is not unique to Singapore. Going back to my observations of the Cambridge (UK) cluster, I observed that it produced a lot of wealthy individuals and serial entrepreneurs, but relatively fewer large companies that would employ a large number of people. Selling out to larger MNCs when the start-up reaches a certain size is quite common too for the Cambridge cluster.

Perhaps a role for the universities, through their continuing education, is to provide hands-on experience for the entrepreneurs in how to build and grow a company, how to prepare for initial public offerings (IPOs), and how to manage big investors and private equity firms. One of the factors that can contribute to the growth of start-ups is to help the entrepreneurs to think regional in Southeast Asia, and global so as to see the world as their potential market and expand their venture internationally beyond the Singapore market. NUS' Overseas Colleges, NTU's Overseas Entrepreneurship Programme and SMU's Global Innovation Immersion programmes have been designed to change and develop this mindset.

However, most importantly, the universities need a few inspiring role models from their alumni, especially those who have built a big and successful private business.

GROOMING HIGH-QUALITY DESIGN TALENT

One of the criticisms of Singapore's ability to be a top innovator is that it is not a top performer in terms of design. In this context, design is much more than a focus on form and aesthetics. It is about broadening the physical design to include end-to-end user experiences, as well as a focus on culture change in the organisations (Dalrymple et al., 2020). Singapore has some good institutions preparing students for a job in design like SUTD, a university that has design in its name and DNA. The government has taken many initiatives to stimulate a focus on design. It has created a Design Council. In 2013, the Singapore Good Design Mark was introduced to reward local efforts in improving designs. It also installed the National Design Centre to document design successes in Singapore and offer courses in design. But really exciting design performance and global leadership in design isn't evident yet. There is a need to improve the structure of arts and design education and research significantly both as a mainstream discipline and embedded as a cross-disciplinary field of study.

Currently, education in arts and design is quite fragmented and dispersed. There is a School of the Arts (SOTA), a pre-tertiary specialised arts school with a six-year integrated arts and academic curriculum, leading to the International Baccalaureate Diploma or Career-related Programme for youth aged 13 to 18 years old. Some of the polytechnics like Temasek, Ngee Ann and Singapore polytechnics offer diplomas in product design. There are two private institutions that are financially supported by the government and that offer diplomas, and degrees, in arts and design related disciplines – LASALLE College of the Arts and the Nanyang Academy of Fine Arts (NAFA). Both institutions offer degrees in collaboration with overseas institutions. For example, LASALLE's degree programmes are validated by Goldsmiths, University of London.[11] NAFA collaborates with several institutions, one example being the Royal College of Music, London, to offer a Bachelor of Music (Hons). While these are no doubt well-recognised partners in their respective fields, they might not all have the same "Ivy League" status as the institutions that the six universities have partnered with.

SUTD has design at the core of its activities and programmes. Its mission reads as follows (SUTD, 2020): "The Singapore University of Technology and Design is established to advance knowledge and nurture technically-grounded leaders and innovators to serve societal needs, with a focus on Design, through an integrated multi-disciplinary curriculum and multi-disciplinary research". The university also has multiple inter-disciplinary design laboratories to develop, prototype and test engineering solutions by understanding social needs. Notwithstanding this, the design focus at SUTD is clearly more technological than for both LASALLE and NAFA.

NTU has an established School of Art, Design and Media to focus on the arts and groom design talent. We quote from its mission (NTU, 2020): "The School of Art, Design and Media seeks to play a weighty role in transforming the island state into a global media city. Our inter-disciplinary courses are designed to mould creative individuals into outstanding artists, designers, animators, new media performers and even business leaders". NUS' Division of Industrial Design in its School of Design and Environment offers also a suite of degree programmes in Industrial Design.

There are also some design initiatives that are driven by Private Education Institutions in Singapore. One of them is the Paris-based Strate School of Design, which launched a Master's degree in Design for Smart Cities in Singapore in 2020 (Strate, 2020).

From these examples, you can conclude that the building blocks to create an integrated educational and research environment for design are in place. Despite these developments, the progress to-date has not placed Singapore as one of the best in the world in arts and design. In the Global Innovation Index (Cornell University et al., 2020) Singapore ranks only 81st for the number of industrial designs by origin per PPP$ Bn GDP. Perhaps one key contributing reason is the fragmentation of the supply of education of design. A reorganisation and a restructuring to create a strong specialised institution with an international partner of superior quality might be the way forward. President Cheong Hee Kiat from SUSS captured this intent as follows:

> We should have a university for the arts to complete the university landscape here. Through this, Singapore can enhance its commitment to arts in its culture. It should probably be smallish. It should bring technology and the digital into art education. It cannot be big or expensive because there may not be that many jobs for the graduates. But as we develop over time into a world class economy, we need experts not just in technology or business. We need graduates with an understanding of culture and history and the arts, and how these interact with the rest of the economy and society.

Early in March 2021, then Minister of Education Lawrence Wong announced that a new University for the Arts will be created by forming an alliance between LASALLE and NAFA and a pro-tem committee was formed to develop the structure and the operating model for this new university. It is believed that this new university will strengthen the focus on arts and groom more design talent.

TAKING A HINT FROM INDUSTRY: DEVELOPING A CULTURE OF INNOVATION AND COLLABORATION

Peter Drucker, the well-known management thinker, once said that "culture eats strategy for breakfast". Similar to the IMF, we believe that what slows Singapore down in becoming a leading nation in innovation output may well be its culture. Companies also recognise the importance of culture in stimulating innovation. The CEO of Microsoft, Satya Nadella, has been able to transform a 148,000-people strong company and changed its organisational culture from a know-it-all culture to a learn-it-all culture. He emphasised that his key role as the CEO of Microsoft was to create a culture that is about listening, learning, and harnessing individual passions and talents that are aligned to the company's mission (Nadella et al., 2017). He also wrote about the importance of employee empowerment, collaboration and the ability to work together across the boundaries of the organisation to drive innovation. In our own work on ecosystems for innovation (De Meyer & Williamson, 2020), we showed that in the face of uncertainty, which is characteristic for leading-edge R&D, new forms of collaborations or ecosystems are more effective for innovation and to scale up.

Universities can probably learn something about reinventing culture. The culture in many of our university departments is often still very siloed. There are some good initiatives to overcome this. For example, at SUTD and SIT, the faculty are seated together to foster collaboration. But the culture at most universities tends to be focused on individual academic achievement. The physical arrangements of the faculty offices are also not conducive for collaboration as individual faculty members are given their own isolated offices. And 'working from home' as a consequence of the lockdown restrictions imposed as a consequence of the COVID-19 pandemic, hasn't helped in breaking down the silos.

From the studies on the sociology of science, we know that scientific exploration is a fundamentally different activity from industrial and commercial R&D. However, we are convinced that universities can adopt some of their methods, for example design thinking, agile methodology or team-based experimentation. These methodologies focus on collaboration, communication and iteration, and have been shown to speed up time-to-market, reduce waste and risks, and can rapidly respond to new trends and opportunities. It would be interesting to explore how these methods could improve the productivity of R&D at our universities and speed up the translation of R&D into innovation.

RECOGNISING THE ROLE OF SOCIAL SCIENCES IN INNOVATION

Many scholars have tried to understand the role of social sciences in innovation. Until recently, it was assumed that this role was rather limited. A recent paper by the OECD (Paunov et al., 2017) suggested that this is to a large extent due to the methodology used in the studies, as the impact on innovation of the different disciplines is typically measured through the number and the analysis of patents. This is one of the primary reasons why the impact of social sciences, where one typically does not patent research results, is under-estimated. Indeed, earlier work at the University of Cambridge showed that the interactions between academia and the industry in the disciplines of social sciences often do not take the form of commercialisation activities such as patenting, licensed research or spinoffs. Rather, they are seen in problem solving activities such as consultancy services and joint research (Hughes et al., 2011). That said, there are two surveys on tertiary education graduates[12] that have shed some light on the contributions from social sciences graduates. In business activities, the bulk of the innovative workforce is composed of graduates in social sciences including business and law studies. This is more pronounced in the services sectors where social sciences graduates who are engaged in innovative activities account for more than 75 percent of the total workforce. In manufacturing industries, more than 50 percent of employees involved in innovative activities are engineering or science graduates. But in manufacturing, social sciences graduates still represent a non-negligible 30 percent of the total (Avvisati et al., 2013). The OECD paper arrives at a conclusion showing that engineers, computer scientists and social scientists all play an important role in driving innovation in the Info-Communication and Technology (ICT) sector. Graduates from each of these disciplines account on average for around 25 percent of the workers with a tertiary education.

We won't go into the details of these studies. But what they tell us is that in order to move from R&D to innovation, we need graduates from the social sciences to work together with their colleagues from the STEM disciplines. In Chapter 8, we highlighted the call from former NUS president Tan Chorh Chuan for more integrated and holistic education and research. Earlier in this chapter, we highlighted former NTU president Bertil Andersson's appeal for more critical thinking to be embedded in education. SUTD president Chong Tow Chong commented that the design capability at SUTD could only be successful if technology is coupled with humanities, arts and social sciences to provide students with a grounding in the practice of inquiry, analysis, interpretation and presentation. If we add our own conviction about the need for integration, there appears to be a strong consensus for social sciences to be integrated with STEM subjects in higher education to guarantee success in innovation.

Yet as we mentioned earlier, the practice of how research is organised is still siloed. Schools, departments or faculties are still organised along disciplines. Other than what's implemented in SUTD, very few programmes bring students from STEM and social sciences together for their education in the other five universities. The collaboration of Duke-NUS with both SMU and SUTD to enable a seamless transition from their undergraduate programmes into the graduate medical school is another small-scale but interesting experiment to bring disciplines together. It also partly explains why joint research programmes between STEM researchers and social scientists are still few and far between in these universities. We are convinced that this move from R&D to innovation will require the allocation of research grants to spur some of these joint research programmes forward.

CONCLUSION

We started this chapter by saying that Singapore wants to be more innovative. Scientific R&D is an input for innovation. According to many observers, Singapore's innovation input is of very high quality. But improving the innovation output will require actions on many fronts. The higher education sector can contribute to this by first creating better performing intermediaries to build a bridge between academic R&D and the industry. Continuing to explore how face-to-face interactions between academics and innovators in the industry are a way forward. Second, innovation has to be nurtured. The push towards innovation will require moving beyond supporting entrepreneurship and start-ups, and guiding and creating an ecosystem for these entrepreneurs to help them to grow. Third, we plead for a concerted effort to improve the development of top-quality designers. Fourth, universities need to embrace a culture of innovation, an area where they can pick up some ideas from commercial organisations. Last but not least, the roles of graduates and researchers in social sciences innovation need to be enhanced and elevated. On a more general level, we are convinced that the allocation of research funding needs to consider the absorptive capacity of the country in order for the "rubber to hit the road".

NOTES

1 The authors of this report are the first to recognise that one should not be obsessed by the absolute ranking and that there are confidence intervals. For example, Singapore scores overall 8, but with a confidence interval of 7 to 12. The interval for innovation input is 1 to 3, and the interval for innovation output is 14 to 23.

2 When it comes to commercialising academic research output, many think of successful start-ups. But the reality is that the bulk of the research results are commercialised by large companies that work closely together with academic institutions.

3 It is important to note that Belgium has few, if any companies specialising in electronics. Most of IMEC's industry partners are located in other countries. But the presence of IMEC has brought some of these MNCs to Belgium and IMEC has had several spinoffs.

4 At the time of writing this book we don't have yet reliable and rigorous studies on the impact of "working from home" and meetings via video-conference platforms on productivity and innovation. But the first indications are that "business as usual" activities can be managed efficiently from home and over these platforms, while innovation, requiring the exchange of fuzzy and sometimes tacit information, requires at least some face-to-face meetings.

5 After the interview and as a consequence of the COVID-19 pandemic and its effects on air traffic, the government has decided to put a pause on the Changi Terminal 5 project for at least two years.

6 The Lean Launchpad Programme is spearheaded by NUS Enterprise with Autonomous Universities such as NTU, SMU and SUTD onboard.

7 This programme was on hold during the pandemic.

8 www.ace.org.sg (Accessed: 4 April 2021).

9 www.sginnovate.com (Accessed: 4 April 2021).

10 Dissenting voices will point out that parents are still not very supportive of their children becoming entrepreneurs. Many of the incubators are populated mainly with foreigners.

11 In 2020 Goldsmiths, University of London was ranked 72nd in the UK by the Complete University Guide and 99th in the UK by *The Guardian*.
12 www.hegesco.org and https://roa.nl/?portfolio=reflex-internationsl-survey-higher-education-graduates (Accessed: 4 April 2021).

BIBLIOGRAPHY

Avvisati, F., Jacotin, G., & Vincent-Lancrin, S. (2013). Educating higher education students for innovative economies: What international data tell us. *Tuning Journal for Higher Education*, 1: p. 223–240.

Beh, S. G. (2017). Singapore's long game in innovation. *The Straits Times*, 23 August. [Online] Available at: www.straitstimes.com/opinion/singapores-long-game-in-innovation (Accessed: 27 February 2020).

Bhaskaran, M. (2018). *Getting Singapore in Shape: Economic Challenges and How to Meet Them*. [Online] Available at: www.lowyinstitute.org/publications/getting-singapore-shape-economic-challenges-and-how-meet-them-0 (Accessed: 15 February 2020).

Bloomberg (2020). *2020 Bloomberg Innovation Index* [Table]. Bloomberg. [Online] Available at: www.aitriz.org/triz-articles/triz-features/790-bloomberg-global-innovation (Accessed: 7 April 2021).

Cohen, W. M., & Levinthal, D. A. (1990). Absorptive capacity: A new perspective on learning and innovation. *Administrative Science Quarterly*, 35(1), p. 128–152.

Cornell University, INSEAD, & WIPO (2020). *The Global Innovation Index 2020: Who Will Finance Innovation?* Ithaca, Fontainebleau and Geneva. [Online] Available at: www.globalinnovationindex.org/Home (Accessed: 15 September 2020).

Dalrymple M., Pickover, S. & Sheppard, B. (2020). Are you asking enough from your design leaders? *McKinsey Quarterly*. February. [Online] Available at: www.mckinsey.com/business-functions/mckinsey-design/our-insights/are-you-asking-enough-from-your-design-leaders# (Accessed: 7 April 2021).

De Meyer, A., & Bhattacharya, L. (2020). *Johnson & Johnson's Choice of Regional Headquarters and Innovation Hub: Why Singapore?* SMU case study SMU-20-0002.

De Meyer, A., & Chan, C. W. (2020). *Schneider Electric: Optimising Business Opportunities from its Regional HQ in Singapore*. SMU Case study SMU-20-0001.

De Meyer, A., & Williamson, P. J. (2020). *The Ecosystem Edge: Sustaining Competitiveness in the Age of Disruption*. Stanford: Stanford University Press.

Hughes, A., Kitson, M., & Probert, J., with Bullock, A., & Milner, I. (2011). *Hidden Connections: Knowledge Exchange between the Arts and Humanities and the Private, Public and Third Sectors*. Cambridge: Arts and Humanities Research Council and the Centre for Business Research.

International Monetary Fund (2017). Staff Report for the 2017 Article IV Consultation with Singapore. *IMF Country Report No 17/240*, July. [Online] Available at: www.imf.org/en/Publications/CR/Issues/2017/07/28/Singapore-2017-Article-IV-Consultation-Press-Release-Staff-Report-45144 (Accessed: 15 February 2020).

JTC (2020). *One North*. [Online] Available at: www.jtc.gov.sg/industrial-land-and-space/Pages/one-north.aspx (Accessed: 3 February 2020).

Lim, C. P. (2016). From research to innovation to enterprise: The case of Singapore. In Cornell University, INSEAD, and WIPO (eds), *The Global Innovation Index 2016: Winning with Global Innovation*. Ithaca, Fontainebleau, and Geneva: Cornell University, INSEAD, and WIPO.

Nadella, S., Shaw, G., & Nicholls, J. T. (2017). *Hit Refresh: The Quest to Rediscover Microsoft's Soul and Imagine a Better Future for Everyone*. New York: Harper Collins.

NTU (2020). *School of Arts Design and Media Mission and Vision*. [Online] Available at: www.adm.ntu.edu.sg/aboutus/Pages/Mission-and-Vision.aspx (Accessed: 20 February 2020).

Paunov, C., Planes-Satorra, S., & Moriguchi, T. (2017). What role for social sciences in innovation? Re-assessing how scientific disciplines contribute to different industries. *OECD Science, Technology and Industry Policy Papers*, No. 45. Paris: OECD Publishing. [Online] Available at: https://doi.org/10.1787/8a306011-en (Accessed: 20 February 2020).

Price, D. (2019). What is a culture of innovation? *Atlassian*, 7 April. [Online] Available at: www.atlassian.com/blog/inside-atlassian/how-to-build-culture-of-innovation-every-day (Accessed: 1 March 2020).

Punggol Digital District (2020). [Online] Available at: https://estates.jtc.gov.sg/pdd (Accessed: 24 March 2020).

Sharma, Y. (2017). The story of how Singapore became a research nation. *University World News*, 15 December. [Online] Available at: www.universityworldnews.com/post.php?story=20171215122350628 (Accessed: 15 January 2020).

Sosa, M. E., & Mihm, J. (2008). Organisation design for new product development. In C. H. Loch and S. Kavadias (eds), *Handbook of New Product Development*. Oxford: Butterworth-Heinemann (Elsevier).

Strate (2020). *Strate's Singapore Campus*. [Online] Available at: www.strate.education/singapore-campus (Accessed: 20 February 2020).

SUTD (2020). *Vision and Mission*. [Online] Available at: www.sutd.edu.sg/About-Us/Mission-and-Values (Accessed: 20 February 2020).

Tang, L. (2018). The Big Read: As ASEAN economies take off, young Singaporeans need to shed misperceptions about the region. *CNA*, 25 September. [Online] Available at: www.channelnewsasia.com/news/singapore/young-singaporeans-asean-southeast-asia-mentality-work-overseas-10751274 (Accessed: 15 February 2020).

The Economist (2014). *All Together Now: What Entrepreneurial Systems Need to Flourish*. Special Report. 16 January.

UKRI (2020). *Innovation and Knowledge Centres*. [Online] Available at: https://epsrc.ukri.org/innovation/business/opportunities/impactschemes/ikcs/ (Accessed: 24 March 2020).

Varma, S., & Boulton, A. (2018). *Investing in Asia: What's behind the Boom?* Boston, MA: Bain & Company.

Zen, S., & Chua, K. H. (2019). Creating an innovation culture – Singapore's not-so-secret formula to becoming a regional tech hub. *South China Morning Post*, 7 September. [Online] Available at: www.scmp.com/tech/enterprises/article/3026044/creating-innovation-culture-singapores-not-so-secret-formula (Accessed: 2 March 2020).

Index

Page numbers in *italics* refer to figures. Page numbers in **bold** refer to tables. Page numbers followed by 'n' refer to notes.

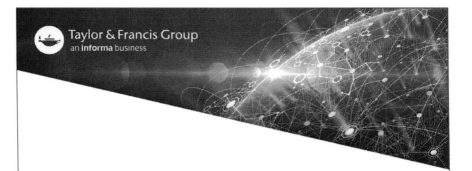

Printed in Great Britain
by Amazon